Foundations of Student Affairs Practice

Foundations of Student Affairs Practice

How Philosophy, Theory, and Research Strengthen Educational Outcomes

Florence A. Hamrick, Nancy J. Evans,

and John H. Schuh

 JOSSEY-BASS
A Wiley Imprint
www.josseybass.com

Published by Jossey-Bass
A Wiley Imprint
989 Market Street, San Francisco, CA 94103-1741   www.josseybass.com

Jossey-Bass books and products are available through most bookstores. To contact Jossey-Bass directly
call our Customer Care Department within the U.S. at 800-956-7739, outside the U.S. at 317-572-3986
or fax 317-572-4002.

Jossey-Bass also publishes its books in a variety of electronic formats. Some content that appears in
print may not be available in electronic books.

Library of Congress Cataloging-in-Publication Data
Hamrick, Florence A. (Florence Aileen)
  Foundations of student affairs practice : how philosophy, theory, and
research strengthen educational outcomes / Florence A. Hamrick, Nancy J.
Evans, and John H. Schuh.
      p. cm. — (The Jossey-Bass higher and adult education series)
Includes bibliographical references (p.   ) and index.
  ISBN 0-7879-4647-8 (alk. paper)
  1. Student affairs services—United States.   2. Education,
Higher—Aims and objectives—United States.   I. Evans, Nancy J., 1947-
II. Schuh, John H.   III. Title.   IV. Series.
  LB2342.9 .H36 2002
  378.1'94—dc21
                            2002011287

Printed in the United States of America
FIRST EDITION
HB Printing 10 9 8 7 6 5 4 3 2 1

Contents

Preface

As calls for improvement and reform in postsecondary education continue to emerge (for example, Wingspread Group on Higher Education, 1993; Levine & Nidiffer, 1996; Kezar, Hirsch, & Burack, 2001), higher education leaders have responded by reasserting traditional arguments in support of higher education (see Lucas, 1996). Nonetheless, advocacy for a richer, more complete, more coherent undergraduate experience continues to come from a variety of sources, and in many ways higher education has not responded well. As the cost of higher education attendance continues to escalate (Clotfelter, 1996; National Commission on the Cost of Higher Education, 1998), some have questioned the value of a baccalaureate degree. This questioning ranges from whether or not individuals are trained well for their first job (Oblinger & Verville, 1998), the extent to which they are prepared for a lifetime of learning and contributing to the larger society (Wingspread Group on Higher Education, 1993), and whether public investment in higher education is well placed (Institute for Higher Education Policy, 1998).

The beginning of the development of the student affairs profession is marked, in the eyes of some, by the 1937 publication of *The Student Personnel Point of View,* or SPPV (*Points of View,* 1989). Although the language of this document is not contemporary, its statements are consistent with the current goals of higher education. In many ways, the SPPV provided a philosophical foundation for the emergence of a variety of student development theories in the 1960s.

Student development theories (works by Chickering, Perry, Kohlberg, and so on) have been employed to explain why students behave the way they do and to develop programmatic and environmental interventions now common on college campuses.

Student development theory helps to explain, for example, why entering, traditional-age, first-year students probably are not ready for a seminar about how to launch a job search after graduation but do need help in dealing with issues related to a changing relationship with their parents or managing their emotions in a stressful situation.

An accelerating number of reports, studies, and analyses released during the past decade or so have focused on delineating the values, activities, and interventions developed by colleges and universities to enrich the undergraduate experiences of students. Among these are the works of Astin (1985, 1993); Pascarella and Terenzini (1991); and Kuh, Douglas, Lund, and Ramin-Gyurnek (1994). This body of literature has yielded solid, empirical evidence for efforts within higher education to emphasize a holistic approach to educating students.

Partly in response to these reports and analyses, the emphasis of student affairs practice has been on offering a beneficial environment that supports the student learning process (American College Personnel Association, 1996) and participating in cross-campus partnerships to craft and offer this rich learning environment. Publications such as *Good Practice in Student Affairs* (Blimling & Whitt, 1999) and *The Handbook of Student Affairs Administration* (Barr, Desler, & Associates, 2000) have asserted that student affairs practitioners would be well served to establish partnerships with other units within an institution of higher education to form a united effort in advancing student learning. As borne out by various evaluation studies (for example, Larrey & Estanek, 1999; Schroeder, Minor, & Tarkow, 1999; Westfall, 1999), these united efforts provide a more powerful educational experience for students.

In response to this convergence of development theory and outcomes literature with the evolving nature of student affairs practice, the experiences of college students will be enriched immeasurably by integrating philosophy, theory, and practice. In this publication, we present philosophy and theory that support informed practice and also identify an array of interventions shown to be successful through rigorous field testing. This integrative approach is attractive to practitioners who are being directed not only to articulate the educational rationale for their program but also to demonstrate the difference the program makes in the lives of their students. Too frequently in the history of student affairs administration, practitioners have relied on publications that discuss philosophy or theory or that describe interventions; this volume attempts to blend these strands with emphasis on frequently cited desirable outcomes for students. Perhaps by serendipity, the opportunity now exists for higher education to focus more clearly than ever on a learning experience for students that is built on an interlocking base of research, theory, and philosophy.

Purpose of the Book

This book is designed to weave together philosophical foundations of higher education and student affairs practice, various developmental theories that have come to frame student affairs practice, and specific interventions—grounded in research—that are designed to enrich the experience of students while they are enrolled at college. In the book, we articulate the prevailing goals and purposes of higher education with respect to student learning outcomes and give the reader the philosophical, theoretical, and empirical background to support implementing a range of interventions designed to promote student learning. Organized on the basis of broad outcomes that are frequently referenced as appropriate goals for educating students, these chapters serve as useful guides for the practicing administrator, faculty member, and higher education leader who desire to enrich the learning environment for students.

Intended Audience

This book is targeted at the practicing student affairs administrator, academic affairs administrator, faculty member, or other institutional leader who is concerned with (1) promoting the growth and development of college students and (2) communicating to various constituent groups the justification for an existing program or a program currently in development. Additionally, faculty and students in a graduate program in student affairs and higher education who wish to link the social expectations of education with theoretical bases underpinning student growth and interventions designed to promote learning will find this volume valuable.

Practitioners can use this book to help inform their daily work. It will assist practitioners in articulating what they are trying to do, why they are trying to do it, and how their efforts are consistent with the educational objectives of their institution. This book also can help those external to the student affairs arena—educational policy makers as well as parents—understand how a variety of experiences available to students inside and outside the classroom contribute to students' learning and development.

Organization of the Book

This book is divided into three parts. Part One is a historical, theoretical, and philosophical overview that frames the remainder of the book. In Part One, we present background chapters addressing the evolution of mission and purpose among higher education institutions, the emergence of student development theories, the current emphasis on student learning by student affairs administrators and others, and the importance of implementing a structured learning environment.

We trace the history of higher education by highlighting how the missions of colleges and universities have changed over time. These changes in mission have strongly influenced the desired outcomes of higher education for students, from the classical curriculum in the antebellum college to today's virtual institution without a campus. The consequence of the ever-evolving mission is that many colleges and universities have become more diverse in terms in their curriculum. What was considered at one time inappropriate for study at the undergraduate level forms the core of the curriculum a generation or two later.

Next, we examine how selected student development theories can be used to describe how students grow and develop. These theories are a useful tool for those concerned about how students learn and grow. Theory can be used to inform pedagogical strategy as well as frame experiences that take place outside of the classroom. In short, it is a powerful tool in developing appropriate experiences for the undergraduate.

Moving to the influence of the campus environment on students, we review environmental theory and how the campus environment affects students. It does so in a variety of ways, and conscious design of the campus environment can lead to developing a supportive learning community, an important ingredient in student success.

Finally, we review how the current emphasis on student learning has affected student affairs practice. Student learning is a primary outcome of the collegiate experience. Colleges and universities increasingly are measured by the extent to which their students learn and how they facilitate the learning process. Familiarity with current literature on this subject helps those responsible for student learning to be more effective in their effort to improve the learning climate on campus.

Although decidedly not intended to be comprehensive in scope, each chapter is included so as to outline recent trends in higher education that support a holistic view of student learning and to reinforce the current and growing call for institutional (as well as departmental and program-level) accountability and demonstration of identifiable results.

In Part Two, we identify and discuss selected desirable student-level outcomes, discuss how student development theories inform our knowledge of these outcomes, and summarize selected student learning opportunities and strategies that have been shown to achieve the respective outcomes. As we deliberated about listing desirable educational outcomes and how such outcomes are best fostered, Newman (1960/1982) presented clear guidance on what did *not* constitute educating students: "Do not say, the people must be educated, when, after all, you only mean, amused, refreshed, soothed, put into good spirits and good humor, or kept from vicious excesses. I do not say that such amusements, such occupations of mind, are not a great gain; but they are not education" (p. 109).

The specific outcomes included in Part Two are (1) a self-aware and interpersonally sensitive individual, (2) a democratic citizen, (3) an educated person, (4) a skilled worker, and (5) a life skills manager. Obviously, these areas are not necessarily distinct from each other, but they are discussed individually for the sake of clarity. Each chapter contains first an overview to briefly define the outcome and provide philosophical or historical warrants for that outcome. Discussion of relevant student development theories and summaries of in-class and out-of-class interventions associated with the outcome follow the introductory section. Guiding principles and implications for practice conclude each chapter.

Although we have identified a set of broad student-level outcomes that we maintain are contemporary foci in higher education, we are also mindful of Dewey's admonition (1916/1985): "Educators have to be on their guard against ends that are alleged to be general and ultimate. Every activity, however specific, is, of course, general in its ramified connections, for it leads one indefinitely into other things. So far as a general idea makes us more alive to these connections, it cannot be too general. But 'general' also means 'abstract,' or detached from all specific context. . . . A truly general aim broadens the outlook; it stimulates one to take more consequences (connections) into account" (p. 116).

In Part Three, we address additional implications for practice and suggest an agenda for future research. We recommend strategies for students to enhance their learning and a research agenda that helps measure student learning. Our view is that an integrated approach to student learning and development affords rich experiences for students and a variety of potential opportunities to investigate the extent to which these experiences are successful in supporting student growth.

Our intent with this book is to help higher education professionals examine desired outcomes for students as well as look at a variety of real-life learning experiences that lead to greater learning and achievement with respect to the outcomes. Higher education professionals will then be better prepared to scan their campus, identify learning experiences, and brainstorm other outcomes and learning experiences that might be crafted to enhance students' learning at a specific campus with its traditions, history, geography, and other characteristics. We hope that this book helps educators "be more alive to these connections" and possibilities at their campus.

A Final Note

Writing this book was a challenge for us. It required a great deal of thinking, reflecting, and synthesizing of information. Our view is that at this time higher education in general and student affairs practitioners in particular will find a discussion of what they are about useful. We hope to extend and enliven the conversation about how the purposes of higher education, the theories that are the foundation for student learning and growth, and the experiences that contribute to student learning complement each other in ways that permit a holistic educational experience for the student.

References

American College Personnel Association (1996). *The student learning imperative: Implications for student affairs in tomorrow's higher education* (online). (http:/www.acpa.nche.edu/sli/sli.htm)

Astin, A. W. (1985). *Achieving educational excellence.* San Francisco: Jossey-Bass.

Astin, A. W. (1993). *What matters in college?* San Francisco: Jossey-Bass.

Barr, M. J., Desler, M. K., & Associates. (2000). *The handbook of student affairs administration* (2nd ed.). San Francisco: Jossey-Bass.

Blimling, G., & Whitt, E. (1999). *Good practice in student affairs: Principles to foster student learning.* San Francisco: Jossey-Bass.

Clotfelter, C. T. (1996). *Buying the best: Cost escalation in higher education.* Princeton, NJ: Princeton University Press.

Dewey, J. (1985). *Democracy and education.* Carbondale, IL: Southern Illinois University Press. (Original work published 1916)

Institute for Higher Education Policy. (1998). *Reaping the benefits: Defining the public and private value of going to college.* Washington, DC: Author.

Kezar, A., Hirsch, D. J., & Burack, C. (2001). Editors' notes. In A. Kezar, D. J. Hirsch, & C. Burack (Eds.), *Understanding the role of academic and student affairs collaboration in creating a successful learning environment.* (New Directions for Higher Education, no. 116, pp. 1–8). San Francisco: Jossey-Bass.

Kuh, G. D., Douglas, K. B., Lund, J. P., & Ramin-Gyurnek, J. (1994). *Student learning outside the classroom.* (ASHE-ERIC Higher Education Report no. 8). Washington, DC: George Washington University, School of Education and Human Development.

Larrey, M. F., & Estanek, S. M. (1999). The Ursuline studies program: A collaborative core curriculum. In J. H. Schuh & E. J. Whitt (Eds.), *Creating successful partnerships between academic and student affairs.* (New Directions for Student Services, no. 87, pp. 63–73). San Francisco: Jossey-Bass.

Levine, A., & Nidiffer, J. (1996). *Beating the odds: How the poor get to college.* San Francisco: Jossey-Bass.

Lucas, C. J. (1996). *Crisis in the academy: Rethinking higher education in America.* New York: St. Martin's.

National Commission on the Cost of Higher Education. (1998). *Straight talk about college costs and prices.* (N.p.): Author.

Newman, J. H. (1982). *The idea of a university.* Notre Dame, IN: Notre Dame University Press. (Original work published 1960)

Oblinger, D. G., & Verville, A. L. (1998). *What business wants from higher education.* Phoenix, AZ: Oryx.

Pascarella, E. T., & Terenzini, P. T. (1991). *How college affects students.* San Francisco: Jossey-Bass.

Points of view. (1989). Washington, DC: National Association of Student Personnel Administrators.

Schroeder, C. C., Minor, F. D., & Tarkow, T. A. (1999). Freshman interest groups: Partnerships for promoting student success. In J. H. Schuh & E. J. Whitt (Eds.), *Creating successful partnerships between academic and student affairs.* (New Directions for Student Services, no. 87, pp. 37–49). San Francisco: Jossey-Bass.

Westfall, S. B. (1999). Partnerships to connect in- and out-of-class experiences. In J. H. Schuh & E. J. Whitt (Eds.), *Creating successful partnerships between academic and student affairs.* (New Directions for Student Services, no. 87, pp. 51–61). San Francisco: Jossey-Bass.

Wingspread Group on Higher Education. (1993). *An American imperative: Higher expectations for higher education.* Racine, WI: Johnson Foundation.

The Authors

Florence A. Hamrick is associate professor of higher education at Iowa State University, Ames. She teaches graduate courses in student development theory and research methods. Previously, she was associate director of the Placement and Career Services Offices at Wichita State University and assistant director of the Department of Student Affairs at Sheldon Jackson College (Alaska).

She earned the Ph.D. in higher education from Indiana University (Bloomington) in 1996, a master of arts in college student personnel from Ohio State University in 1983, and a bachelor of arts in English from the University of North Carolina, Chapel Hill, in 1981.

Hamrick has served two terms on the editorial board of the *Journal of College Student Development* and is a former assistant editor of the American College Personnel Association's Media Board. She has authored or coauthored eight book chapters, eleven refereed journal articles, four invited publications, and fifteen nonrefereed articles and reports. She has made more than forty conference presentations and speeches, including a plenary address to the 2000 International Educational Research for Empowerment Conference in Chiang Mai, Thailand. Her two dozen presentations to national conferences include the American Educational Research Association, the Association for the Study of Higher Education, the American College Personnel Association, and the National Association for Student Personnel Administrators. Her research interests include college students, nondominant groups within American higher education, and the student affairs profession.

She has served on the directorates of the Commission for Career Planning and Placement and the Commission for Professional Preparation of the American College Personnel Association;

she is a past national coordinator for the New Professionals Network of the National Association of Student Personnel Administrators. In 2001, the American College Personnel Association named Hamrick an emerging scholar.

Nancy J. Evans is a professor in the Department of Educational Leadership and Policy Studies and coordinator of the higher education program at Iowa State University. She teaches courses on student development theory, campus environments and cultures, and sexual orientation issues in higher education. She previously served on the faculty of student affairs preparation programs at Penn State University, Western Illinois University, and Indiana University. Earlier, she held positions in the counseling centers at Bowling Green State University and the University of Iowa, in residence life and student activities at Stephens College, and as assistant dean of students at Tarkio College.

She received the Ph.D. in counseling psychology from the University of Missouri-Columbia in 1978, an M.S. Ed. in higher education and college student personnel from Southern Illinois University-Carbondale in 1972, an M.F.A. in theatre from Western Illinois University in 1991, and a B.A. in social science from the State University of New York-College at Potsdam in 1970.

She has edited, coedited, and coauthored several books, among them *Encouraging the Development of Women* (1985); *Beyond Tolerance: Gays, Lesbians and Bisexuals on Campus* (1991, with Vernon Wall); *The State of the Art of Professional Preparation and Practice: Another Look* (1998, with Christine Phelps Tobin); *Student Development in College: Theory, Research, and Practice* (1998, with Deanna Forney and Florence Guido-DiBrito); and *Toward Acceptance: Sexual Orientation Issues on College Campuses* (2000, with Vernon Wall). She is also a member of the editorial board for the *Journal of College Student Development*. In addition, Evans has numerous journal articles and book chapters to her credit and has presented more than one hundred programs and papers at professional association meetings. Her research interests include gay, lesbian, and bisexual issues; the impact of the campus environment on students; student development; and diversity in higher education.

Evans has an extensive record of service to student affairs professional associations, most recently serving as president of the

American College Personnel Association in 2001–02. She was named an annuit coeptis senior professional by ACPA in 1989, an ACPA senior scholar in 1998, and an ACPA diamond honoree in 2002. In recognition of her scholarly work, Evans was given the ACPA Contribution to Knowledge Award in 1998.

John H. Schuh is professor of educational leadership at Iowa State University in Ames, where he is also department chair. Previously he held administrative and faculty assignments at Wichita State University, Indiana University (Bloomington), and Arizona State University. He earned his bachelor of arts degree in history from the University of Wisconsin-Oshkosh, and his master of counseling and Ph.D. degrees from Arizona State.

He is the author, coauthor, or editor of more than 175 publications, including 16 books and monographs, more than 45 book chapters, and 90 articles. His most recent previous publication, *Assessment Practice in Student Affairs* (with Lee Upcraft), was released in 2001. He has served as editor and chair of the ACPA Media Board and as a member of the editorial board of the *Journal of College Student Development.* Currently he is editor in chief of the *New Directions for Student Services* Sourcebook Series and is associate editor of the *Journal of College Student Development.* Schuh has made more than 170 presentations and speeches to campus-based, regional, and national meetings. He received a Fulbright award to study higher education in Germany in 1994.

Schuh has served on the governing boards of the American College Personnel Association, the National Association of Student Personnel Administrators (twice), and the Association of College and University Housing Officers (twice). He is a member of the Evaluator Corps of the North Central Association of Colleges and Schools and served as convention chair of the 2000 NASPA annual conference in Indianapolis.

Schuh has received the Contribution to Knowledge Award and the Presidential Service Award from the American College Personnel Association, the Contribution to Research or Literature award from the National Association of Student Personnel Administrators, and the Leadership and Service Award and S. Earl Thompson Award from the Association of College and University Housing Officers-International. He has been elected as a senior scholar diplomate by the American College Personnel Association, was chosen as one of seventy-five diamond honorees by ACPA in 1999, and named a pillar of the profession by NASPA in 2001.

Foundations of Student Affairs Practice

Part One

Historical, Theoretical, and Philosophical Foundations

In this first part (Chapters One through Four), we present the historical, theoretical, and philosophical background for our later examination of specific learner outcomes. Understanding the context in which learning occurs is critical to developing a program or intervention that assists students in becoming self-confident, mature individuals who lead fulfilling lives and make a positive contribution to their community and to society. Learner outcomes are greatly affected by the type and mission of the institution in which a student enrolls, the processes by which the student develops in college, aspects of the campus environment, and the attention given to learning by student affairs staff and other educators.

Institutional type and mission largely determine the educational outcomes that a college or university stresses and how it attempts to accomplish them. In Chapter One, we trace the evolution of higher education institutions in the United States from their inception to the present, noting the increasing variation of institutional mission and purpose that has occurred in response to the needs of society. We also discuss the implications of institutional mission and goals for creating a unique culture and emphasis in various types of institutions.

In Chapter Two, we lay out a comprehensive overview of student development theories that currently inform educational practice. These theories focus on how students grow and change in college and how their development interacts with and influences their achievement of specific learning outcomes. These theories are particularly instructive in designing appropriate experiences to accomplish specific educational goals.

The campus environment has a powerful impact on student development and learning. In Chapter Three, we review campus environment theories and how the campus can be intentionally constructed to positively contribute to educational outcomes. We examine physical, structural, human-aggregate, and perceptual aspects of the environment, introduce models of environmental assessment and redesign, and suggest environmental interventions that can further student learning.

In recent years, leading student affairs associations have called for renewed emphasis on student learning in student affairs practice. Stressing that student learning is the primary outcome of college, they suggest that student affairs educators have an important role to play in its achievement. In the final chapter in Part One, we examine current literature on this subject with the goal of helping student affairs practitioners better understand their role as educator, as well as the importance of collaboration between student affairs and academic affairs to improve the learning climate on campus.

After completing the four chapters in Part One, you should have a comprehensive understanding of the institutional, developmental, and environmental factors influencing the outcomes of college. This overview of the historical, theoretical, and philosophical underpinnings of student affairs and higher education should be of great assistance as you explore the complexity and dynamic interplay of variables that contribute to positive educational outcomes for your students. We revisit salient concepts and ideas presented in Part One when we explore specific learner outcomes in the second part of this book.

Chapter One

Examining Institutional Missions

What are institutions of higher education about? Why do they exist? What do they attempt to accomplish? What is or should be the nature of the task(s) of higher education? These questions and others have been contemplated and debated virtually as long as higher education has existed in the United States. Through examining institutional mission statements, one finds an impressive array of purposes articulated by colleges and universities. This chapter is an overview of evolving, characteristic purposes of higher education as illustrated by mission statements from a variety of institutions. Such institution-level analysis is critical because an institutional mission statement identifies the salient and desirable outcome characteristics of graduates.

By no means should this chapter be construed as presenting either a comprehensive historical overview of higher education or a complete taxonomy of institutional purposes and characteristics. Instead, in this chapter we illustrate how various representative institutions approach higher education and trace some of the historical developments in the United States that have informed evolving notions of the purpose of higher education. What emerges is a multiplicity not only of institutional types but also evolving purposes that now coexist or are articulated in some combination.

This range of missions and purposes is related to a similarly wide range of student learning outcomes, which have broadened over the centuries as institutions added dimensions to their mission and purpose that in a previous era would never have been considered to have a place in higher education. The mission of an

3

institution "influences all aspects of the day-to-day institutional life and the future and development of the college or university" (Barr, 2000, p. 25). Kuh, Schuh, Whitt, and Associates (1991) asserted: "Together, mission and philosophy provide a rationale for the institution's educational programs, policies, and practices" (p. 41). One of the best ways to understand what an institution of higher education desires to accomplish is to study the mission statement and compare what it says about the institution's aspirations with what it actually accomplishes.

Higher Education's Roots: The Liberal Arts College

As Weingartner (1992) pointed out, "since the days of Plato and Protagoras, someone has always written about and prescribed how the young should be educated" (p. 1). Documentation of higher education mission and purpose in the United States begins with the colonial colleges, of which Harvard, founded in 1636, was the first. Others followed over the years, among them William and Mary, Yale, the College of New Jersey (now Princeton University), and King's College (now Columbia University). These colleges were founded to offer an educational experience for young men preparing to become leaders in their community. Most students came from affluent families, and religious education was a central part of the collegiate experience for these young men. All of the colonial colleges had a religious affiliation, and, to apply a contemporary label, all were private.

The curriculum of these colleges was prescribed; that is, all students took the same classes. No major or minor fields existed, and the curriculum was classical in nature. Such courses as Greek, Latin, rhetoric, and mathematics dominated the curriculum. No attempt was made to offer "practical" courses such as engineering or business management, since these did not fit with the purposes of higher education. Brubacher and Rudy (1997) asserted that "it is useless to argue whether the colonial colleges were intended to be theological seminaries or schools of higher culture for laymen. They were clearly designed to perform both functions" (p. 6).

After the revolutionary war ended, liberal arts colleges continued down the course charted for them, although Brubacher and

Rudy (1997) pointed out that preparation for the ministry had declined somewhat. The classical curriculum continued until the notable debate triggered by the Yale Report of 1828. This document, issued to quell a growing call for colleges to teach more practical subjects, vigorously defended the status quo: "Undergraduate education, the argument continued, should *not* attempt to include professional studies" (Lucas, 1994, p. 133, italics in original), but should instead be a foundation for all of the professions. Lucas (1996) added that the liberal arts college's function was "one of academic, intellectual and moral preparation for professional life. . . . The point needs to be emphasized that students' specific career goals notwithstanding, broad liberal learning was *thought to be* the best possible preprofessional training" (p. 53).

The roots of a liberal arts education are deep, and the philosophy is clear: the undergraduate experience is to impart broad knowledge about a wide range of subjects—not training for a specific professional career. A liberal education was intended to help students better understand the world around them, communicate lucidly, solve problems, and become better learners. Echoes of this form of education abound in contemporary higher education. Consider, for example, these excerpts from institutional publications:

> Harvard College adheres to the purposes for which the Charter of 1650 was granted: "The advancement of all good literature, arts, and sciences; the advancement and education of youth in all manner of good literature, arts and sciences; and all other necessary provisions that may conduce to the education of the . . . youth of this country." In brief: Harvard strives to create knowledge, to open the minds of students to that knowledge, and to enable students to take best advantage of their educational opportunities. [Harvard University Website, citing Harry L. Lewis, dean of Harvard College, Feb. 23, 1997; see the references at the end of this chapter for the date on which Websites were accessed].

> The Royal Charter formally establishing King's College in 1754 defined the institution's goal as "the Instructions and Education of Youth in the Learned Languages and Liberal Arts and Sciences." This mandate has not essentially changed, even with the transformation of King's College into Columbia, one of the world's foremost research universities [Columbia University Website].

> The mission of Occidental College is to provide a gifted and diverse group of students with a total educational experience of the highest quality—one that prepares them for leadership in an increasingly complex, interdependent and pluralistic world. The distinct interdisciplinary and multicultural focus of the College's academic program seeks to foster both the fulfillment of individual aspirations and a deeply-rooted commitment to the public good [Occidental College Website].

Each statement builds on its respective founding assertion that a liberal, broadly-based approach to undergraduate education serves students best over a lifetime. This philosophy of education also was the earliest model for higher education in this country; it is the one to which other models for higher education are frequently compared. The enduring power of the liberal arts legacy should not be underestimated. In some institutions, a form of liberal arts curriculum is the substantive academic undergraduate experience. In almost all other colleges and universities, the liberal arts approach to undergraduate education is echoed instead in the "general education," "core," or "foundational" requirements for all undergraduate students.

Nevertheless, the definition of what constitutes a liberal education can vary dramatically from institution to institution. For example, Seattle University has a prescribed core curriculum, and all students must take certain courses in order to graduate. On the other hand, although Grinnell College requires that students participate in a first-year seminar and declare a major, curricular requirements for all students are minimal (Grinnell College Website). Both institutions profess a strong liberal arts education. Which is better? This question has no answer, since quality is measured by the extent to which students' needs are met within the context of each institution's definition of a liberal education.

The Emergence of the State University

Exactly which was the first state university in the country is a matter of dispute, according to Brubacher and Rudy (1997), although they concede that the University of Virginia, founded in 1819, was "America's first real state university" (p. 147). Although other universities were founded in the antebellum period, one should not confuse these institutions with the contemporary state university. These institutions were modest in nature, often receiving minimal funding from state government, and "the level of instruction seems to have been far below what would have been deemed university work in Europe" (Brubacher & Rudy, 1997, p. 155).

As these institutions developed, the debate intensified about the extent to which the curriculum should offer a practical form of education leading to the professions. Whether this was a function of the development of state universities, a matter of timing, or a combination of these two factors or others, the fact is that "a disproportionate number of leaders in all of the major professions from the 1820s onward *were* college graduates notwithstanding that lack of formal academic credentials did not necessarily preclude professional attainment" (Lucas, 1994, p. 136, italics in original).

At this point in time (just before the Civil War), the debate over the curriculum was also in many ways a debate about the purpose and corresponding outcomes of a college education: Should higher education train the mind and result in a liberally educated person, or should higher education incorporate practical knowledge and thus have a vocational dimension? As one example, Lucas (1994) pointed to California's superintendent of public instruction, who demanded to know in 1858 for which occupations a college prepared students, amid others' assertions that an institution of higher learning was never intended to supply technical skills needed for practicing any occupation. Increasing demands for including practical knowledge in the curriculum were met with the passage of federal legislation that led to land-grant colleges.

In 1916, John Dewey observed: "Liberal education aims to train intelligence for its proper office: to know. The less this knowledge has to do with practical affairs, with making or producing, the more adequately it engages intelligence" (1916/1985, p. 262). The establishment and evolution of the land-grant college served to challenge the perspective that intelligence is not optimally engaged by practical study at an institution of higher education. Early land-grant colleges began to coexist with institutions advancing the more traditional liberal arts approach, and some institutions attempted to offer both kinds of education.

Development of the Land-Grant College

Named for U.S. Rep. Justin Morrill from Vermont, the Morrill Land Grant Act of 1862 made grants of land to support institutions of higher education. In such states as Wisconsin, Illinois, and Missouri, the land grants enhanced the state's existing public universities. In others such as Iowa and Kansas, the land grants led to establishing new institutions. The land-grant act mandated a practical curriculum; subjects included mechanics (engineering) and agriculture. Although in contemporary higher education circles few would challenge the appropriateness of these fields as areas of study within higher education, at the time the act was passed many scholars had serious doubts about the legitimacy of this curriculum. Concern surrounding the nature of the curriculum and the ultimate purpose of higher education was a weighty issue of the times and was debated vigorously even within the newly organized land-grant colleges: "Confusing the situation still further was the chronic disagreement that existed over the proper balance to be struck within a land-grant institution between traditional classical studies and technical specialties" (Lucas, 1994, p. 151).

Concomitant with the development of a broad-based curriculum, the land-grant ideal also included attention to economic and social development. The land-grant college literally belonged to the citizens of the state; extension services ensured the college's presence throughout the state. For example, the history of extension in Wisconsin indicates "the Wisconsin Idea": "extension education programs to address the relevant social, economic, environmental and cultural issues of its citizens" (University of Wisconsin Extension History Website). The contemporary mission includes strengthening "the economy of Wisconsin and the economic interests of working people" (University of Wisconsin Extension Mission Website).

These and other unique features of the land-grant college were reflected in an institutional mission statement that differed greatly from the mission statement of the liberal arts college. Here are two statements that contrast markedly with those of the liberal arts colleges cited earlier:

> Kansas State University is a comprehensive, research, land-grant institution first serving students and the people of Kansas and also the nation and the world [Kansas State University Website].

> Colorado State University has a unique mission in the state of
> Colorado. The land-grant concept of a balanced program of
> teaching, research, extension, and public service provides the
> foundation for the University teaching and research programs,
> Agricultural Experiment Station, Cooperative Extension, and
> Colorado State Forest Service [Colorado State University Website].

Attention to the practical aspects of higher education was assured
with the development of the land-grant university, and the
espoused purposes of higher education were broadened to include
at least two identifiable and somewhat conflicting purposes. Some
institutions emphasize their goal to liberally educate students for
further learning and for positions of responsibility in later life—
the legacy of the liberal arts college. Others primarily foster preparing students with the vocational and professional knowledge they
need for a career—a product of the land-grant institution. As
Dewey observed in 1916, "Our actual system is an inconsistent
mixture. . . . In the inherited situation, there is a curious inter-
mingling, in even the same study, of concession to usefulness and
a survival of traits once exclusively attributed to preparation for
leisure" (Dewey, 1916/1985, p. 266).

With the development of the extension model, the means of
delivering knowledge was also altered, along with the nature of the
"students" who would learn. This outreach method of knowledge
delivery is also discussed later in this chapter as it relates to development of specialized institutions of higher education.

Graduate Education and Research

As the land-grant colleges were developing in the post–Civil War
period, interest in research and creative activity was growing at
many universities. As a consequence of their exposure to European
education in general and German universities in particular, university presidents in this country began to press for development
of research activities and graduate education. Developing graduate education became one of several factors that eventually distinguished a university from a college. Introducing research as an
important dimension of university work was taken especially seriously in some quarters, as some doubted whether undergraduate

education even belonged in the university. Clark University, for example, refused admission to undergraduates for the first fifteen years of its existence (Lucas, 1996).

Perhaps the most noteworthy example of the development of graduate education in the United States was the founding of Johns Hopkins University, which started as a graduate institution and only later developed an undergraduate educational program. Even today, graduate students outnumber undergraduates at selected institutions. MIT is one example of this enrollment pattern, with approximately 55 percent of the student body consisting of graduate students (Massachusetts Institute of Technology Website).

The development of the graduate dimension of higher education adds to institutional complexity and signifies yet another purpose of higher education. To be sure, not all students at these universities seek to be admitted to graduate school or become a researcher, but research institutions point out that their research activity benefits all through its integration into the undergraduate experience. Note the role of research in undergraduate education in these statements:

> The unique educational philosophy of Johns Hopkins was first articulated more than a century ago by Daniel Coit Gilman, the university's first president. Gilman believed that the highest quality education must be carried out in a research environment and that the best training, whether undergraduate or graduate, takes place under the supervision of an active researcher [Johns Hopkins Website].

> Caltech conducts instruction at both the undergraduate and graduate levels and, including its off-campus facilities, is one of the world's major research institutions. Its mission to train creative scientists and engineers is achieved by conducting instruction in an atmosphere of research, accomplished by the close contacts between a relatively small group of students (approximately 900 undergraduates and 1,100 graduate students) and the members of a relatively large faculty (approximately 280 professorial faculty and 130 research faculty) and a postdoctoral population of approximately 400 [California Institute of Technology Website].

Student Diversity in Higher Education

With the passage of time and the development of several social movements in the United States came the advent of colleges designed to serve specific, previously underserved groups of students. Colleges were founded to serve historically underrepresented populations as denoted by race, gender, and economic means. A brief discussion of these institutions follows.

Development of Colleges for African Americans

Even now, educational opportunities for African Americans lag far behind those for whites by a variety of measures, not the least of which is the percentage of high school graduates who attend a postsecondary institution. Description of this national tragedy has been discussed widely in other publications (see, for example, Bowen & Bok, 1998; Cuyjet, 1997; Fleming, 1984), but it is important to remember that only modest opportunities for higher education were available for African Americans before the Civil War, followed by a thirty-year growth period in colleges for African Americans (Brubacher & Rudy, 1997). The need was great, since before the Emancipation Proclamation just twenty-seven individuals were listed in a roster of all black graduates (Lucas, 1994).

The growth of colleges for African Americans was stimulated by reformers from the North and by the second Morrill Act. Lucas (1994) estimated that approximately two hundred colleges for African Americans were established in the 1870s and 1880s, though only forty private institutions and seventeen public ones survived to the turn of the century. The educational quality of these institutions was poor, "offering virtually nothing in the way of defensible college-level instruction" (p. 162).

The passage of the second Morrill Act led to establishment of land-grant institutions in the South and border states for African Americans. The strategy followed by southern states in founding institutions under the second Morrill Act was to keep higher education segregated; a total of nineteen black institutions were eventually founded under its auspices (Hoffman, Snyder, & Sonnenberg, 1996). In an era of "separate but equal" educational opportunity in the southern states, this approach was an understandable strategy. Lamentably, the institutions were not equivalent. As Lucas (1994) concluded, "separation, not equality, was the reality so far as institutions of higher learning were concerned" (p. 165). Despite the lack of financial support by state legislatures and state educational agencies and predominant curricular emphasis on skilled trades (Brubacher & Rudy, 1997), the surviving colleges persisted, and many have become outstanding institutions of higher education.

The purposes of these institutions (now termed historically black colleges and universities, or HBCUs) have evolved to mirror many of the same educational purposes of other colleges and universities, but service to African Americans clearly continues as the primary focus. As the proportion of African Americans enrolled at traditionally white institutions has increased over the past twenty-five years, the proportion of African American students enrolling at HBCUs has declined. However, even though HBCUs as a group enrolled only 2 percent of all postsecondary students in 1994 (including more than 230,000 African American students), they awarded 28.5 percent of the baccalaureate degrees and 15.3 percent of the master's degrees earned by African Americans in that same year (Nettles & Perna, 1997).

The development of institutions of higher education for African Americans added a diversity of institutions and missions to the higher education landscape. Consider the mission statements of two of them:

> Founded in 1895 as an institution to serve primarily the educational needs of Black students, the University provides instruction, research and public extension services, consistent with its land-grant and public functions, for all segments of the population to achieve their personal, educational and professional goals [Fort Valley State University Website].

> Wilberforce University is the nation's oldest private African-American University. It has a deep commitment to provide academically excellent and relevant higher education, particularly for African-American men and women. This commitment aims at increasing the probabilities of success in college and subsequent careers for individuals previously excluded from the mainstream American society [Wilberforce University Website].

Higher Education for Women

As was the case for African Americans, limited higher education opportunities for women were available until the nineteenth century. With some exceptions, higher education for women came about through establishment of seminaries and colleges for women. Of the estimated three thousand women enrolled in college in 1870, twenty-two hundred were students at women's colleges and the remaining eight hundred were enrolled at coeducational colleges and state universities. An additional eight thousand women were enrolled in women's seminaries (Newcomer, cited in Horowitz, 1984). Women's colleges strived to offer high-quality education for young women; Vassar College's liberal arts curriculum was comparable to that of Yale (Horowitz, 1984). Brubacher and Rudy (1997) pointed out, though, that objectives for women's education included "preparing women for home duties and cultivating their grace and gentility" (p. 69). Religious objectives also were important at many women's colleges.

Despite such stated goals, however, opposition to women's colleges was strong. Among the charges identified by Brubacher and Rudy (1997) were the questionable value of higher education for women, concern that higher education could have an adverse effect on the health of women, and convictions that women were intellectually inferior to men. Horowitz (1984) cited additional opposition concerning women entering a public career or calling upon graduation from a women's college. Depending upon the college, women clearly did not enjoy the range of curricular or career choices available to men; their curricular options were often limited to teaching, nursing, or home economics. Although this may no longer be the case, women are still underrepresented in many traditionally male professions, notably the professoriate, where they make up approximately one-third of full-time faculty members (Glazer-Raymo, 1999; "The American College Teacher: National Norms for the H.E.R.I Faculty Survey," cited in Magner, 1999; U. S. Department of Education, 1997, Table 227).

Nevertheless, the influence of women's colleges grew along with enrollment until the era of the First World War (Horowitz, 1984). Lucas (1994) estimated that by 1900 about three-quarters of all institutions of higher education admitted men and women, although women would not become the majority of entering first-year students until 1976 (U.S. Department of Education, 1997).

Contemporary women's colleges bring a unique dimension to the higher education landscape. Consider these mission statements:

> Regis College is a Catholic, liberal arts and sciences college for women. As a liberal arts college, Regis College accepts the responsibility for providing an environment in which the student can gain a breadth of knowledge in the humanities, the natural sciences and the social sciences as well as an in-depth understanding of one sector of learning [Regis College Website].

> Mills is an independent liberal arts college for women, with graduate programs for both women and men. The curriculum fosters excellence: Mills educates its students to think critically and communicate responsibly and effectively, to accept the challenges of their creative visions, and to acquire the knowledge and skills necessary to understand the natural world and effect thoughtful changes in society [Mills College Website].

Additionally, the College of St. Catherine, the largest Catholic college for women in the United States, has adopted as its vision statement "to be the world's pre-eminent Catholic college educating women to lead and influence" (College of St. Catherine Website).

Tribal Colleges

Native Americans have the lowest rate of educational attainment of any racial or ethnic group in the United States. Very few matriculate in an institution of higher education and fewer still graduate (Cunningham & Parker, 1998). Many factors militate against the pursuit of higher education by American Indians, including a long history of mistreatment in white-run educational institutions, significant incidence of poverty, geographic isolation, and cultural barriers (Cunningham & Parker, 1998; Pavel, Swisher, & Ward, 1995).

Ironically, educating native populations was a stated goal of our earliest institutions of higher education; Harvard, Dartmouth, and the College of William and Mary all included provisions for educating native youth (Boyer, 1997). However, their purpose in giving American Indians the opportunity to obtain an education was to convert them to Christianity and hasten their assimilation into European American culture. Few Indians chose to pursue education under these conditions, and many who did enroll soon left. Later attempts were made to educate Indian children in boarding schools away from their tribes, again with the goal of eradicating Indian culture. The education that Indians received in these institutions was poor; the minority who did graduate were ill-prepared for employment either on or off their reservation.

In 1928, the Meriam report, a scathing indictment of government policy with regard to native populations, produced evidence of mismanagement in government-run boarding schools and criticized both the quality and content of the curriculum at these institutions (Boyer, 1997). Many schools were closed, and some attempts at educational reform were begun. During Franklin Roosevelt's administration, efforts were made to initiate community-based schools on the reservations, but control still remained in the hands of white administrators. Scholarships and federal loan programs became available for Native Americans to attend college, but poor educational preparation and cultural barriers prevented many from enrolling. According to Boyer (1997), many tribes had no college graduates at the start of World War II.

After that war, programs were cut as funding was diverted to postwar recovery (Boyer, 1997). Attempts were made to terminate federal government involvement in Indian affairs, to eliminate reservations, and to relocate Indians to metropolitan areas. These efforts did great damage to Indian self-sufficiency and self-esteem, but they also led to greater resolve on the part of Native Americans to control their own destiny. The Self-Determination Act of 1975 gave tribes greater autonomy as well as support for technical training.

Native American leaders saw the need for members to obtain advanced education to assume new responsibility on the reservation and to successfully manage tribal affairs (Boyer, 1997). Many tribes encouraged their young people to attend college, but the results were disappointing. The dropout rate for Native Americans was as high as 75 percent in 1970 (Fuchs & Havighurst, 1973). Throughout the decade of the 1960s, American Indian leaders, particularly those of the Navajo nation, discussed the possibility of establishing their own colleges. These discussions eventually led to establishment of Navajo Community College, now called Diné College, in 1968 (Boyer, 1997). Over the next few years, several other tribal colleges were established.

A total of twenty-eight tribally chartered colleges now exist in twelve states. There are also three federally chartered Indian colleges and one Canadian tribal college (American Indian Higher Education Consortium, 1999). All the tribal colleges are either fully accredited or, in the case of three new institutions, candidates for accreditation. All offer the associate's degree as well as certificates for programs that are less than two years in length. Four colleges also offer the bachelor's degree and two offer the master's degree.

The tribal colleges modeled themselves after community colleges, stressing local control and commitment to the needs of the population they serve (Boyer, 1997). In addition to their academic programs, they offer community services such as literacy programs, counseling, child care, cultural enrichment initiatives, and programs designed to encourage economic development (Cunningham & Parker, 1998). Unlike other community colleges, they have a dual academic mission: first, to recognize and honor the heritage of the tribe through using culturally based teaching techniques; and second, to offer traditional coursework based on Western models of learning that transfer to four-year institutions and prepare students to function in European American society (Tierney, 1992). Boyer (1997) noted that "graduates leave with both a better understanding of their own culture and the ability to take part in the larger American society. For the first time, they do not have to make the painful choice between one culture and the other" (pp. 25–26). The tribal colleges also afford a personalized atmosphere and emphasize close relationships between faculty and students (Cunningham & Parker, 1998; Tierney, 1992).

The tribal college is succeeding despite many obstacles. The greatest problem is funding. Because the colleges are located on federally controlled land, funding is available only from federal appropriations and from tuition (Cunningham & Parker, 1998). Little or no state or local support exists. Because federal appropriations have never equaled the amount of money authorized for the support of tribal colleges, they receive only about two-thirds of the financial support available to other community colleges. Lack of funds has resulted in a number of other problems for tribal colleges, among them inadequate facilities and equipment as well as low salaries for faculty.

The success of the tribal college, despite these challenges, is indicated by rapid expansion (American Indian Higher Education Consortium, 1999). Enrollment has increased from twenty-one hundred in 1982 (O'Brien, 1992) to almost twenty-five thousand in 1995–96 (American Indian Higher Education Consortium, 1999). Enrollment in tribal colleges has increased more rapidly than that of Native American students at other institutions of higher education (American Indian Higher Education Consortium, 1999). In Montana, North Dakota, and South Dakota, more Native American students are enrolled in tribal colleges than are enrolled in predominantly white institutions.

Although data are limited, Native American students at tribal colleges seem to be obtaining a degree in higher numbers than are Native American students in other institutions of higher education (American Indian Higher Education Consortium, 1999). In addition, a significant number of these two-year graduates are transferring to four-year colleges, where they earn a higher GPA and have a higher graduation rate than their peers who started at a four-year college. Tribal college graduates also have a high rate of employment, ranging from 85 to 93 percent (Boyer, 1997). A large majority of these graduates stay on their reservation, contributing meaningfully to the well-being of their tribe (Cunningham & Parker, 1998).

The unique character and contributions of the tribal college can be seen in the mission statements of two of these institutions:

The mission of Northwest Indian College is to provide post-secondary educational opportunities for Northwest Indian people. The college curriculum will include academic, vocational, continuing, cultural, community service, and adult basic education. Specific courses of study and activities will be offered in accordance with identified needs and interests of the various Native American communities. The college will also provide in-service training, planning, research, and evaluation services to tribal institutions and departments as needed. The college will provide opportunities for individuals to gain self-sufficiency in a rapidly changing, technological world while recognizing and nurturing their cultural identity [Northwest Indian College Website].

The College of the Menominee Nation (CMN) is founded from the highest ideals of the Menominee Indian Tribe and the Menominee people. Its first emphasis is upon its students: to provide a quality environmental and educational experience which will allow those choosing to pursue their individual goals to achieve a significant position in the world's economy and social structure. This overall goal will be pursued out of the history, traditions, values and aspirations of the Menominee Indian Tribe, thus strengthening and preserving the Tribe's history, traditions, values, and aspirations [College of the Menominee Nation Website].

The Hispanic-Serving Institution

Hispanics are the fastest growing minority population in the United States (Benítez, 1998). Unfortunately, their participation in higher education lags behind their numbers in the general population. Although more Hispanic youths are attending college than in past years, they are not doing so at a rate equivalent to other ethnic groups. The gap between Hispanic and white college graduates actually increased from 15 to 21 percentage points between 1992 and 1996 (National Education Goals Panel, 1996). They now make up almost 8 percent of all students in postsecondary education, an increase from 4.5 percent in 1985 (U.S. Department of Education, 1998a). However, the number of degrees awarded has remained static since the 1980s, at around 6 percent of all associate's degrees and 4 percent of all bachelor's degrees awarded in 1993 (President's Advisory Commission, 1996).

Around half of all Hispanic students in the United States attend one of about 177 colleges and universities with more than 25 percent Hispanic enrollment (U.S. Department of Education, 1998b). Hispanic-serving institutions (HSIs) were formally designated as such in Title III of the Higher Education Act of 1965 (HEA) as amended (Benítez, 1998). This act was designed to extend assistance to low-income and underrepresented populations in higher education. To be recognized as an HSI under this act, an institution has to meet three criteria:

- Have at least 25 percent Hispanic undergraduate full-time equivalent enrollment
- Provide assurances that no less than 50 percent of its Hispanic students are low-income individuals *and* first-generation college students
- Provide assurances that an additional 25 percent of its Hispanic students are low-income individuals or first-generation college students (Title III, Sect. 316, HEA, as cited in Benítez, 1998, pp. 59–60)

Currently, 131 institutions meet these criteria; 50 are located in Puerto Rico (Benítez, 1998). Most of them are two-year colleges. Because they have limited endowments and rely heavily on federal and state funds, many of these schools are underfunded. As a result, their ability to provide adequate facilities, current technology, and competitive salaries is problematic.

Students choose HSIs because they are close to home and inexpensive (Benítez, 1998). Most Hispanic students must work while attending college and usually take longer to complete a degree than white students do. The dropout rate of Hispanic students nationwide is 33 percent higher than for whites, but students who attend HSIs are more likely to complete a degree than those who attend other institutions (U.S. Department of Education, 1997, as cited in Benítez, 1998).

Because the number of Hispanic youths in the United States is rapidly increasing, Hispanic-serving colleges and universities play an increasingly important role in educating this population (Benítez, 1998). Despite the fact that many of these colleges have become Hispanic-serving by default rather than design, most are aware of their unique mission in serving this underrepresented population. The mission statements of two Hispanic-serving colleges underscore this commitment:

UTB/TSC advances economic and social development, enhances the quality of life, fosters respect for the environment, provides for personal enrichment, and expands knowledge through programs of research, service, continuing education and training. It convenes the cultures of its community, fosters an appreciation of the unique heritage of the Lower Rio Grande Valley and encourages the development and application of bilingual abilities in its students. It provides academic leadership to the intellectual, cultural, social and economic life of the binational urban region it serves [University of Texas at Brownsville and Texas Southmost College Website].

WNMU recognizes as a strength the multilingual, multinational population of the region and state as it accepts the responsibility to be particularly mindful and supportive of the unique opportunities afforded by this diversity. The University aspires to promote increased access to all levels of education and to help people better understand and appreciate diversity, tolerance and cooperation. The University is committed to help preserve and enhance the rich cultural heritage of the region it serves and to broaden its student diversity by reaching out to students from other states and regions [Western New Mexico University Website].

Development of colleges for historically underrepresented students added another dimension to the overall purposes of higher education: social justice. Higher education was seen as a means by which members of groups who had been or were still systematically excluded from the benefits of American society could take their rightful place. Before establishment of these institutions, very few members of a nondominant population had any opportunity for postsecondary education. Establishment, then, of these institutions played a crucial role in underscoring how important educating all citizens was to the nation. Although these institutions did not necessarily broaden the curriculum of higher education, they added an important element to the purposes of higher education.

The Community College

The development of the community college continued the theme of broadening access to higher education for individuals who had few or no postsecondary educational options. In this respect, the community college exemplified the tradition of improving access to higher education that began with the founding of the land-grant institutions and continued with colleges for people of color and women. Consistent with a college transfer mission, many community colleges offered a wide range of liberal arts coursework. However, community colleges also expanded the higher education curriculum by including subjects for academic study that heretofore were excluded.

Community colleges are the most rapidly growing sector of higher education. Relatively few existed prior to World War II (Lucas, 1996), but toward the close of the twentieth century community colleges enrolled more than one-third of all students in the United States (U.S. Department of Education, 1997, Table 173) and accounted for more than half of all undergraduate students in public institutions (Table 198). The community college permits greater access for members of historically underrepresented groups, including returning adult students and students of color (U.S. Department of Education, 1997); it is a low-cost local option for higher education.

The community college serves a variety of purposes, among them vocational training, college transfer preparation, enrichment, certification programs, and direct links with local industry. The community college has a service mission to the local municipality and is designed to enrich the lives of the local citizens, as the following mission statements illustrate. Moreover, with a wide-ranging curriculum, students can take a variety of special courses geared not necessarily toward career preparation but instead toward life skills building and general interests, as shown by general automotive repair at Mesa (Arizona) Community College (Mesa Community College Website) and basic dog obedience at Miami-Dade Community College (Miami-Dade Community College Website). Offering these courses side by side with more traditional academic offerings demonstrates the dramatic range of coursework at a community college. In this case, various curricula provide vocational education, enrichment and skill development courses not leading to a degree, and college transfer programs.

Community colleges welcome virtually all students, and high school completion is often not required for admission (Lucas, 1996). Tuition and fees—especially at a public two-year college—are typically very modest in comparison with a four-year institution. Development of the community college permitted greater access for students, who were characterized by Lucas (1994) as those "lacking the means or desire to embark upon a four-year curriculum directly from high school, or those who sought relatively inexpensive instruction within commuting distance" (p. 221). With the emergence of the community college, courses of study that departed even further from the traditional liberal arts education became part of higher education, and the student body further diversified. Consider these community college mission statements:

> Compton Community College is dedicated to providing the residents of its service region with diverse education, careers and cultural opportunities. The college is committed to offering a comprehensive curriculum in a safe, friendly and accessible environment that prepares students to achieve their personal and professional goals [Compton Community College Website].

> The mission of Scottsdale Community College (S.C.C.) is to create accessible, effective and affordable environments for teaching and learning for the people of our communities in order that they may grow personally and become productive citizens in a changing multicultural world [Scottsdale Community College Website].

The Municipal University

The municipal university, originally operated by a local municipality, represents another variation on the theme of increased access to higher education. Brubacher and Rudy (1997) noted that six contemporary institutions (the universities of Louisville, Akron, Charleston, Toledo, and Cincinnati; and Wichita State University) were each founded by an act of city government. As a contemporary institution, the municipal university tends to be part of a state system of higher education while keeping its mission focused on the urban area and its needs. Citing Title XI of the Higher Education Act of 1980, Rothblatt (1988) noted that "today higher education institutions are defined as urban if their location is in a city, if their student body is recruited locally, if improved access is emphasized, if professional or specialized programs of study are featured, and if the institution repeatedly shows itself sensitive to urban social and economic problems" (p. 130).

Therefore, even though a number of institutions are located in a municipal setting, the defining characteristic of the municipal university is that it is materially of the city rather than merely being located in the city.

Brubacher and Rudy (1997) also pointed out that these institutions offer educational opportunities for greater metropolitan residents in the same way that the state university or land-grant college increased access for students from small towns and rural areas; "the net result was to accelerate and broaden the already powerful movement for democratic higher learning" (p. 168). According to Lucas (1994), those who attend such institutions include returning adult students, people seeking a second career, students who had dropped out of college, those with families and children, or those who were unable to afford a full-time residential college experience. Municipal university students often maintain their local professional and personal responsibilities during their college experience. As has been the case with so many of the institutions identified in this section of this chapter, the municipal institution broadened access to higher education to groups of people who simply had no other alternative and, without its existence, would not have had the advantage of higher education.

Additionally, it is common for such an institution to develop specialized curricula and institutes to meet the needs of the urban area served. Examples of this are Wichita State University's National Institute for Aviation Research, which helps serve the local aviation industry; and the link between the Urban Studies Institute of the University of Louisville and metropolitan Louisville. Clearly, the relationship between the institution and the urban area's economic needs results in a variety of activities with a veneer of vocationalism attached. No one pretends that vocationalism is an unacceptable focus at a municipal institution; in fact, just the opposite is true.

Mission statements from such institutions illustrate not only their educational services but also their close ties to the metropolitan area. Consider two mission statements:

> The role of and mission of the University of Nebraska at Omaha
> reflect a distinctly metropolitan emphasis. Accordingly, many
> of the academic majors, research activities and public service
> programs respond to its urban/suburban environment
> [University of Nebraska at Omaha Website].

> The University of Louisville shall serve as Kentucky's urban/
> metropolitan university. Located in the Commonwealth's largest
> metropolitan area, it shall serve the specific education, intellectual,
> cultural, service and research needs of a diverse population,

including many ethnic minorities and placebound, part-time, nontraditional students [University of Louisville Website].

The Special-Purpose Institution

Rounding out the constellation of higher education settings is the special-purpose institution of higher education, which often has a relatively narrow curriculum designed to produce graduates with a specialty in a narrow academic discipline or professional skill. Among these are the Colorado School of Mines, Embry Riddle Aeronautical University, the Culinary Arts Institute, the Fashion Institute of Technology, and the military service academies. Curricula are tied narrowly to vocational outcomes, as in becoming a mining engineer, aerospace engineer, or military officer. Consider these mission statements:

> Mission statement of The School of the Art Institute of Chicago: To establish and conduct comprehensive programs of education including preparation of visual artists, teachers of art, and designers; to provide education services in written, spoken and media formats [School of the Art Institute of Chicago Website].

> The mission of the South Dakota School of Mines and Technology is
>
> • To prepare men and women for an enhanced quality of life by providing a broad educational environment which fosters a quality educational experience leading to baccalaureate and post-baccalaureate degrees emphasizing science and engineering.
> • To contribute to the expansion of knowledge through programs of basic and applied research, scholarship and other creative endeavors.
> • To utilize the special capabilities and expertise on the campus to address regional, national, and international needs [South Dakota School of Mines and Technology Website].

The Virtual University

With the start of a new century, the concept of what education is and how it is acquired has been broadened to the point where a case can be made that higher education is virtually everywhere. With the development of educational delivery systems that use television and the Internet, students can participate in postsecondary education anywhere with a technological link. For example, the University of Phoenix has focused its online classes on the needs of working adult students. Here is the mission statement:

> The University of Phoenix is a private, for-profit higher education institution whose mission is to provide high quality education to working adult students [University of Phoenix Website].

This example, then, illustrates how the site at which one participates in higher education has become nearly irrelevant. Just as important, what constitutes higher education has evolved as well.

Discussion

Over a period of more than 350 years, higher education in the United States has evolved from a narrow experience designed to prepare young men for a lifetime of leadership, and perhaps civic service, to offering a variety of educational experience to virtually all citizens. Access over the centuries has broadened dramatically; although not every person can enroll in any institution, there is an institution available to serve virtually every citizen. From narrow purposes in the beginning, higher education institutions now exist for wide-ranging purposes often defined by institutional history and culture, geography, market niche, financing, or a combination of these factors and others. All institutions, however, have the potential to make an important contribution to the growth of students.

In tracing the emergence of various institutional types in higher education, we see clearly not only that a diversity of institutional purposes exists but that an evolving sense of appropriate delivery systems for higher education has emerged as well. In terms of purpose, any one institution may adopt one or a combination: liberally educating students, providing career or vocational preparation, furthering social justice, enhancing personal development, or participating in economic development.

The purposes of an institution also inform its curricular emphasis and academic opportunities and in turn suggest a sense of the kind of student-level outcome the institution intends to promote. For example, the rate of student job placement is regarded as a central indicator of institutional effectiveness for a vocationally oriented institution or program, while the rate at which students gain acceptance to graduate study is an important success indicator for a liberal arts institution.

Not all institutions pursue each outcome with equal vigor. As Howard Bowen (1977) noted before introducing his taxonomy of higher education's goals for college students, "each of the goals is, to a degree, considered an important responsibility of higher education. But this does not mean that every institution pursues every one of these goals or gives the same emphasis to all of them. There is room for variety among institutions in their goal patterns" (p. 54).

The second strand of evolution implicit in this chapter involves the kind of learning experience employed to foster the student-level outcomes described. No longer limited to the lecture as the traditional knowledge-delivery method, learning now includes a range of experiences: individual or group distance learning (for example, through Web-based courses); and—broadly defined—laboratory experiences such as internship, externship, service learning, credit for life experience, and other forms of out-of-class experience. For instance, Jacoby and Associates (1996) identified a variety of credit-bearing experiences that only a few decades ago would have been considered inappropriate for college students. Self-paced as well as self-directed learning has become increasingly accepted in higher education. Although in one sense these new delivery systems are made possible by technological advances in travel, communication, and information, educational experiences such as distance education and internship nonetheless maintain roots in earlier educational programs, as with apprenticeship for the study of professions such as law and medicine, and Chautauqua programs that afforded a distance learning opportunity in the nineteenth century.

In summary, not only has the appropriate content for a college education evolved, so has what is considered to be appropriate delivery and experience for facilitating desired learning. In light of these multiple educational purposes, myriad student-level outcomes are also increasingly desired along with demonstration that such outcomes are being realized. In the chapters immediately following, selected aspects of student development theory, environment theory, and student learning are examined as they inform discussion of student outcomes and assessment of outcomes. The second part of the book is devoted to discussing the outcomes themselves, developmental insights into each of them, and effective learning interventions designed to promote and realize these outcomes among students.

References

American Indian Higher Education Consortium, and the Institute for Higher Education Policy. (1999). *Tribal Colleges: An introduction.* Retrieved Dec. 28, 1999. (www.aihec.org/intro.pdf)

Barr, M. J. (2000). The importance of institutional mission. In M. J. Barr, M. K. Desler, & Associates, *The handbook of student affairs administration* (2nd ed., pp. 25–49). San Francisco: Jossey-Bass.

Benítez, M. (1998). Hispanic-serving institutions: Challenges and opportunities. In J. P. Merisotis & C. T. O'Brien (Eds.), *Minority-serving institutions: Distinct purposes, common goals* (New Directions for Higher Education, no. 102, pp. 57–68). San Francisco: Jossey-Bass.

Bowen, H. R. (1977). *Investment in learning.* San Francisco: Jossey-Bass.

Bowen, W. G., & Bok, D. (1998). *The shape of the river: Long term consequences of considering race in college and university admissions.* Princeton, NJ: Princeton University Press.

Boyer, P. (1997). *Native American colleges: Progress and prospects.* Princeton, NJ: Carnegie Foundation for the Advancement of Teaching.

Brubacher, J. S, & Rudy, W. (1997). *Higher education in transition: A history of American colleges and universities* (4th ed.). New Brunswick, NJ: Transaction.

California Institute of Technology Website. Accessed May 13, 1999. (www.caltech.edu/catalog/98CAT1.html)

College of the Menominee Nation Website. Accessed Dec. 28, 1999. (www.menominee.com/cmn/MISSION.HTM)

College of St. Catherine Website. Accessed Sept. 13, 1999. (www.stkate.edu)

Colorado State University Website. Accessed May 12, 1999. (www.colostate.edu/catalog/theuniv.pdf)

Columbia University Website. Accessed May 12, 1999. (www.columbia.edu/cu/aboutcolumbia/mission.html)

Compton Community College Website. Accessed July 29, 1999. (www.compton.cc.ca.us/homepage.htm)

Cunningham, A. F., & Parker, C. (1998). Tribal colleges as community institutions and resources. In J. P. Merisotis & C. T. O'Brien (Eds.), *Minority-serving institutions: Distinct purposes, common goals* (New Directions for Higher Education, no. 102, pp. 45–56). San Francisco: Jossey-Bass.

Cuyjet, M. J. (1997). *Helping African-American men succeed in college* (New Directions for Student Services, no. 80). San Francisco: Jossey-Bass.

Dewey, J. (1985). *Democracy and education*. Carbondale, IL: Southern Illinois University Press. (Original work published 1916).

Fleming, J. (1984). *Blacks in college: A comparative study of students' success in black and white institutions*. San Francisco: Jossey-Bass.

Fort Valley State University Website. Accessed May 13, 1999. (http://fvsu.edu/pages/home.htl)

Fuchs, E., & Havighurst, R. J. (1973). *To live on this earth: American Indian education*. Garden City, NY: Doubleday.

Glazer-Raymo, J. (1999). *Shattering the myths: Women in academe*. Baltimore, MD: Johns Hopkins University Press.

Grinnell College Website. Accessed Oct. 10, 1999. (www.grinnell.edu/www/catalog/acadprogs/acadreq/html)

Harvard University Website. Accessed May 12, 1999. (www.harvard.edu/help/faq_index.html)

Hoffman, C. M., Snyder, T. D., & Sonnenberg, B. (1996). *Historically black colleges and universities: 1976–1994*. (NCES 96–902.) Washington, DC: U.S. Department of Labor, Office of Educational Research and Improvement, National Center for Education Statistics.

Horowitz, H. L. (1984). *Alma mater: Design and experience in the women's colleges from their nineteenth-century beginnings to the 1930s* (2nd ed.). Amherst, MA: University of Massachusetts Press.

Jacoby, B., & Associates. (1996). *Service-learning in higher education*. San Francisco: Jossey-Bass.

Johns Hopkins University Website. Accessed May 13, 1999. (http://jhu.edu/~admis/catalog/intro/unique.html)

Kansas State University Website. Accessed May 12, 1999. (www.ksu/edu/provost/planning/mission.html)

Kuh, G. D., Schuh, J. H., Whitt, E. J., & Associates. (1991). *Involving colleges*. San Francisco: Jossey-Bass.

Lucas, C. J. (1994). *American higher education*. New York: St. Martin's Press.

Lucas, C. J. (1996). *Crisis in the academy*. New York: St. Martin's Press.

Magner, D. K. (1999). The graying professoriate. *Chronicle of Higher Education, 46*(2), A18–A19.

Massachusetts Institute of Technology Website. Accessed May 13, 1999. (www.mit.edu/admissions/whynot/index.html)

Mesa Community College Website. Accessed May 13, 1999.
(http://mcinfo.mc.maricopa.edu/sis/schedule.new?AUT&1996&s
ite=all)

Miami-Dade Community College Website. Accessed May 13, 1999.
(www.kendall.mdcc.edu/otis/bspecial.htm)

Mills College Website. Accessed May 12, 1999. (http://www.mills.edu)

National Education Goals Panel. (1996). *The National Education Goals
Report: Building a nation of learners.* Washington, DC: Government
Printing Office.

Nettles, M. T., & Perna, L. W. (Eds.). (1997). *The African American education data book. Vol. 1: Higher and adult education.* Fairfax, VA: Freder-
ick D. Patterson Research Institute of the College Fund/UNCF.

Northwest College Website. Accessed Dec. 28, 1999. (www.nwic.edu/)

O'Brien, E. M. (1992). *American Indians in higher education.* (American
Council on Education Research Brief, vol. 3, no. 3.) Washington,
DC: American Council on Education.

Occidental College Website. Accessed May 12, 1999.
(www.oxy.edu/oxy/welcome/mission.htm)

Pavel, M., Swisher, K., & Ward, M. (1995). Special focus: American Indian
and Alaska Native demographic and educational trends. In D. J.
Carter & R. Wilson (Eds.), *Minorities in higher education 1994: Thir-
teenth annual status report* (pp. 33–56). Washington, DC: American
Council on Education.

President's Advisory Commission on Education Excellence for Hispanic
Americans (1996). *Our nation on the fault line: Hispanic American education.* Washington, DC: Government Printing Office.

Regis College Website. Accessed May 12, 1999.
(http://www.regiscollege.edu)

Rothblatt, S. (1988). London: A metropolitan university? In T. Bender
(Ed.), *The university and the city: From medieval origins to the present*
(pp. 119–149). New York: Oxford University Press.

School of the Art Institute of Chicago Website. Accessed May 12, 1999.
(www/artic/edu/saic/about/mission)

Scottsdale Community College Website. Accessed July 29, 1999.
(www.sc.maricopa.edu/info/aboutscc.htm)

South Dakota School of Mines and Technology Website. Accessed May
12, 1999. (www/sdsmt/edu/catalog97/mission.htm#mission)

Tierney, W. (1992). *Official encouragement, institutional discouragement:
Minorities in academe—The Native American experience.* Norwood, NJ:
Ablex.

University of Louisville Website. Accessed May 12, 1999.
(http://www.louisville.edu)

University of Nebraska at Omaha Website. Accessed May 12, 1999. (http://www.unomaha.edu)

University of Phoenix Website. Accessed May 27, 1999. (www.uophx.edu/uop/_gettokn.htm)

University of Texas at Brownsville and Texas Southmost College Website. Accessed Dec. 30, 1999. (www.utb.edu/about/index.html)

University of Wisconsin Extension History Website. Accessed May 28, 1999. (www.uwex.edu/exthist/html)

University of Wisconsin Extension Mission Website. Accessed May 28, 1999. (www.uwex.edu/mission/html)

U.S. Department of Education. (1997). *Digest of education statistics 1997.* (NCES 98–105.) Washington, DC: National Center for Education Statistics.

U.S. Department of Education. (1998a). *The condition of education 1998.* (NCES 98–013.) Washington, DC: National Center for Education Statistics.

U.S. Department of Education (1998b). *Fact sheet: Title III institutions.* Washington, DC: Government Printing Office.

Weingartner, R. H. (1992). *Undergraduate education: Goals and means.* New York: ACE/Macmillan.

Western New Mexico University Website. Accessed Dec. 30, 1999. (www.wnmu.edu/univ/intrwnmu.htm#Mission)

Wilberforce University Website. Accessed May 13, 1999. (www.wilberforce.edu/uni/mission.htm)

Chapter Two

Putting Student Development in Context

Student development theories focus on the interpersonal and intrapersonal changes that occur while a student is in college and the factors that contribute to these changes (Knefelkamp, Widick, & Parker, 1978). Development is viewed as a positive growth process in which the individual becomes able to deal with increasingly complex experiences (Sanford, 1967). Rodgers (1990) defined *student development* as "the ways that a student grows, progresses, or increases his or her developmental capabilities as a result of enrollment in an institution of higher education" (p. 27). This chapter is an overview of the evolution of student development theory, the aspects of development that theorists have explored, and the major theoretical work that has guided the practice of student affairs. A general overview of how student development theory can guide student affairs practice and enhance student learning concludes the chapter.

Student development theory emerged from the disciplines of psychology and sociology, as student affairs became a profession in the midtwentieth century (Evans, Forney, & Guido-DiBrito, 1998). Faced with significant changes occurring on college campuses, particularly those related to the social upheaval caused by the Vietnam War, the civil rights movement, and the women's movement, student affairs administrators sought guidance in understanding their increasingly diverse student population. Their end goal was to learn how an institution of higher education could best serve the needs of its clientele. Psychologists such as Erik Erikson (1950, 1968) and Jean Piaget (1952) posed a picture of human development over the life span, while sociologists and social psychologists (for example, Lewin, 1936) contributed an understanding of environmental and group influences that affect human interaction. Later theorists, notably Nevitt Sanford (1967), Douglas Heath (1968), Roy Heath (1964), and Kenneth Feldman and Theodore Newcomb (1969), built on this early work, specifically examining the experiences of students in college.

Arthur Chickering's *Education and Identity* (1969) was a comprehensive overview of the developmental issues faced by students in college and factors in the college environment that affected outcomes. A contemporary publication, William Perry's *Forms of Intellectual and Ethical Development in the College Years: A Scheme* (1968), introduced a theory that purported to explain the cognitive development of students in college. Kohlberg's theory of moral development (1976) rounded out the "big three" theoretical examinations of young adult development that became the mainstay of developmentally based student affairs practice through the 1980s.

A drawback of these early student development theories, however, was that they were based on white, middle-to-upper-class, largely male populations aged eighteen to twenty-two. Patricia Cross (1971) was one of the first theorists to point out that not all students fit this profile and that educators have to understand the characteristics and needs of a broader range of students. Beginning in the 1980s, a number of writers began to question the generalizability of existing theories, and new approaches were introduced that explored the experiences and perceptions of women; people of color; and gay, lesbian, and bisexual individuals. Gilligan's examination, in 1982, of women's moral development was the first widely recognized work with this focus. Other theorists examined gender differences in cognitive development, among them Belenky, Clinchy, Goldberger, and Tarule (1986) and Baxter Magolda (1992), and identity development (Josselson, 1987, 1996). Theories of adult development, including work by Levinson (1978), Levinson and Levinson (1996), Neugarten (1979), Schlossberg, Waters, and Goodman (1995), Baltes (1987), Perun and Bielby (1980), and Elder (1995), have also been influential in calling attention to the issues that may be experienced by older students in college. In recent years, theorists have written about the development of racial and ethnic identity (for example, Atkinson, Morten, & Sue, 1993; Cross, 1991, 1995; Helms, 1993, 1995; Helms & Cook, 1999; Phinney, 1990); gay, lesbian, and bisexual identity (for example, Cass, 1979; D'Augelli, 1994; McCarn & Fassinger, 1996); and gender identity (Downing & Roush, 1985; O'Neil, Egan, Owen, & Murry, 1993; Ossana, Helms, & Leonard, 1992).

Several theorists have focused on specific domains of development. In addition to the work of Kohlberg (1976) and Gilligan (1982) on moral development and the identity development theories already noted, theorists have addressed faith development (Fowler, 1981; Parks, 1986, 2000) and career development (Holland, 1985/1992; Krumboltz, 1981; Super, 1990, 1992). Broader conceptualizations of development include theories examining ego development (Loevinger, 1976), orders of consciousness (Kegan, 1982, 1994), and maturity (Heath, 1968, 1977).

The move toward a student learning focus in student affairs, described later in this volume, led to interest in how students learn and process information. A number of theorists have examined this process. Kolb's experiential learning model (1984) was one of the first to be used in student affairs. Gardner's theory of multiple intelligences (1987, 1993) has recently received attention.

Major theories that have influenced the practice of student affairs are reviewed here. They are grouped under the developmental domain that they address.

Psychosocial Development

Psychosocial development theories focus on the developmental issues that individuals must address over the course of their life span, related to how they define themselves, how they relate to others, and what they choose to do with their lives. Psychosocial theorists posit that at various points throughout the life course, different concerns will take precedence and become major challenges the individual must resolve in order to advance. Included in this grouping are the developmental theory of Erikson (1959, 1968) and the work on identity development done by Marcia (1966) and Josselson (1987, 1996) that grew out of his approach; Chickering's seminal work (1969; Chickering & Reisser, 1993) on the developmental issues of college students; adult development theories; theories specifically examining racial, ethnic, sexual orientation, and gender identities; and career development theories.

Erikson

Erik Erikson (1959) was the first psychologist to discuss development across the life span. He also differed from earlier psychologists by placing development in a social context and considering the role played by the external environment in addressing the developmental issues faced by people throughout the course of their lives. Erikson stressed that historical-cultural values and norms influence identity development (Widick, Parker, & Knefelkamp, 1978b).

Erikson (1959, 1968) posited that individuals pass through eight stages, each of which is characterized by a specific developmental task. Each new stage appears when internal biological and psychological changes intersect with environmental conditions that require action; for example, a girl reaching puberty is confronted with social norms concerning the role expectations for teenage girls in American culture. Although these stages are not necessarily age-linked, they do arise in an invariant sequential order. Erikson labeled each of his stages by identifying the basic attitude, or life orientation, that results from successful or unsuccessful resolution of the associated developmental issues, which Erikson called crises. Three of these stages occur during the preschool period: trust versus mistrust, autonomy versus shame and doubt, and initiative versus guilt. The next stage, industry versus inferiority, arises during childhood. Identity versus role confusion and intimacy versus isolation occur during adolescence and young adulthood. During middle adulthood, generativity versus stagnation is addressed. The final stage, integrity versus despair, occurs in late adulthood.

The speed with which an individual moves through each stage varies; in some instances, a person's development may become arrested in a particular stage, resulting in failure to move further. In addition, as an adult, an individual may revisit earlier stages to resolve a particular conflict differently. For instance, a woman who married at an early age and later divorced may need to reconsider issues of intimacy and identity as she begins to make a new life for herself as a single person.

The developmental crisis associated with each stage presents the individual with opportunity while at the same time increasing vulnerability (Erikson, 1968). When a developmental crisis is successfully resolved, the person gains new skills and a positive self-concept is acquired. Less successful resolution of crisis, however, can lead to lowered self-esteem and interfere with the person's ability to successfully address issues in the future. Regression to a previous stage often occurs as the individual attempts more successful resolution of a previous crisis.

Although Erikson (1959, 1968) did not specifically address the developmental issues facing college students, his work has great utility for educators working with students of all ages who are facing various developmental crises. In addition, a number of theorists built on Erikson's ideas while focusing on the development of college students. The work of several of these theorists is discussed here.

Marcia

Using a sample of college men, James Marcia (1966) empirically examined the identity development process in young adults, basing his work on Erikson's theory (1959, 1968). He focused on the role of exploration and commitment in identity formation. Marcia (1980) referred to exploration as a "crisis, defined in terms of the presence or absence of a decision-making period" (p. 161). Decision making results in commitment: a personal investment in the decision. Marcia examined three areas in which crisis and commitment occur: political ideology, vocational choice, and religion. In a later study of college women, Schenkel and Marcia (1970) added sexual values and standards as a fourth component of identity.

Marcia (1966) proposed four styles of identity resolution:

1. *Identity diffusion.* A crisis may or may not have been experienced, but in either case no commitment has been made; however, the person is not concerned about lack of direction.
2. *Foreclosure.* No crisis has been experienced, but a commitment has been made on the basis of the values of significant others, particularly parents.
3. *Moratorium.* The person is in the midst of a crisis and is actively attempting to make a commitment.

4. *Identity achievement.* The person has experienced a crisis and has worked through it, making a commitment.

These styles of identity resolution are not necessarily hierarchical; nor does an individual always reach identity achievement.

Marcia's work (1966, 1980) underscores the various approaches that students take in resolving identity issues. Student affairs professionals need to be aware of the differing needs of students using each style and design interventions accordingly.

Josselson

Using Marcia's model (1966) as a starting point, Josselson (1987) examined the identity development of women. She first interviewed women during their senior year in college and then re-interviewed them twelve years later; she continued to follow these women as they moved into midlife (Josselson, 1996). Josselson found that, for women, social, sexual, and religious values were more significant areas of crisis and commitment than were occupational and political values. Her findings also suggested that women's identity was determined, to a large extent, by the degree to which they accepted or deviated from the value system held by their parents, particularly by their mother.

More than any other factor, crisis in relationships, particularly relationships with men, led to growth and change in the lives of the women Josselson (1987) interviewed. Relationships with men were an opportunity for either self-validation and support or fulfilled dependency needs for women. For the women in this study, work was less central in their lives than relationships.

Josselson's work (1987, 1996) highlights the important roles played by relationships in the lives of women. An educator must keep in mind that how a woman constructs her relationship with her parents as well as with significant others in her life is a salient factor in her self-definition.

Chickering

Like Marcia (1966, 1980) and Josselson (1987, 1996), Chickering (1969) built on the work of Erikson (1959, 1968). Seeing establishment of identity as central during the college years, Chickering sought to further delineate the issues involved in this process. To acknowledge recent research findings and to be more inclusive of various student populations, in 1993 Chickering and Reisser revised Chickering's original theory.

Taking into account social, emotional, and intellectual aspects of well-being, Chickering and Reisser (1993) identified seven "vectors of development." Chickering (1969) used the term vectors "because each seems to have direction and magnitude—even though the direction may be expressed more appropriately by a spiral or by steps than by a straight line" (p. 8). Chickering noted that students move through the vectors at differing rates and often need to recycle through particular vectors as they are confronted with new situations. Issues associated with one vector may affect those of another vector; for instance, a student's sense of intellectual competence affects how she or he approaches career decision making.

Chickering's vectors are not rigidly hierarchical, but they do build on each other, leading to greater complexity, stability, and integration as issues associated with each vector are resolved. Chickering and Reisser's revised vectors of 1993 are developing competence, managing emotions, moving through autonomy toward interdependence, developing mature interpersonal relationships, establishing identity, developing purpose, and developing integrity.

Chickering and Reisser (1993) posited that environmental factors play an important role in achievement of the developmental tasks noted here. They proposed that seven aspects of the college environment influence development: institutional objectives, institutional size, faculty-student interaction, curriculum, teaching practices, diverse student communities, and student affairs programs and services. Three principles undergird these factors: integration of work and learning, recognition and respect for individual differences, and acknowledgement of the cyclical nature of learning and development.

Chickering's theory (Chickering & Reisser, 1993) serves as a powerful reminder of the issues faced by students in college. It makes some suggestions for designing the college environment to facilitate the development of students. In addition to assisting educators in their work with individual students, programming and policy are both informed by Chickering's theory.

Adult Development

As noted earlier, Erikson (1959) was the first psychologist to recognize that development occurred over the entire life span rather than just during childhood and adolescence. Many theorists since Erikson have explored growth and change during adulthood and factors that contribute to this process. These theories are of increasing relevance for individuals who work with college students, not only because the theories forecast the process of development for traditional-aged students but also because educators must be aware of the issues faced by the increasing number of older adults attending college. Adult development theories can be broadly grouped into three categories by the degree to which attention is focused on psychological processes versus sociological influences on development. Moving from internally focused to externally oriented, these categories are life stage, life events and transition, and life course. Integrative approaches form a fourth category.

Life Stage Perspectives

Life stage theorists see development as following a predictable pattern over the life course. As he or she moves through childhood, adolescence, and adulthood, the individual addresses similar developmental tasks that build on each other, contributing to growing complexity and leading to individuation. Internal maturational processes, influenced to some degree by environmental factors, trigger the appearance of each task. Levinson and Levinson (1996) identified differences on the basis of gender in how components of each stage were carried out; for example, marriage roles were separated into the homemaker role for women and the provider role for men. Life stage theories can be subdivided into two approaches: those in which stages of development are presented as age-linked (for example, Gould, 1978, Levinson, 1978; Levinson & Levinson, 1996) and those in which stages are viewed as sequential but not necessarily tied to a specific age (Erikson, 1959; Vaillant, 1977).

In addition to Erikson's theory (1959), the life stage theory of Daniel Levinson (1978) is among the best known and most used of these approaches. He saw a person's life as having an underlying structure or design at any given point. Key components of the life structure include relationships with significant others, such as life partners, children, or work colleagues; or with a significant social group, such as a church or club.

According to Levinson (1978), throughout one's life periods of stability alternate with periods of transition during which life is examined and change is likely to occur. He saw lives as divided into twenty-five-year eras, each having a distinct character, separated by major transitions. In Levinson's model, each era is divided into three stages, beginning with a novice phase, in which the person tests out an initial life structure; a mid-era transition, in which this initial structure is evaluated; and a culminating phase, during which the life structure is modified and improved.

During the first era of a person's life, which lasts from approximately age twenty-two to age forty, the first major life structure is created. The novice phase of this era, labeled "entering the adult world," is characterized by two elements: forming a relationship with a mentor and establishing a dream. A mentor is a somewhat older person who offers advice, support, and sponsorship, while the dream is an imagined picture of what one wants to become. During the "age-thirty transition," the novice life structure is evaluated and modified. The culminating phase of the first era, "settling down," involves finding a comfortable place in society and working to achieve one's dream.

A major transition occurs at midlife, from age forty to forty-five. At this time, a person considers such questions as, What have I accomplished in life? and What do I want in the future? This transition may or may not involve a crisis, depending on how the person answers these questions. "Entering middle adulthood" may involve creating a totally new life structure or slightly modifying the previous structure. Similar patterns of reassessment and recreation occur as the individual moves into later life.

Life Events and Transition Perspectives

Theorists within this category (for example, Bridges, 1991; Fiske & Chiriboga, 1990; Schlossberg, Waters, & Goodman, 1995; Sugarman,

1986; and Whitbourne, 1985) suggest that what shapes a person's life are the significant individual events (marriage, birth, death) and cultural events (war, economic conditions, social movements) that they experience. Unlike the life stage theorists, life events theorists do not link a life event to a specific age or period. Rather, the life event itself is the focus. Life events theorists examine the meaning an event holds for the individual and how it is negotiated. Factors that may influence how a person experiences an event, such as its timing and probability, are also considered. Rather than being a point in time, a life event is viewed as a transition that the individual must negotiate over a period of time (Schlossberg et al., 1995).

The transition theory of Schlossberg and her associates (1995) is particularly helpful to educators working with students who experience many transitions during their time in college. Schlossberg and colleagues defined a transition as "any event, or non-event, that results in changed relationships, routines, assumptions, and roles" (p. 27). They were careful to point out that a transition exists only when a person labels it as such.

How an individual makes sense of a transition depends on its type, context, and impact. With regard to *type,* Schlossberg (1989) discussed the importance of examining whether a transition is anticipated or not. She also suggested that a nonevent—that is, an event that is expected but doesn't happen (such as failure to graduate from college, or inability to find a life partner)—can be as significant as an event that actually occurs. *Context* refers to the individual's relationship with the transition and the setting in which it occurs. A transition can be personal or it can happen to a significant other; both can affect the individual. The setting of a transition might be one's work environment, a personal relationship, community, and so forth. *Impact* involves how much an event affects the person and changes his or her life. An indicator of impact is the degree of stress one feels, which is dependent on "the ratio of the individual's assets and liabilities at the time" (Evans et al., 1998, p. 112).

Schlossberg, Waters, and Goodman (1995) stressed that a transition is a process, during which one moves from preoccupation with the transition to integration of the transition into one's life. The time needed to complete this process varies for each person, as does the outcome. The degree to which one successfully accomplishes this task is contingent on four sets of factors: situation, self, support, and strategies. The balance of deficits and resources within these categories determines "why different individuals react differently to the same type of transition and why the same person reacts differently at different times" (Schlossberg et al., 1995, p. 49).

Situation refers to aspects of the transition itself, such as what triggered it, the timing, how much control the individual has over it, whether a role change is involved, its duration, previous experience with a similar transition, concurrent stress, and the person's perception of who or what is responsible for the transition. *Self* includes personal and demographic characteristics (gender, age, stage of life, state of health, ethnicity). Psychological factors such as ego development, self-efficacy, determination, and values are also involved. *Support* includes intimate relationships, family, friends, and other sources of support found in an institution or community. Support may be emotional in nature or it may involve validation, aid, or feedback. It is important to assess whether the support is stable, role-dependent, or likely to change. *Strategies* refer to the approaches used to address the transition. The individual may attempt to modify the situation, control its meaning, or manage the stress incurred. Coping modes may include seeking information, direct action, inhibition of action, or changing one's thinking.

Life Course Perspectives

Life course perspectives use a sociological, rather than psychological, framework to examine life events. This approach includes theorists who associate development with social role taking (Hughes & Graham, 1990), the timing of life events (Bengston, 1996; Neugarten, 1979), and how people select and construct their environments (Elder, 1995). These theorists examine the socially constructed beliefs people hold about how such roles as parent, worker, life partner, and friend are to be played out. Factors such as modification of role (say, redefining the student role when one moves from high school to college), assumption of a new role (becoming a parent), and loss of a certain role (having a parent die) are seen as contributing to a shift in how individuals view themselves. The timing of life events is also a key factor in how the individual perceives and reacts to those events. According to these theorists, every society creates expectations about age-appropriate behavior. Events that are "off-time" (such as starting college at age forty) are more likely to cause stress than events that occur "on time"(Neugarten, 1979).

The life course perspective of Elder (1995), for example, helps the educator understand factors that affect development across the life span. Elder defined the social life course as "the interweave of age-graded trajectories, such as work and family careers, that are subject to changing conditions and future options; and to short-term transitions, ranging from birth and school entry to retirement" (p. 105). He emphasized "the social pathways of human lives, their sequence of events, transitions, and social roles" (p. 103). Four key concepts associated with this theory are historical change, human agentry, linked lives, and timing.

Elder (1995) contended that social forces shape the course of life. Both historical time and place affect development. For example, the Vietnam War certainly affected the decisions made by college men at that time; living near the World Trade Center on September 11, 2001, had an equally profound effect.

Elder (1995) also stressed that people actively plan their lives and make choices that affect their life course. These choices are influenced by their personal situation and how they interpret it. Facing the possibility of going to war during the Vietnam era, for example, required that young men take some action. Some chose to move to Canada while others enlisted or went in the service when they were drafted. Their personal belief systems and values, as well as their family circumstances, influenced their decision.

Elder (1995) pointed out that people's lives are intertwined; "personal actions have consequences for others, and the actions of others impinge on the self" (p. 112). A young woman whose fiancé chose to move to Canada, or who went to war and was killed, would obviously be affected by his decision.

Elder (1995) identified four aspects of timing that influence the life course: historical time, social timing, synchrony of the trajectories of oneself and significant others, and one's life stage at the point of social change. He defined social timing as "the incidence, duration, and sequence of roles and the related age expectations and beliefs" (p. 114). The influence of life stage at the point of social change is evident if one thinks about the varying degrees of influence the Vietnam War had on young babies versus college-age men.

Integrative Perspectives

Several theorists (Baltes, 1982, 1987; Magnusson, 1995; Perun & Bielby, 1980; Peters, 1989) have attempted to integrate biological, psychological, and sociological aspects of development into an inclusive model. For example, Baltes (1982) hypothesized that biological and environmental factors were the major determinants of development. These factors, he suggested, were influenced by forces related to the person's age, by historical events in the experience of particular cohorts, and by nonnormative influences important to specific individuals. Developmental changes over the life span, Baltes believed, occur as a result of the interaction of these factors. Baltes (1987) pointed out that there is no single direction for change in adulthood, with both growth and decline occurring. Magnusson (1995) also saw the individual functioning as an integrated organism—psychological, biological, and behavioral processes interacting continuously with situational factors in the environment.

Perun and Bielby (1980) viewed adulthood as consisting of a series of temporal progressions, sequences of events that follow unique timetables. Some of these life experiences are internal (physical maturation, intellectual development, moral development) while others are external (change in family, new work role). A timetable might be inevitable, such as the occurrence of biological change; or it may be more variable and self-determined, as when one attends college or the career one follows. Thus, for each individual the life path varies depending on how these factors intertwine. Societal norms and conditions that exist during a particular historical period also influence the timetables.

Perun and Bielby (1980) introduced the concept of asynchrony, which occurs when one or more dimensions are off-time in relation to the others. Asynchrony creates stress, but it can also induce change. Perun and Bielby noted that "synchronous movement through developmental progressions is contingent . . . on timing schedules established by the social structure with individuals experiencing rewards and punishments both intra-psychically

and socially relative to their lives' continuity with externally prescribed age norms" (pp. 105–106). This idea is particularly helpful
when working with students who are feeling societal pressure for
being off-time in attending college, establishing a career, or forming a significant relationship.

Adult development theories guide the educator in working
with students of all ages. They point out the aspects of life that are
important to people and how individuals are influenced by life
changes. Each approach focuses on an aspect of the process of
adult development; as such, each brings rich understanding of factors that an educator must consider in guiding students individually and in developing programs to assist them.

Racial and Ethnic Identity Theories

A number of theorists have examined how individuals come to
understand their racial and ethnic heritage and the role played by
ethnicity in their lives. These models can be divided into two categories: those focusing on the identity development process (Atkinson et al., 1993; Cross, 1991, 1995; Helms, 1993, 1995; Helms &
Cook, 1999; Phinney, 1990) and those exploring acculturation and
its impact on development (Isajiw, 1990; Rowe, Bennett, & Atkinson, 1994; Sodowsky, Kwan, & Pannu, 1995).

Minority Identity

Atkinson, Morten, and Sue (1993) introduced a model of minority identity development that they believe is applicable to all racial
and ethnic groups. Other models specific to particular racial and
ethnic groups (for instance, that of Cross, 1991, 1995) demonstrate
a similar progression in development.

The Atkinson, Morten, and Sue model consists of five stages
centering on how individuals feel about their own racial or ethnic
groups, how they perceive the white majority, and how they relate
to other minority groups. In *conformity,* the first stage, individuals
view their own racial or ethnic group as well as other minority
groups negatively, taking on the stereotypes and attitudes of the
majority culture. They demonstrate a preference for majority cultural values and behaviors. In the second stage, *dissonance,* indi-

viduals are confused and conflicted about beliefs and values, usually because of negative experience on the basis of race or ethnicity. The third stage, *resistance*, is characterized by rejection of white culture and embracing one's own culture. Other cultural groups are still viewed ambivalently, however, since individuals at this stage are quite ethnocentric.

Introspection follows as people begin to see themselves as unique individuals apart from their racial or ethnic group. They begin to realize that not everything about the dominant culture is bad and not everything about one's own culture is good. This is a period of evaluation and reflection. *Synergistic awareness*, the final stage in the model, is reached once a person achieves identity that incorporates appreciation and valuing of one's own culture, a sense of self-worth, willingness to acknowledge that some aspects of the majority culture are positive, and appreciation of other cultures. Atkinson, Morton, and Sue viewed development through these stages as a continuous process influenced by the types of positive and negative experience that individuals have with their own cultural group, the dominant cultural group, and other cultural groups.

Ethnic Identity

Phinney (1990) examined the process of ethnic identity development, basing her work on that of Erikson (1968) and Marcia (1966). Ethnic identity includes aspects of culture learned from one's family and community; it can include religion, language, social norms, and customs. Isajiw (1990) divided ethnic identity into two aspects. The first is external: observable social and cultural behavior, such as language, friendship, and participation in ethnic group functions and activity. The second is internal: a state of mind or feeling (including such cognitive components as self-image and an image of one's ethnic group, knowledge of the heritage and history of that ethnic group, and understanding of its values), moral components (such as feelings of group obligation and commitment to the group), and affective components (among them feelings of attachment to one's ethnic group, a preference for associating with members of that group, and comfort with its cultural patterns).

Phinney (1990) identified three stages of development. The first, *unexamined ethnic identity,* can take two forms. Diffusion consists of lack of interest in or concern with ethnicity, while foreclosure involves drawing on the interpretations of others for one's understanding of ethnicity. The second stage in Phinney's model, *ethnic identity search* (also called moratorium), is characterized by exploration and a desire to understand the role played by ethnicity in one's life. In the third stage, *achieved ethnic identity,* individuals have a clear, secure sense of their ethnicity.

In their bidirectional model of ethnicity, Sodowsky, Kwan, and Pannu (1995) suggested that there are two dimensions of ethnicity: the extent to which the individual has adopted a white identity and the degree to which he or she has retained identity associated with the ethnic heritage. The researchers proposed four orientations: bicultural, strong-ethnic, strong-white, and culturally marginalized identity. Their model is not linear; rather, individuals can move from one orientation to another over time depending on the situation. In their home communities, for example, students may exhibit a strong ethnic identity, while at college they may present as bicultural.

White Identity

The most recent iteration of Helms's model of white identity development is presented in Helms and Cook (1999). It focuses on the process by which individuals overcome internalized racism. There are two major phases of this process: giving up a racist identity, and creating a nonracist identity.

The entire process includes seven statuses. In the first status, *contact,* individuals are unaware of the racist nature of their actions and happy with the status quo. In *disintegration,* individuals experience conflict and distress as they become aware of their whiteness and the implications of some of their actions for other racial groups. *Reintegration* involves belief in the racial superiority of whites and engagement in acts of prejudice against those of other races. *Pseudoindependence* is characterized by an "intellectualized commitment to one's own socioracial group and subtle superiority and tolerance of other socioracial groups as long as they can be helped to conform to white standards of merit" (p. 92). An individual in *immersion* seeks out information about racial and ethnic groups, racism, and cultural understanding in an attempt to redefine what it means to be white. In this status, "the focus shifts from trying to change blacks to trying to change whites" (Evans, et al., 1998, p. 79). *Emersion* encompasses pride in developing a new white identity and interacting with other white people who share similar views. The final status, *autonomy,* is exemplified by internalization of a multicultural perspective and deep personal commitment to work to overcome racial oppression.

Rowe, Bennett, and Atkinson (1994) also examined white identity development, focusing on the attitude of the individual about being white and how attitude affects relationships with nonwhite people. Basing their work on Phinney's theory (1990), they identified seven types, using as a basis for categorization exploration of racial attitudes and commitment to them. *Avoidant* persons have not considered their own race and are not concerned about racial and ethnic matters. *Dependent* individuals have minimal awareness that being white is a racial identity but have not personally considered the implications of being white. Because of conflict between recent experiences and previously held attitudes, *dissonant* persons are often conflicted and confused about racial and ethnic issues and about how to view members of a racial or ethnic minority.

People who hold the fourth type of view, *dominative,* believe in the superiority of the majority culture and its legitimate right to dominate racial or ethnic minority peoples. An individual with *conflictive* views opposes obvious discrimination but does not support programs, such as affirmative action, designed to lessen the effects of discrimination. *Integrative* people believe that right intention and rational action will overcome past problems related to race and ethnicity. Finally, *reactive* individuals actively oppose racism and discrimination and identify strongly with racial or ethnic minority groups; however, they are sometimes paternalistic and come at issues from a largely white point of view. Both direct interaction with people of color and the opportunity to learn about individuals of other racial and ethnic backgrounds can lead to attitude change, according to Rowe, Bennett, and Atkinson.

As global consciousness increases and as the diversity of our country and college student population grows, racial and ethnic identity becomes salient. For a student who is a member of a nondominant population, gaining a clear sense of self as a racial and ethnic being and determining how one wishes to present oneself and relate to others often takes precedence over other developmental issues (Cross, 1991). Students who are members of dominant groups are also being challenged to consider their own identities in relation to those of the diverse individuals with whom they are in relationship (Helms, 1995). An educator must be cognizant of the important roles played by race and ethnicity in the lives of students and create opportunity for development to occur in this arena.

Gay, Lesbian, and Bisexual Identity

Levine and Evans (1991) reviewed a number of models of gay, lesbian, and bisexual identity development (for example, Cass, 1979; and Troiden, 1989) from both the psychological and the sociological literature that suggest this process moves through a series of stages. Later work by McCarn and Fassinger (1996) and D'Augelli (1994) presented alternative views of the developmental process. Some models focus on the internal process of coming to know oneself, while others concentrate on the external process of interaction with others and self-presentation.

Stage Models

In summarizing the models they reviewed, Levine and Evans (1991) identified four general stages of gay, lesbian, and bisexual identity. In level one, *first awareness*, "individuals are becoming conscious of homoerotic feelings and behaviors, generally with no sense of these feelings being 'okay'" (p. 11). The second level, *self-labeling*, "centers around individuals beginning to identify themselves as being gay and having early contacts with the gay community" (p. 11). The third level, *community involvement and disclosure*, is characterized by increased self-acceptance and greater willingness to share one's identity with others. The final level, *identity integration*, involves incorporation of one's sexual identity into one's overall sense of self. At this point, individuals are comfortable with who they are and how they interact with both heterosexual and nonheterosexual others.

Cass (1979) suggested that development through these stages depends on the interaction of psychological and environmental factors. The process by which a student experiences and interprets same-sex attraction is internal. However, development is facilitated by such external factors as positive interaction with individuals who are openly gay, lesbian, or bisexual; opportunities to socialize with gay, lesbian, and bisexual peers; and support from heterosexual allies.

McCarn and Fassinger

McCarn and Fassinger (1996) studied lesbian identity development. They saw development as occurring in two areas: individual sexual identity and group membership identity. With regard to both, the individual goes through stages from nonawareness to (1) awareness, (2) exploration, (3) deepening and commitment, and (4) internalization and synthesis. Individual sexual identity first involves feelings of being different, then having strong sexual feelings for a woman (or women). At the third stage the woman acknowledges, accepts, and acts on her sexual attractions, and in the final stage she weaves her sexual identity into her total identity.

Group membership identity focuses on interaction with other gay, lesbian, and bisexual people. The first step is becoming aware that people have differing sexual orientations. Then one explores one's own potential role and interaction with regard to the lesbian, gay, and bisexual communities. At the third stage, one becomes personally involved in the gay, lesbian, or bisexual community and is willing to accept the pluses and minuses of such involvement. Finally, one openly accepts the identity associated with being a member of a sexual minority group in the various contexts of one's life. The separation of psychological and social processes of identity development is an important contribution of McCarn and Fassinger's theory in that it underscores that people are not always at the same stage in each area.

D'Augelli

D'Augelli (1994) introduced a life span model of gay, lesbian, and bisexual identity development stressing that development is affected in important ways by the environment. According to D'Augelli, three sets of variables are influential: (1) the individual's actions and subjective interpretation of experiences, (2) interactions with important people in his or her life; and (3) the larger environment, including social norms, historical time, and geographical setting. He argued that identity is not fixed; rather, people change and develop across their entire life span in response to environmental conditions in which they find themselves, as well as physical and biological changes that they experience. Thus, no two individuals develop in the same way. He also stressed that the individual plays a role in his or her own development by making choices and interpreting the outcomes.

D'Augelli (1994) identified six intersecting identity processes that an individual must address. Every gay, lesbian, or bisexual person must exit the heterosexual identity that she or he and others have assumed. This process may involve telling others that one is not heterosexual and choosing to give up the privileges associated with this identity. The person must at the same time determine what it means to be gay, lesbian, or bisexual and how to present this new identity to others and interact with people in a variety of settings. Individuals must determine whether to reveal this identity to their parents, and if so, how to handle the parents' reactions and relate to them. Learning how to relate intimately to a significant same-sex partner is another challenge for a gay, lesbian, or bisexual person since there are few positive open role models of such relationships and little available information. A final aspect of gay, lesbian, and bisexual identity development is determining how one wishes to relate to the larger lesbian, gay, and bisexual community, including the extent to which one desires to be an activist in seeking rights for the entire community.

Gay, lesbian, and bisexual students and students who are questioning their sexual identity are increasingly visible on the college campus. Often the environment for these students is hostile (Evans & D'Augelli, 1996). If all students, including those who are gay, lesbian, and bisexual, are to be given equal opportunity for growth and development, services must be available to assist them in negotiating the challenges they face. The college must address the developmental needs of gay, lesbian, and bisexual students through counseling, support groups, and social outlets as well as educate heterosexual students about this population.

Gender Identity

Gender identity "concerns how one comes to see and understand oneself as a woman or a man in this society" (McEwen, 1996, p. 202). It is heavily influenced by societal norms and cultural expectations as well as by internal maturation and personal decision making (Ross-Gordon, 1999). McEwen (1996) contended that sexism is the foundation of various models of gender identity, in that both men and women must decide to what extent they will adhere to traditional expectations regarding the dominance of men and the submission of women. McEwen pointed out that "the experience and process of becoming aware of sexism, abandoning a sexist identity, and developing a nonsexist identity is different for women, the oppressed group, than it is for men, the dominant group" (p. 202).

O'Neil, Egan, Owen, and Murry (1993) introduced a model of gender identity applicable to both men and women, which they entitled the "gender role journey" (p. 167). They identified transitions in individuals' lives related to sexism and gender roles. These transitions are (1) acceptance of traditional gender roles; (2) ambivalence about gender roles; (3) anger, characterized by expression of negative feelings about sexism; (4) activism, which involves immersing oneself in learning about gender roles and reestablishing a gender identity that is nonsexist; and (5) celebration and integration of these new nonsexist gender roles into one's life.

Two models examine the development of women's gender identity: Downing and Roush's feminist identity model (1985) and Ossana, Helms, and Leonard's womanist identity model (1992). They are similar in that each starts with a stage in which traditional gender roles are unconsciously accepted. Then women become aware of the sexist nature of these roles as a result of personal experience. The third stage involves actively seeking out information about what it means to be a woman in our society. In the fourth stage, women develop a positive sense of themselves as women and integrate this new gender identity into their overall self-concept. Downing and Roush added a fifth stage, in which women take on an activist role in working to achieve a nonsexist society. Ossana, Helms, and Leonard, in contrast to Downing and Roush, permit greater personal choice with regard to whether or not a feminist ideology is adopted and suggest that it is not requisite for a healthy gender identity.

Rapidly changing gender roles often leave young people confused about who they are and what is expected of them as a man or woman. Choices concerning gender identity often become particularly salient during college as a student develops intimate relationships and makes decisions about a career. College and universities have an obligation to provide educational opportunities to explore aspects of gender and the implications of gender role choice through classes, programs, and personal and career counseling.

Career Development

The choice of a career and determining the role that career plays throughout one's life are major developmental issues people face. Over the years, theorists have presented many interpretations of the career development process. Osipow (1973) grouped various career development theories into four categories: trait-and-factor, sociological, developmental, and personality. Montross (1981) added a fifth category, social learning, to this list. Representative theories from each category are reviewed here.

Trait-and-Factor Theory

The earliest models of vocational choice (Parsons, 1909; Paterson & Darley, 1936; Williamson, 1939, 1965) viewed the individual as having specific identifiable traits, such as interests and aptitude, that could be matched with the requirements of a particular occupation to determine the field in which the individual would be happy and successful. These theorists suggested that career choice is successful when individuals know themselves well, have a clear picture of the requirements of various occupations, and are able to identify a good match. Rounds and Tracey (1990) characterized the trait-and-factor approach as a theory of person-environment fit, suggesting that this approach still has merit for assisting an individual in determining an appropriate career choice.

Sociological Theory

Sociological career theories focus on environmental factors that influence career decision making (Herr & Cramer, 1988). Such socioeconomic factors as parental occupation and income, family characteristics, educational and community environment, race, and gender have been hypothesized to play an important role in career selection (Blau & Duncan, 1967; Hotchkiss & Borow, 1990). Economic conditions, including job availability, awareness of opportunities and trends in the labor force, availability of training for various career options, and salaries associated with various employment options, also influence career decisions (Asbury, 1968; LoCascio, 1967; Schmeiding & Jensen, 1968).

Several theorists have suggested that chance is an important factor in career selection (Bandura, 1982; Caplow, 1954; Miller & Form, 1951). Osipow (cited in McDaniels & Gysbers, 1992, p. 42) noted that "people follow the course of least resistance in their educational and vocational lives. . . . People do react to their environments and follow those avenues educationally and vocationally which they perceive to be open to them with a minimum of difficulty."

Developmental Theory

In the 1950s, Donald Super began to formulate a theory that has evolved over time to include fourteen propositions suggesting how personal and societal variables intersect in the process of career development over the life span (McDaniels & Gysbers, 1992). Super (1992) suggested that there are nine overlapping life roles that contribute to a person's career and that have prominence to varying degrees over the life span: child, student, leisurite, citizen, worker, spouse, homemaker, parent, and retired person. Social determinants (the economy, labor market, community, peer groups, family, and the like) as well as personal determinants (needs, aptitudes, values, interests, and so on) influence each role and contribute to the career decision-making process as well as to the evolution of one's career.

Super (1990) viewed the individual's career as moving through five stages: growth, exploration (which is further broken down into fantasy, tentative, and realistic phases), establishment (which has trial and stable phases), maintenance, and decline. During a transition from one stage to the next, or during a period of uncertainty or instability in a person's career, additional growth, reexploration, and reestablishment occur.

Super (1990) noted that people's personal characteristics qualify them for a variety of occupations and that preferences, situations, and self-concepts evolve over the course of the life span, leading to various levels of satisfaction and choices over time. Fulfillment and successful adjustment in a particular setting, according to Super (1983), is related to the concept of career maturity (which he labeled "career adaptability" in adulthood)—"a readiness to engage in the developmental tasks appropriate to the age and level at which one finds oneself" (McDaniels & Gysbers, 1992, p. 48).

Personality Theory

On the basis of interests that people identify, John Holland (1985/1992) introduced a typology of six vocational personalities and six corresponding work environments, which he labeled *realistic* (concrete, practical, technical), *investigative* (scientific, intellectual, analytical), *artistic* (creative, spontaneous, expressive), *social* (people-oriented, helpful, empathic), *enterprising* (persuasive, extraverted, entrepreneurial), and *conventional* (orderly, conforming, data-oriented). Few people or environments are a "pure" type (say, entirely social). People are generally assigned a three-letter code (such as SAI) that represents their three strongest interests. Likewise, an environment is given a three-letter code that indicates the three types most strongly represented there.

According to Holland (1985/1992), career satisfaction, achievement, and persistence are contingent on the extent to which there is a match between the individual's vocational type and the work environment in which one finds oneself—in Holland's terms, a *congruent* situation. Holland believed that people seek out settings where they can use their skills and where their values and attitudes are appreciated. Thus they look for an environment that consists of people similar to them. (Holland's theory has been used to examine person-environment interaction as well as vocational decision making; this is examined in the next chapter).

Holland (1985/1992) arranged the six types around a hexagon, with adjoining types being most similar. The order of the letters around the hexagon is RIASEC. Holland used the term *consistency* to describe any three-letter code made up of similar types of people and environment (that is, those adjacent to each other on the hexagon). For example, a person whose three-letter code is SEC (letters next to one another on the hexagon) has interests that are quite consistent. The behavior and career aspirations of such a person would be more predictable and stable than those of a person whose interests were less consistent—say, having a code of RAE.

Holland (1985/1992) used the term *differentiation* to describe the strength of a person's interests in one area. A high score on one dimension (for instance, artistic) and low scores on other dimensions suggest highly differentiated interests. Scores that are more evenly distributed across dimensions indicate a variety of interests. Persons whose interests are highly differentiated are likely to be happy in a narrower range of occupations than those who have undifferentiated interests that can be adapted to a variety of careers. An individual with undifferentiated interests may have a harder time choosing a career than someone who has clearly differentiated interests.

Social Learning Theory

John Krumboltz and his associates (Mitchell, Jones, & Krumboltz, 1979) used social learning principles to explain the process of career decision making and adjustment. According to Krumboltz (1981), there are four factors that influence career decision making. The individual is born with a particular *genetic endowment* (race, sex, physical characteristics, and so on) and *special abilities* (such as intelligence, musical ability, and muscular coordination). How the person chooses to use these characteristics is influenced by *environmental conditions and events* (job opportunities, training opportunities, remuneration for various jobs, environmental and community conditions). The interaction of these personal and environmental variables creates particular *learning experiences,* either instrumental (the individual acts on the environment to produce a certain outcome, as in giving a speech that is well received) or associative (the person reacts to something that occurs in the environment—perhaps observing a play that has an emotional impact). *Task approach skills*—attitudes, skills, and work habits that affect career planning and job performance—develop as a result of the three influences just listed.

In addition to task approach skills, two other outcomes result from the interaction of these four influences. *Self-observation generalizations* are the opinions individuals hold of their abilities and traits–how individuals see themselves. These self-perceptions may or may not be accurate. *Action* refers to a specific step the person takes toward involvement in a career, such as applying for a job.

Learning is an important component of Krumboltz's model (1979). Success at a particular task as well as positive feedback from others about one's performance increase the probability that the activity will be repeated and that, as a result, skills at performing the task will improve. Positive reinforcement also increases an individual's preference for certain activities. Negative experience and feedback, by contrast, discourage repetition of behaviors and skills do not develop. The individual's desire to pursue a negatively reinforced activity is low. People tend to pursue career options in which they can use skills that they are good at and where significant others reinforce their performance or participation in that activity. Observing valued others being reinforced performing certain tasks is a positive influence as well. Krumboltz (1981) also stressed the importance of exposure to information about career options and related training and employment opportunities. He saw career development as a lifelong process, with each experience building on the previous ones (Minor, 1992).

These career development theories offer guidance for the educator in working with students who are engaged in career exploration and decision making. Each points to certain variables that warrant consideration in this process: external influences (sociological and social learning theory), person-environment fit (trait-and-factor and personality theories), and self-concept (developmental theory). Looking at career development through a number of lenses assists the student in making a well-considered decision about his or her life's work.

Cognitive Structural Theories

Cognitive-structural theorists consider how people interpret their experience and make meaning out of concepts to which they are exposed. Cognitive-structural development occurs in stages, in which persons gradually move from using simplistic assumptions about how the world operates in making a decision or interpreting experience, to basing their understanding on complex principles. Progression through this hierarchy of increasingly complex stages occurs as they engage in new experiences, are exposed to differing perspectives, and must resolve cognitive conflict.

Cognitive-structural theories can be grouped into categories, depending on the specific aspect of cognitive-structural development being considered. The categories are (1) epistemological reasoning, including the work of Perry (1968); King and Kitchener (1994); Belenky, Clinchy, Goldberger, and Tarule (1986); and Baxter Magolda (1992); (2) moral reasoning, such as the theories of Kohlberg (1976) and Gilligan (1982); (3) faith development, exemplified by the work of Fowler (1981) and Parks (1986, 2000); (4) ego development (Loevinger, 1976); (5) orders of consciousness (Kegan, 1982, 1994); and (6) maturity (Heath, 1968).

Epistemological Development

A number of theorists have explored how intellectual development occurs. The first theorist to systematically do so in the college setting was William Perry (1968). King and Kitchener (1994) extended his work to explore how people approach ill-structured problems. Belenky, Clinchy, Goldberger, and Tarule (1986) and Baxter Magolda (1992) were particularly interested in gender-related patterns of epistemological development.

Perry

Perry (1968) proposed a scheme of intellectual and ethical development made up of nine positions, or points of view, from which individuals consider the world around them. These nine positions can be grouped into four levels that represent fundamental differences in the process of meaning making: dualism, multiplicity, relativism, and commitment (King, 1978). *Dualism* consists of dichotomous thinking, in which information, ideas, and concepts are viewed as either right or wrong. People in a position of authority are assumed to have all the answers, and their role is to supply those answers. An authority who does not give answers is viewed as incompetent. In *multiplicity,* the individual comes to understand that not all knowledge is known but assumes that it will be eventually. Until the answers are found, all points of view are considered equally valid and each person is entitled to his or her own opinion. The individual at this level is unable to evaluate arguments and does not understand the importance of supporting evidence when stating a position.

Movement to *relativistic thinking* occurs when individuals come to recognize that in many areas there are no right answers. Knowledge is seen as contextual and relative. At this level, individual are able to think analytically and to evaluate their own ideas as well as those of others. An authority is viewed as a guide or source of information. The last level in the Perry scheme, *commitment,* involves making personal commitments within a relativistic context. Alternatives are weighed and options are considered on the basis of a clear sense of identity. These commitments are tested, evaluated, and modified as necessary.

Perry (1968) focused only minimally on the process of developmental change. He suggested that progression through the stages of cognitive reasoning results from integrating new information into existing ways of thinking, thereby rounding out a particular stage, and then creating new ways of thinking when new stimuli can no longer be explained using the old approach.

Perry's theory (1968) has had significant impact both in and out of the classroom (Evans et al., 1998). For example, the Developmental Instruction model (Knefelkamp, 1984) gives guidance for supporting and challenging students at various stages of development through differential use of structure, diversity, experiential learning, and personalism (see Evans et al., 1998). The Perry scheme informs educators about the lenses through which the student interprets experience. It also guides them in structuring appropriate learning experiences that support students at their current level of reasoning and encourage them to develop cognitively.

King and Kitchener

The work of Patricia King and Karen Kitchener (1994) has focused on understanding the development of reflective judgment. Believing that Perry (1968) had confused intellectual and psychosocial development in later stages, King and Kitchener studied the relationship between epistemology (assumptions about learning) and judgment only. They were interested in what happened to cognitive development beyond relativism, a topic that they believed Perry's theory did not adequately address. King and Kitchener's theory describes how an individual solves an ill-structured problem—that is, one without a clear answer (how to address racism, how to curb pollution).

King and Kitchener (1994) identified seven stages of development, divided into three levels. Each stage represents an understanding of knowledge and how knowledge is acquired, as well as an approach to solving ill-structured problems. As people move through the stages, their thinking becomes increasingly complex.

Prereflective thinking (stages one through three) is characterized by lack of awareness that knowledge is uncertain, failure to recognize that some problems don't have a right answer, and inability to use evidence in reasoning toward a conclusion. Individuals using *quasi-reflective thinking* (stages four and five) recognize that ill-structured problems exist and that there may be uncertainty associated with conclusions; they use evidence but have trouble drawing a reasoned conclusion and justifying beliefs. *Reflective thinking* (stages six and seven) includes awareness that knowledge must be actively constructed, that conclusions must be viewed in context, that judgment must be based on relevant data, and that any conclusion is open to reevaluation. Individuals tend to use a range of reflective judgment stages rather than just one at a time, and their performance varies depending on the degree of support and feedback they experience (Kitchener, Lynch, Fischer, & Wood, 1993).

Progression through the reflective judgment stages is facilitated by exposure to topics that are controversial. The individual needs an opportunity to grapple with complex problems, along with training and practice in using evidence to draw conclusions and support interpretations (King, 1996). Most of the issues that college students face are ill-structured problems (which activities to engage in, whom to become intimate with, what major and career to pursue). Educators need to challenge students to consider the ramifications of their decisions and provide evidence-based rationales for the choices they make. The educator also has to help students understand that any ill-structured problem can be reevaluated when new evidence becomes available.

Belenky, Clinchy, Goldberger, and Tarule

Mary Belenky and her colleagues (1986) were the first researchers to examine systematically the intellectual development of women. Drawing on information obtained from in-depth interviews with a group of women who were diverse with regard to age, concerns, and educational level, Belenky and colleagues compared the results they obtained with those reported by Perry (1968), whose findings were from interviews with men. Belenky and coauthors identified differences in the extent to which women and men actively engaged authorities and knowledge itself.

Belenky, Clinchy, Goldberger, and Tarule (1986) outlined five perspectives on knowing that were apparent in their research. Because their study was not longitudinal in nature, they cautioned that they could not determine if these perspectives were sequential stages. They also noted that because of the limitations of their study they were unable to determine how or why shifts in perspective occur. The five perspectives are silence, received knowledge, subjective knowledge, procedural knowledge, and constructed knowledge.

Belenky and her colleagues (1986) suggested that a collaborative approach in the classroom and respect for individual learners enhance intellectual development. They advocated use of teaching methods that encourage connection and acceptance rather than evaluation. Their theory should remind educators that women's cognitive development differs in important ways from that of men and that a variety of learning approaches must be considered to reach all students.

Baxter Magolda

Marcia Baxter Magolda's theory of epistemological reflection (1992) extended the work of Perry (1968) and Belenky, Clinchy, Goldberger, and Tarule (1986). Because her research consisted of periodic interviews with equal numbers of male and female students over a five-year period (a total of 101 students participated), Baxter Magolda was able both to compare the cognitive reasoning of men and women and also study the development of epistemological reflection over time.

Baxter Magolda (1992) described four "qualitatively different ways of knowing each characterized by a core set of epistemic assumptions"(p. 29). The first stage is *absolute knowing*, where knowledge is viewed as certain, authorities are seen as having all the answers, and the student's role is to reproduce information presented by the instructor so that it can be evaluated as right or wrong. In the second stage, *transitional knowing*, the individual acknowledges that some knowledge is uncertain and that authorities do not always have all the answers. Understanding and being able to use information is emphasized over merely memorizing.

The third stage is *independent knowing*. At this stage, knowledge is viewed as being mostly uncertain. Instructors are valued if they create a positive environment in which learning can occur. Students expect an opportunity to engage in independent thinking and share their opinions; they want to be evaluated on the strength of their thinking. The final stage in the epistemological reflection model is *contextual knowing*. Here students recognize that context plays a strong role in determining the validity of knowledge and that supporting one's position with evidence is crucial. They seek the opportunity to apply learning and to have their arguments critiqued by their classmates and instructors.

Gender-related patterns were identified in the first three stages, with a higher percentage of women demonstrating a relational pattern of knowing and a greater proportion of men using an impersonal pattern. Baxter Magolda (1995) suggested that the gender-related patterns of knowing come together in the final stage of epistemological reasoning: "When young adults in this study faced the limitations of their pattern of knowing, they learned how to use the alternative and then integrate the two" (p. 215).

Baxter Magolda (1992) noted that socialization and the extent to which a student is placed in a subordinate role affect movement through the four stages. She stressed the need to transform educational practice to encourage intellectual development, suggesting that the educator needs to validate the student as knower, situate learning in the student's experience, and define learning as jointly constructed meaning. These guidelines are valuable for both classroom teachers and student affairs professionals who are engaged in creating a learning environment.

Moral Development

Moral development is defined as "the transformations that occur in a person's form or structure of thought" (Kohlberg & Hersh, 1977, p. 54) with regard to what is considered right or necessary. Many of the decisions that college students must make with regard to interacting with others have moral implications. The two leading approaches to moral development are those of Kohlberg (1976) and Gilligan (1977, 1982).

Kohlberg

Lawrence Kohlberg's theory of moral development (1976) built on Piaget's investigation of the moral development of children (1932/1977). Kohlberg viewed morality as being centered on the concept of justice, which he defined as "the primary regard for the value and equality of all human beings, and for reciprocity in human relations" (Kohlberg, 1972, p. 14).

Kohlberg (1976) identified six stages of moral judgment, which he grouped into three levels. At the *preconventional* level, the individual's reasoning process is concrete and self-focused. Societal rules and expectations are not yet understood. Individuals are concerned only with what they will personally get out of any action. At the *conventional* level, the rules of society and the opinions of others, especially authorities, are paramount. Being a good member of society is the major criterion for any action. *Postconventional or principled* reasoning is based on self-determined principles and values. At this level, individuals are able to step away from the rules and expectations established by others and choose their own directions.

Progression to more advanced stages of reasoning requires the ability to see others' viewpoints and to reason logically (Walker, 1988). Development is enhanced if individuals are exposed to high-stage thinking and if they experience cognitive conflict. (This kind of conflict is induced when individuals face situations that point out contradiction in their existing reasoning structures or when they discover that their reasoning is different from that of important people in their lives (Kohlberg, 1976).

Gilligan

Carol Gilligan, a colleague of Kohlberg's, studied the moral development of women and introduced an alternative model that took into account their relational concerns (Gilligan, 1982). The principles that underscore moral decision making, according to Gilligan, are care and responsibility rather than justice. The dilemma involved in making a moral judgment is balancing the individual's needs in relation to the needs of others. Like Kohlberg (1976), Gilligan (1977) identified three levels of reasoning; a transition occurs between each pair of levels. At the first level, *orientation to individual survival,* individuals are focused on their own needs and survival. In level two, *goodness as self-sacrifice,* acceptance by others is the primary concern and the goal is achieved by putting the needs of others before one's own. At the third level, the *morality of nonviolence,* the individual "asserts a moral equality between self and other" (Gilligan, 1977, p. 504). Personal needs are weighed against the concerns of others; the underlying principle for making decisions is that of nonviolence.

Research (see Evans et al., 1998) has supported the existence of two moral orientations, one based on justice and rights as presented by Kohlberg (1976) and the other built upon care and responsibility as suggested by Gilligan (1982). Although women are likely to use a care-based approach and men are likely to use a justice-oriented approach, both men and women have been found to use both approaches (Gibbs, Arnold, & Burkhart, 1984). The educator should keep in mind that men and women may use differing value systems when making a moral decision and take into account what is important to each gender in asking students to consider key questions.

Many moral dilemmas face college students today. Whether to cheat on an exam, make alcohol available to an underage student, charge a trip to Florida on a parent's credit card, or vote against a minority student organization's request for funding are only a few examples. Moral development theory can help the educator understand how students reason about such decisions. It also suggests ways of encouraging development of complex forms of moral judgment.

Faith Development

Students often confront issues of faith as they move away from home and experience a new environment, perhaps for the first time. Exposure to different belief systems, as well as complex challenges, often results in questioning of existing beliefs and a desire to explore the spiritual realm in depth. The theories of Fowler (1981) and Parks (1986, 2000) focus on this developmental process.

Fowler

James Fowler (1981) was the first theorist to examine faith from a developmental perspective. He saw faith as being relational in nature, founded on a felt sense of relationship between self and others, as well as a commitment to a larger center of meaning and purpose (God). Fowler suggested that faith is "a universal feature of human living, recognizably similar everywhere despite the remarkable variety of forms and contents of religious practice and belief" (p. 14).

According to Fowler (1981), faith development progresses through six stages that parallel the individual's intellectual (Piaget, 1950) and moral (Kohlberg, 1971) development. These stages focus on how beliefs and values come to be important to the individual, not on the specific beliefs and values he or she adopts. Like other cognitive stages, Fowler's stages are sequential, hierarchical, and universal. Transitions from one stage to the next are caused by crisis and can be prolonged and painful. Each stage is more complex than the one preceding it, with later stages being a more mature expression of faith than earlier ones.

Parks

Building on the work of Fowler (1981), Perry (1968), and Gilligan (1982), Sharon Daloz Parks (1986) introduced a theory that addresses faith development during the college years. Parks argued that Fowler's theory does not describe the experience of traditional college students well because they are neither adolescents nor adults and therefore do not belong in Fowler's third (adolescent) or fourth (adult) stage.

Parks (1986, 2000) stressed the interconnections of affective, cognitive and social/cultural factors in faith development. She believed that faith results from the intersection of self, other, world, and God. As faith develops, how each component is viewed and how it interacts with the others changes and becomes more complex. According to Parks (2000), how students interpret their experiences in college depends on three factors: the form of knowing (cognitive process), the form of dependence (affective and relational aspects), and the form of community (social and cultural context). These forms combine in unique ways to produce four stages of faith. The *adolescent or conventional* stage is dualistic in nature. Students in this stage rely on authorities for information and look to others for self-definition. Being part of a community that has answers about how to be and what to believe is important.

Most students are in the *young adult* stage, the second in Parks's model. At this point, individuals begin to make independent decisions and tentative commitments; they need a community in which to explore. Older students may be in the *tested adult* stage, where individuals are more secure and confident about their decisions and values. The goal is finding a community with a compatible belief system. Parks's final stage, *mature adult,* is rarely achieved before midlife. At this level, individuals connect with and commit themselves to the larger world and its challenges.

Parks saw the most important task of young adulthood as forming a dream (Parks, 1986). In this process, imagination is a key factor. It is imagination that assists the individual experiencing what is often a difficult transition from one form of faith to another. Five steps contribute to an act of imagination (Parks, 2000). *Conscious conflict* involves acknowledgment that something in one's world is out of balance. *Pause* consists of reflection and examination. *Image* (or *insight*) is the "a-ha" moment when an answer becomes evident. *Repatterning and release of energy* involves reconstructing one's world to incorporate the new insight and releasing the tension that accompanied the dilemma. The final step, *interpretation*, is the process of trying out the new direction.

Parks (2000) saw the role of the educational environment as supporting development of imagination. In her view, every experience a student has is an opportunity to make meaning. The college environment, then, can be a positive or a negative force in a student's development of faith. A positive environment is one with opportunity for reflection and testing new ways of being.

Ego Development

Within the cognitive structural tradition, Jane Loevinger (1976) explored the process of ego development in studies involving girls and women. Loevinger saw ego as the key aspect of the self that determines how individuals perceive and engage their world. She considered ego development the "master trait" encompassing moral development, cognitive complexity, and development of the capacity for interpersonal relationships (p. 41). She defined the ego's "frame of reference" as "structure" (p. x). The particular structure of the individual's ego "determines how he [or she] interacts with the environment by a) selecting what he [or she] will respond to and b) by choosing a response that accommodates the varying demands of different environments" (Knefelkamp, Parker, & Widick, 1978, p. 70). Development is defined as acquiring increasingly complex structures that result when the person and the environment interact (Loevinger, 1976).

Loevinger identified ten stages in her model of ego development. Like other cognitive structural stages, Loevinger's build on each other and follow an irreversible, invariant, hierarchical sequence. In order of increasing complexity, her stages are presocial, symbiotic, impulsive, self-protective, conformist, self-aware, conscientious, individualistic, autonomous, and integrated. In the earlier stages, individuals tend to be concerned about only the specific others who can meet their needs. Later, individuals sees themselves in relation to the larger group and constantly seek to gain approval within this context. At the most advanced stages of development, individuals come to see that they have a role in determining what happens in their environment and in making choices about how to interact with others and how to address the inevitable conflicts that arise from multiple roles and responsibilities. Although individuals progress through these stages in order, they are not age-linked.

Although Loevinger's model (1976) is primarily cognitive in nature, her definition of ego as a holistic concept is for the educator an important reminder that human beings should not be compartmentalized. An intervention designed to address intellectual development may also have an impact on moral or social development.

Orders of Consciousness

Robert Kegan (1982, 1994) also looked at development inclusively, taking into account cognitive and affective components. He considered himself a neo-Piagetian and is therefore generally grouped with the cognitive structural theorists. His first book (1982) was concerned with the evolution of the self, particularly in its relationship with the other. In it, Kegan "describes the processes of differentiating *self* from *other* and then integrating *self* with *other* as the ego evolves throughout the life course" (Rodgers, 1990, p. 39). In his more recent work (1994), Kegan examined the demands placed on adults by the challenges of modern life.

Kegan (1994) introduced six "orders of consciousness" that determine how persons make sense of their experiences. They think, feel, define themselves, and relate to others differently at each level. Though not strictly hierarchical, these orders of consciousness develop along a continuum from simple to complex; later experiences are based on earlier ones, as is the case in other cognitive structural theories. In addition to their cognitive dimension, however, Kegan's orders also have intrapersonal and interpersonal aspects that determine how individuals view themselves and relate to others.

Kegan (1994) used Sanford's challenge and support concepts (1966) to explain how development through his orders occurs. He argued that society presents more challenges than it does supports, and that additional supports must be introduced into the environment to encourage growth. "Sympathetic coaches" (p. 43) are needed, who validate the individual as he or she currently is while also introducing new information that encourages reflection and movement to a new order. Kegan stressed that an educator must offer a bridge between old and new ways of being.

Kegan's theory (1982, 1994) helps educators understand the tensions that exist between a student's desire for connection to others and the need to be independent. As a student progresses through college, one need may take precedence over the other. These needs are apparent in how students relate to their peers and to others in their environment. The educator can be of assistance by recognizing these tensions and helping the student find the supports needed to move to a higher order of consciousness.

Maturity Theory

Douglas Heath (1968) believed that to encourage maturity in college students, an educator must have a comprehensive understanding of the nature of maturity and the factors of which it consists. Though not strictly cognitive-structural in nature, Heath's model delineates characteristics of the mature person and paints a picture of development from immature to mature ways of functioning in the world. Heath identified four self systems (intellect, values, self-concept, and interpersonal relationships) and five developmental growth dimensions (becoming able to represent experience symbolically, becoming other-centered, becoming integrated, becoming stable, and becoming autonomous). Maturation, according to Heath, "involves movement along the growth dimensions in each of the four areas of the self" (Widick, Parker, & Knefelkamp, 1978a). Heath viewed development as an adaptive process. If the individual's internal equilibrium is disrupted, a self-regulating principle causes the person to seek new responses that restore balance. Depending on conditions, these new responses either encourage greater maturity or result in regression to immature states. Thus, the environment can either enhance maturing or retard it.

Heath's model (1968) is rather abstract, but it does suggest some of the factors involved in developing maturity and can be useful in delineating ideal outcomes of educational practice. Like Kegan (1982, 1994), Heath stressed the interconnectedness of cognitive and psychosocial development. Specifically, Heath's research suggested that intellectual maturity is necessary for self-growth in other areas (Widick et al., 1978a). The current focus on learning as the basis for student affairs practice is certainly supported by Heath's work.

Learning Style Theory

Learning style theorists point out that individuals vary in how they approach learning; each style must be honored for its particular contributions and strengths. Rather than focusing on one or two approaches to learning, the educator should strive to develop all the various means that contribute to people's understanding of, and interaction with, their world. Although a number of learning styles are informative (see King, 1996), those of Kolb (1984) and Gardner (1987, 1993) are particularly applicable in the higher education setting.

Experiential Learning

Learning, according to Kolb (1984), is "the process whereby knowledge is created through the transformation of experience" (p. 38). He viewed learning as a cyclical process involving four components that build on each other: concrete experience (CE), reflective observation (RO), abstract conceptualization (AC), and active experimentation (AE). In describing this process, Evans, Forney, and Guido-DiBrito (1998) wrote that "to be effective, learners need the abilities represented by each of these four components of the learning cycle. They need to be able to involve themselves fully and without bias in learning experiences (CE), observe and reflect on these experiences from multiple perspectives (RO), formulate concepts that integrate their observations into theories (AC), and put such theories to use in making decisions and solving problems (AE)" (p. 209).

These four modes of learning fall along two dimensions (Kolb, 1984). Concrete experience and abstract conceptualization are both ways of taking in information, while reflective observation and active experimentation are means of processing it. Every individual tends to prefer one adaptive mode of learning over the other on each dimension. As a result, four learning styles emerge. *Divergers* (CE and RO) are people-oriented, focusing on feelings and values; they are imaginative and good at generating alternatives. *Assimilators* (AC and RO) are idea-oriented, analytical, and good at creating models and organizing information. *Convergers* (AC and AE) are technically oriented, good at problem solving and decision making, and excellent at practical application of ideas. *Accommodators* are action-oriented, risk-taking, and good at carrying out plans.

Kolb (1984) viewed learning styles not "as fixed traits but as stable states" (Evans et al., 1998, p. 212). They are influenced by heredity, life experiences, and the requirements of one's current environment. In the college setting, the student's area of specialization, career choice, current employment, and out-of-class activities are all influential.

Multiple Intelligences

Gardner (1987, 1993) suggested that intelligence is a complex phenomenon, which he defined as "an ability to solve a problem or to fashion a product which is valued in one or more cultural settings" (Gardner, 1987, p. 25). He identified eight domains of intelligence: linguistic, logical-mathematical, musical, spatial, bodily-kinesthetic, interpersonal, intrapersonal, and naturalist (Gardner, 1993; Shores, 1995). People's skills at using each of these multiple intelligences vary. For example, a person may be very good at picking up the harmony in a song (musical intelligence) but quite clumsy on the basketball court (bodily-kinesthetic intelligence). Development of each intelligence proceeds independently and at its own pace.

Gardner (1993) argued that educators must attend to development of each type of intelligence rather than focusing mainly on linguistic and logical-mathematical skills, as has been traditionally the case. He pointed out that typical educational approaches disadvantage students whose skills lie in the bodily-kinesthetic or interpersonal arenas.

Understanding learning styles is helpful for both faculty and student affairs administrators. Such knowledge enables them to design activities that require a variety of styles and to assign students to tasks that draw on their strengths. Challenging students to develop skills in less preferred areas is also important and can be accomplished if an educator establishes appropriate levels of support and validation.

Implications

As educators consider the outcomes of college, developmental theory is useful both in suggesting which outcomes are most salient and therefore should be encouraged and in imparting direction as to how to achieve those outcomes. For instance, psychosocial theories such as those of Erikson (1959) and Chickering (Chickering & Reisser, 1993) offer a comprehensive overview of the developmental issues that people must resolve throughout their lives. Certainly, a college education should prepare individuals to address concerns such as finding purpose for their lives, developing meaningful relationships, and giving back to society. In addition, cognitive structural theorists such as Perry (1968), King and Kitchener (1994), and Kohlberg (1976) have suggested that development of complex patterns of intellectual and moral reasoning is an important goal of higher education. Acknowledging that students learn differently, as noted by Kolb (1984) and Gardner (1987, 1993), is also important if all students are to maximize their potential.

Several factors seem to encourage positive developmental outcomes. Dissonance created by exposure to new situations and information is a necessary condition for change to occur (Erikson, 1968; Kohlberg, 1972). Individuals must do something to resolve the conflict they experience in such a situation. The student must also have an opportunity to actively confront real dilemmas and make decisions about them (King & Kitchener, 1994; Kohlberg, 1972). These assertions suggest, for example, that an overly protective college environment might be comfortable but may not lead to positive developmental outcomes. Colleges that wish to enhance development must create a stimulating environment that poses new challenges and diverse perspectives while also maintaining appropriate support structures (Chickering & Reisser, 1993; Sanford, 1966).

Student development theory is useful in working with individual students, in designing and carrying out programs, and in establishing policy and practices on campus. Having an understanding of the developmental issues typically experienced by students and how they reason about their experiences can help the educator read and relate to individual students. For instance, knowing that respect for elders is an important value in Asian American cultures (Sue & Sue, 1990) may be of assistance when discussing family issues with a Korean-American student. Likewise, understanding that many eighteen-year-old students use preconventional moral reasoning (Rest, 1986) may be helpful in explaining the sanctions for underage drinking in the residence hall.

Theory can also be useful when developing a program or workshop on a college campus. For instance, a program may be more successful if its content and timing are matched to Chickering's developmental vectors (Evans et al., 1998). Since first-year students are often concerned about developing academic competence, an academic skills program is likely to benefit them. Seniors, by contrast, would benefit more from a program discussing transition from college to the workforce. Cognitive structural theories offer guidance concerning how to present a program (Evans et al., 1998). Dualistic thinkers, for example, need much more structure than do relativistic thinkers. Learning style theory generates information on how students take in information. For instance, some students learn best through active engagement while others learn more effectively when given the opportunity to reflect on information provided.

Policy formation is also enhanced by considering theory. For example, knowing that the issues faced by adult students differ from those of eighteen-to-twenty-two-year-olds (Chickering & Reisser, 1993) may lead to the conclusion that regulations concerning eligibility for a college-awarded short-term loan or the requirement that students live in a residence hall during the first year of study might need to be modified. Cognitive structural theory also suggests that younger students, who tend to be dualistic thinkers, need more specific rules and structure in their living situation than do older students who approach a situation from a relativistic perspective (Evans et al., 1998). Involving students in developing policies is also a way to challenge their thinking and encourage cognitive and moral development.

In each of these instances, theory helps student affairs educators be proactive in their work. As Evans (1996) noted: "Theory suggests questions to ask, avenues to explore, and hypotheses to test. It provides shortcuts to exploring students' concerns and analyzing how they are addressing them" (p. 183). Use of student development theory can also facilitate evaluation of interventions. As already noted, important learning outcomes are presented in the various developmental theories. The purpose of evaluation should be to assess the extent to which these outcomes are achieved, both with regard to specific programs and also in a global sense by the educational experience as a whole.

In future chapters, relevant developmental theory is introduced as it relates to specific outcomes of higher education. In some instances, theory has guided design and evaluation of interventions to enhance these outcomes, while in other cases reference to theory is noticeably missing. In each case, conclusions are drawn concerning the contributions of various theoretical perspectives to our understanding of the outcome and the strategies for ensuring that it is achieved.

References

Asbury, F. A. (1968). Vocational development of rural disadvantaged eighth grade boys. *Vocational Guidance Quarterly, 17,* 109–113.

Atkinson, D. R., Morten, G., & Sue, D. W. (1993). *Counseling American minorities: A cross-cultural perspective* (4th ed.). Madison, WI: Brown and Benchmark.

Baltes, P. B. (1982). Life-span development psychology: Some conveying observations on history and theory. In K. W. Schaie & J. Geiwitz (Eds.), *Readings in adult development and aging* (pp. 12–25). Boston: Little, Brown.

Baltes, P. B. (1987). Theoretical propositions on life-span developmental psychology: On the dynamics between growth and decline. *Developmental Psychology, 23,* 611–626.

Bandura, A. (1982). The psychology of chance encounters and life paths. *American Psychologist, 37,* 747–755.

Baxter Magolda, M. B. (1992). *Knowing and reasoning in college: Gender-related patterns in students' intellectual development.* San Francisco: Jossey-Bass.

Baxter Magolda, M. B. (1995). The integration of relational and impersonal knowing in young adults' epistemological development. *Journal of College Student Development, 36,* 205–216.

Belenky, M. F., Clinchy, B. M., Goldberger, N. R., & Tarule, J. M. (1986). *Women's ways of knowing: The development of self, voice, and mind.* New York: Basic Books.

Bengston, V. L. (Ed.). (1996). *Adulthood and aging: Research on continuities and discontinuities.* New York: Springer.

Blau, P. M., & Duncan, O. D. (1967). *The American occupational structure.* New York: Wiley.

Bridges, W. (1991). *Managing transitions: Making the most of change.* Reading, MA: Addison-Wesley.

Caplow, T. (1954). *The sociology of work.* Minneapolis: University of Minnesota Press.

Cass, V. C. (1979). Homosexual identity formation: A theoretical model. *Journal of Homosexuality, 4,* 219–235.

Chickering, A. W. (1969). *Education and identity.* San Francisco: Jossey-Bass.

Chickering, A. W., & Reisser, L. (1993). *Education and identity* (2nd ed.). San Francisco: Jossey-Bass.

Cross, K. P. (1971). *Beyond the open door: New students to higher education.* San Francisco: Jossey-Bass.

Cross, W. E., Jr. (1991). *Shades of black: Diversity in African American identity.* Philadelphia: Temple University Press.

Cross, W. E., Jr. (1995). The psychology of Nigrescence: Revising the Cross model. In J. G. Ponterotto, J. M. Casas, L. A. Suzuki, & C. M. Alexander (Eds.), *Handbook of multicultural counseling* (pp. 93–122). Thousand Oaks, CA: Sage.

D'Augelli, A. R. (1994). Identity development and sexual orientation: Toward a model of lesbian, gay, and bisexual development. In E. J. Trickett, R. J. Watts, & D. Birman (Eds.), *Human diversity: Perspectives on people in context* (pp. 312–333). San Francisco: Jossey-Bass.

Downing, N. E., & Roush, K. L. (1985). From passive acceptance to active commitment: A model of feminist identity development for women. *Counseling Psychologist, 13,* 695–709.

Elder, G. H., Jr. (1995). The life course paradigm: Social change and individual development. In P. Moen, G. H. Elder, Jr., & K. Lüscher (Eds.), *Examining lives in context: Perspectives on the ecology of human development* (pp. 101–139). Washington, DC: American Psychological Association.

Erikson, E. H. (1950). *Childhood and society.* New York: Norton.

Erikson, E. H. (1959). Identity and the life cycle. *Psychological Issues, 1,* 1–171.

Erikson, E. H. (1968). *Identity: Youth and crisis.* New York: Norton.

Evans, N. J. (1996). Theories of student development. In S. R. Komives, D. B. Woodard, Jr., & Associates, *Student services: A handbook for the profession* (3rd ed., pp. 164–187). San Francisco: Jossey-Bass.

Evans, N. J., & D'Augelli, A. R. (1996). Lesbians, gay men, and bisexual people in college. In R. C. Savin-Williams & K. M. Cohen (Eds.), *The lives of lesbians, gays, and bisexuals* (pp. 201–226). New York: Harcourt Brace.

Evans, N. J., Forney, D. S., & Guido-DiBrito, F. (1998). *Student development in college: Theory, research, and practice.* San Francisco: Jossey-Bass.

Feldman, K. A., & Newcomb, T. M. (1969). *The impact of college on students.* 2 vols. San Francisco: Jossey-Bass.

Fiske, M., & Chiriboga, D. A. (1990). *Change and continuity in adult life.* San Francisco: Jossey-Bass.

Fowler, J. W. (1981). *Stages of faith: The psychology of human development and the quest for meaning.* San Francisco: Harper & Row.

Gardner, H. (1987). The theory of multiple intelligences. *Annals of Dyslexia, 37,* 19–35.

Gardner, H. (1993). *Multiple intelligences: The theory in practice.* New York: Basic Books.

Gibbs, J. C., Arnold, K. D., & Burkhart, J. E. (1984). Sex differences in the expression of moral judgment. *Child Development, 55,* 1040–1043.

Gilligan, C. (1977). In a different voice: Women's conceptions of self and morality. *Harvard Educational Review, 47,* 481–517.

Gilligan, C. (1982). *In a different voice: Psychological theory and women's development.* Cambridge, MA: Harvard University Press.

Gould, R. (1978). *Transformations: Growth and change in adult life.* New York: Simon and Schuster.

Heath, D. (1968). *Growing up in college.* San Francisco: Jossey-Bass.

Heath, D. (1977). *Maturity and competence: A transcultural view.* New York: Gardner.

Heath, R. (1964). *The reasonable adventurer.* Pittsburgh, PA: University of Pittsburgh Press.

Helms, J. E. (1993). *Black and white racial identity: Theory, research and practice.* Westport, CT: Praeger.

Helms, J. E. (1995). An update of Helms's white and people of color racial identity models. In J. G. Ponterotto, J. M. Casas, L. A. Suzuki, & C. M. Alexander (Eds.), *Handbook of multicultural counseling* (pp. 181–198). Thousand Oaks, CA: Sage.

Helms, J. E., & Cook, D. A. (1999). *Using race and culture in counseling and psychotherapy: Theory and process.* Needham Heights, MA: Allyn & Bacon.

Herr, E. L., & Cramer, S. H. (1988). *Career guidance and counseling through the life span.* Glenview, IL: Scott, Foresman.

Holland, J. L. (1992). *Making vocational choices: A theory of vocational personalities and work environments* (2nd ed.). Odessa, FL: Psychological Assessment Resources. (Original work published 1985)

Hotchkiss, L., & Borow, H. (1990). Sociological perspectives on career choice and attainment. In D. Brown, L. Brooks, & Associates, *Career choice and development: Applying contemporary theories to practice* (2nd ed., pp. 262–307). San Francisco: Jossey-Bass.

Hughes, J. A., & Graham, S. W. (1990). Adult life roles: A new approach to adult development. *Journal of Continuing Higher Education, 38* (2), 2–8.

Isajiw, W. W. (1990). Ethnic-identity retention. In R. Breton, W. W. Isajiw, W. E. Kalbach, & J. G. Reitz (Eds.), *Ethnic identity and equality* (pp. 34–91). Toronto: University of Toronto Press.

Josselson, R. (1987). *Finding herself: Pathways to identity development in women.* San Francisco: Jossey-Bass.

Josselson, R. (1996). *Revising herself: The story of women's identity from college to midlife.* New York: Oxford University Press.

Kegan, R. (1982). *The evolving self.* Cambridge, MA: Harvard University Press.

Kegan, R. (1994). *In over our heads: The mental demands of modern life.* Cambridge, MA: Harvard University Press.

King, P. M. (1978). William Perry's theory of intellectual and ethical development. In L. L. Knefelkamp, C. Widick, & C. A. Parker (Eds.), *Applying new developmental findings* (New Directions for Student Services, no. 4, pp. 35–51). San Francisco: Jossey-Bass.

King, P. M. (1996). Student cognition and learning. In S. R. Komives, D. B. Woodard, Jr., & Associates, *Student services: A handbook for the profession* (3rd ed., pp. 218–243). San Francisco: Jossey-Bass.

King, P. M., & Kitchener, K. S. (1994). *Developing reflective judgment: Understanding and promoting intellectual growth and critical thinking in adolescents and adults.* San Francisco: Jossey-Bass.

Kitchener, K. S., Lynch, C. L., Fischer, K. W., & Wood, P. K. (1993). Developmental range of reflective judgment: The effect of contextual support and practice on developmental stage. *Developmental Psychology, 29,* 893–906.

Knefelkamp, L. L. (1984). *A workbook for the practice-to-theory-to-practice model.* Unpublished manuscript, University of Maryland, College Park.

Knefelkamp, L. L., Parker, C. A., & Widick, C. (1978). Jane Loevinger's milestones of development. In L. L. Knefelkamp, C. Widick, & C. A. Parker (Eds.), *Applying new developmental findings* (New Directions for Student Services, no. 4, pp. 69–78). San Francisco: Jossey-Bass.

Knefelkamp, L. L., Widick, C., & Parker, C. A. (1978). Editors' notes: Why bother about theory? In L. L. Knefelkamp, C. Widick, & C. A. Parker (Eds.), *Applying new developmental findings* (New Directions for Student Services, no. 4, pp. vii–xvi). San Francisco: Jossey-Bass.

Kohlberg, L. (1971). Stages of moral development. In C. M. Beck, B. S. Crittenden, & E. V. Sullivan (Eds.), *Moral education: Interdisciplinary approaches* (pp. 23–92). Toronto: University of Toronto Press.

Kohlberg, L. (1972). A cognitive-developmental approach to moral education. *Humanist, 6,* 13–16.

Kohlberg, L. (1976). Moral stages and moralization: The cognitive-developmental approach. In T. Lickona (Ed.), *Moral development and behavior: Theory, research, and social issues* (pp. 31–53). Austin: Holt, Rinehart & Winston.

Kohlberg, L., & Hersh, R. H. (1977). Moral development: A review of the theory. *Theory into Practice, 16,* 53–59.

Kolb, D. A. (1984). *Experiential learning: Experience as the source of learning and development.* Englewood Cliffs, NJ: Prentice Hall.

Krumboltz, J. D. (1979). A social learning theory of career decision making. In A. M. Mitchell, G. B. Jones, & J. D. Krumboltz (Eds.), *Social learning and career decision making* (pp. 19–49). Cranston, RI: Carroll.

Krumboltz, J. D. (1981). A social learning theory of career selection. In D. H. Montross & C. J. Shinkman (Eds.), *Career development in the 1980s: Theory and practice* (pp. 43–66). Springfield, IL: Charles C. Thomas.

Levine, H., & Evans, N. J. (1991). The development of gay, lesbian, and bisexual identities. In N. J. Evans & V. A. Wall (Eds.), *Beyond tolerance: Gays, lesbians and bisexuals on campus* (pp. 1–24). Alexandria, VA: American College Personnel Association.

Levinson, D. J. (1978). *The seasons of a man's life.* New York: Ballantine.

Levinson, D. J., & Levinson, J. D. (1996). *The seasons of a woman's life.* New York: Ballantine.

Lewin, K. (1936). *Principles of topological psychology.* New York: McGraw-Hill.

LoCascio, R. (1967). Continuity and discontinuity in vocational development theory. *Personnel and Guidance Journal, 46,* 32–36.

Loevinger, J. (1976). *Ego development: Conceptions and theories.* San Francisco: Jossey-Bass.

Magnusson, D. (1995). Individual development: A holistic, integrated model. In P. Moen, G. H. Elder, Jr., & K. Lüsher (Eds.), *Examining lives in context: Perspectives on the ecology of human development* (pp. 19–60). Washington, DC: American Psychological Association.

Marcia, J. E. (1966). Development and validation of ego-identity status. *Journal of Personality and Social Psychology, 3,* 551–558.

Marcia, J. E. (1980). Identity in adolescence. In J. Adelson (Ed.), *Handbook of adolescent psychology* (pp. 159–187). New York: Wiley.

McCarn, S. R., & Fassinger, R. E. (1996). Revisioning sexual minority identity formation: A new model of lesbian identity and its implications for counseling and research. *Counseling Psychologist, 24,* 508–534.

McDaniels, C., & Gysbers, N. C. (1992). *Counseling for career development: Theories, resources, and practice.* San Francisco: Jossey-Bass.

McEwen, M. K. (1996). New perspectives on identity development. In S. R. Komives & D. B. Woodard, Jr. (Eds.), *Student services: A handbook for the profession* (pp. 188–217). San Francisco: Jossey-Bass.

Miller, D. C., & Form, W. H. (1951). *Industrial sociology.* New York: Harper & Row.

Minor, C. W. (1992). Career development theories and models. In D. H. Montross & C. J. Shinkman (Eds.), *Career development: Theory and practice* (pp. 7–34). Springfield, IL: Charles C. Thomas.

Mitchell, A. M., Jones, G. B., & Krumboltz, J. D. (Eds.). (1979). *Social learning theory and career decision making.* Cranston, RI: Carroll.

Montross, D. H. (1981). Introduction. In D. H. Montross & C. J. Shinkman (Eds.), *Career development in the 1980s: Theory and practice* (pp. xi–xv). Springfield, IL: Charles C. Thomas.

Neugarten, B. L. (1979). Time, age, and the life cycle. *American Journal of Psychiatry, 136,* 887–894.

O'Neil, J. M., Egan, J., Owen, S. V., & Murry, V. M. (1993). The Gender Role Journey Measure: Scale development and psychometric evaluation. *Sex Roles, 28,* 167–185.

Osipow, S. H. (1973). *Theories of career development* (rev. ed.). Englewood Cliffs, NJ: Prentice Hall.

Ossana, S. M., Helms, J. E., & Leonard, M. M. (1992). Do "womanist" identity attitudes influence college women's self-esteem and perceptions of environmental bias? *Journal of Counseling and Development, 70,* 402–408.

Parks, S. (1986). *The critical years: Young adults and the search for meaning, faith, and commitment.* San Francisco: Harper San Francisco.

Parks, S. D. (2000). *Big questions, worthy dreams: Mentoring young adults in their search for meaning, purpose, and faith.* San Francisco: Jossey-Bass.

Parsons, F. (1909). *Choosing a vocation.* Boston: Houghton Mifflin.

Paterson, D. G., & Darley, J. G. (1936). *Men, women, and jobs: A study in human engineering.* Minneapolis: University of Minnesota Press.

Perry, W. G., Jr. (1968). *Forms of intellectual and ethical development in the college years: A scheme.* New York: Holt, Rinehart & Winston.

Perun, P. J., & Bielby, D. D. (1980). Structure and dynamics on the individual life course. In K. W. Back (Ed.), *Life course: Integrative theories and exemplary populations* (pp. 97–119). Boulder, CO: Westview.

Peters, J. M. (1989). Programming through the client's lifespan. In D. J. Blackburn (Ed.), *Foundations and changing practices in extension* (pp. 84–93). Guelph, Ontario: University of Guelph.

Phinney, J. S. (1990). Ethnic identity in adolescents and adults: Review of research. *Psychological Bulletin, 108,* 499–514.

Piaget, J. (1950). *The psychology of intelligence.* San Diego, CA: Harcourt Brace Jovanovich.

Piaget, J. (1952). *The origins of intelligence in children.* New York: International Universities Press.

Piaget, J. (1977). *The moral judgment of the child* (M. Gabain, Trans.). Harmondsworth, England: Penguin. (Original work published 1932)

Rest, J. R. (1986). *Moral development: Advances in research and theory.* New York: Praeger.

Rodgers, R. F. (1990). Recent theories and research underlying student development. In D. G. Creamer & Associates, *College student development: Theory and practice for the 1990s* (pp. 27–79). Alexandria, VA: American College Personnel Association.

Ross-Gordon, J. M. (1999). Gender development and gendered adult development. In M. C. Clark & R. S. Caffarella (Eds.), *An update on adult development theory: New ways of thinking about the life course* (New Directions for Adult and Continuing Education, no. 84, pp. 29–37). San Francisco: Jossey-Bass.

Rounds, J. B., & Tracey, T. J. (1990). From trait-and-factor to person-environment fit counseling: Theory and process. In W. B. Walsh & S. H. Osipow (Eds.), *Career counseling: Contemporary topics in vocational psychology* (pp. 1–44). Hillsdale, NJ: Erlbaum.

Rowe, W., Bennett, S. K., & Atkinson, D. R. (1994). White racial identity models: A critique and alternative proposal. *Counseling Psychologist, 22,* 129–146.

Sanford, N. (1966). *Self and society.* New York: Atherton Press.

Sanford, N. (1967). *Where colleges fail: A study of the student as a person.* San Francisco: Jossey-Bass.

Schenkel, S., & Marcia, J. E. (1970). Attitudes toward premarital intercourse in determining ego identity status in college women. *Journal of Personality, 40,* 472–482.

Schlossberg, N. K. (1989). *Overwhelmed: Coping with life's ups and downs.* San Francisco: Lexington.

Schlossberg, N. K., Waters, E. B., & Goodman, J. (1995). *Counseling adults in transition* (2nd ed.). New York: Springer.

Schmeiding, O. A., & Jensen, S. (1968). American Indian students: Vocational development and vocational tenacity. *Vocational Guidance Quarterly, 17,* 120–123.

Shores, E. F. (1995). Howard Gardner on the eighth intelligence: Seeing the natural world. *Dimensions of Early Childhood, 23*(4), 5–9.

Sodowsky, G. R., Kwan, K. K., & Pannu, R. (1995). Ethnic identity of Asians in the United States. In J. G. Ponterotto, J. M. Casas, L. A. Suzuki, & C. M. Alexander (Eds.), *Handbook of multicultural counseling* (pp. 123–154). Thousand Oaks, CA: Sage.

Sue, D., & Sue, D. W. (1990). *Counseling the culturally different: Theory and practice* (2nd ed.). New York: Wiley.

Sugarman, L. (1986). *Life-span development: Concepts, theories and interventions.* New York: Methuen.

Super, D. E. (1983). Assessment in career guidance: Toward truly developmental counseling. *Personnel and Guidance Journal, 61,* 555–562.

Super, D. E. (1990). A life-span, life-space approach to career development. In D. Brown, L. Brooks, & Associates, *Career choice and development: Applying contemporary theories to development* (2nd ed., pp. 197–261). San Francisco: Jossey-Bass.

Super, D. E. (1992). Toward a comprehensive theory of career development. In D. H. Montross & C. J. Shinkman (Eds.), *Career development: Theory and practice* (pp. 35–64). Springfield, IL: Charles C. Thomas.

Troiden, R. R. (1989). The formation of homosexual identities. *Journal of Homosexuality, 17*(1–2), 43–74.

Vaillant, G. (1977). *Adaptation to life.* Boston: Little, Brown.

Walker, L. J. (1988). The development of moral reasoning. *Annals of Child Development, 5,* 33–78.

Whitbourne, S. K. (1985). The psychological construction of the life span. In J. E. Birren & K. W. Schaie (Eds.), *Handbook of the psychology of aging* (2nd ed., pp. 594–618). New York: Van Nostrand Reinhold.

Widick, C., Parker, C. A., & Knefelkamp, L. (1978a). Douglas Heath's model of maturing. In L. Knefelkamp, C. Widick, & C. A. Parker (Eds.), *Applying new developmental findings* (New Directions for Student Services, no. 4, pp. 79–91). San Francisco: Jossey-Bass.

Widick, C., Parker, C. A., & Knefelkamp, L. (1978b). Erik Erikson and psychosocial development. In L. Knefelkamp, C. Widick, & C. A. Parker (Eds.), *Applying new developmental findings* (New Directions for Student Services, no. 4, pp. 1–17). San Francisco: Jossey-Bass.

Williamson, E. G. (1939). *How to counsel students: A manual of techniques for clinical counselors.* New York: McGraw-Hill.

Williamson, E. G. (1965). *Vocational counseling.* New York: McGraw-Hill.

Chapter Three

How Campus Environments Influence Student Outcomes

One of the essential factors influencing learning and the eventual outcomes of a student's learning experience is the campus environment. It can vary considerably from one place to the next; that is, the features of the campus environment can differ dramatically. For example, contrast the environment of a college located in a small town, removed from the bustle of everyday life, with the environment of a campus located in a major metropolitan area. Each campus can ensure an excellent education for a student, but the manner in which that education is obtained depends on what the campus offers.

This chapter is designed to address selected issues related to how the campus environment affects student learning. We start with an overview of theories that address person-environment interaction and then discuss features of the campus environment that affect the student experience. In the final section of this chapter, we examine how a positive learning environment can be created on campus.

A Theoretical Perspective on Person-Environment Interaction

Kurt Lewin (1936) presented a foundation for understanding the impact of the environment on student development and learning with his famous equation, $B = f (P \times E)$. Translated into words, Lewin's premise is that any behavior is a result of the interaction of an individual with his or her environment. If the behavior that educators wish to encourage is student learning, for example, to begin with they must consider factors that characterize the student, such as educational and social background, academic ability, developmental level, and personality type. In addition, they must also acknowledge the role played by aspects of the college environment, including the physical surroundings, the organizational structure of the institution, the human aggregate, and the social climate.

Most important, they must consider the *interaction* of person and environment. Each person finds some environmental conditions supportive and others aversive. Likewise, a specific environment is welcoming to some students but not to others. A student from an affluent suburban high school who has excelled in advanced placement courses may adjust easily to a selective private college honors program, while a student from a small rural high school who has had only basic college preparatory courses may find such a program extremely challenging.

Several theorists have discussed how person-environment interaction shapes student development. The ideas of Nevitt Sanford (1966, 1967), Alexander Astin (1984), Nancy Schlossberg (1989), and Laura Rendón (1994) are reviewed here.

Challenge and Support

Nevitt Sanford (1966) suggested that three conditions enhance student growth and development: readiness, challenge, and support. Readiness relates to the person; Sanford hypothesized that individuals cannot change until they are ready to do so. Readiness results from internal processes associated with maturation or from beneficial environmental conditions.

Sanford also observed that for students to grow they must be presented with environmental challenges: "For a change to occur, there must be internal or external stimuli which upset [the student's] existing equilibrium, which cause instability that existing modes of adaptation do not suffice to correct, and which thus require the person to make new responses and so to expand his [sic] personality" (1967, p. 51). For development to occur, finding the optimal level of challenge is crucial (Sanford, 1966). If students experience too much dissonance, they may resort to a not-so-beneficial coping strategy, such as exhibiting previous, less adaptive behaviors; using existing behaviors inflexibly; escaping the challenge by leaving the environment; or ignoring the challenge if they cannot escape it. On the other hand, if too little challenge is present in the environment, they do not develop or learn, although they may be comfortable and enjoy their experiences in college.

To achieve an optimal level of dissonance, challenge in the environment must be balanced by support. The necessary ratio of challenge to support depends on the personality and background of the individual (Sanford, 1966). Self-sufficient students who are clear about their career direction need less guidance from an adviser than do students who are undecided about a major and feel challenged by the range of options available.

Using Sanford's thinking (1966, 1967) as a framework, an educator finds many opportunities to stimulate student learning and growth through the environment. For instance, residence hall living can be a challenge for students who may have to reach a compromise with a roommate, or dealing with people with vastly different values. In the academic arena, faculty may challenge a student to support a point of view through a paper or oral presentation. Other students may take contrasting perspectives in analyzing literature, historical events, and so on. Experiences such as these, both inside and outside the classroom, can enrich a student's educational experience. Some challenges can be purposefully structured by the institution through policies and practices, as with setting a moratorium on roommate change for the first two weeks of the academic year. Others may simply emerge, perhaps through an intense discussion in class or through students in a club determining whether or not to devote some of their resources to support a local philanthropic activity.

Sanford (1967) suggested caution in crafting challenges for students: "Surely we can afford to be deliberate about introducing young people to the major challenges of adult life, but there would be no advantage in this unless the time thus gained were actually filled with experiences that develop the personality" (p. 56). Using this assertion as guidance, purposeful challenges have to be developed in the context of the student's readiness to face them and with appropriate support available. As an illustration, many traditional students would not be ready to deal with the problems of group living, as in a residence hall, unless staff guidance is available. Or they might not be ready to plan their entire academic program without the assistance of an academic adviser. The growth and development that occur from circumstances such as those described by Sanford can result in greater independence on the part of students, as was demonstrated in one study of residence hall students in which close supervision by residence hall staff led to development of autonomy (Kuh & Schuh, 1983).

Involvement

Astin (1984) proposed that for learning to occur, students must become actively involved in the college environment. He defined involvement as "the amount of physical and psychological energy that the student devotes to the academic experience" (p. 297). Energy can be invested in the academic experience as a whole or in a specific event or activity, such as working in a professor's lab or being a member of a Greek organization. Astin stressed that involvement must be quantitative and qualitative in nature; it refers both to the actual amount of time a student devotes to an activity and also to the seriousness with which the student takes the experience. Astin hypothesized that "the amount of student learning and personal development associated with any educational program is directly proportional to the quality and quantity of student involvement in that program" (p. 298). Continuing that line of thinking, he went on to state that "the effectiveness of any educational policy or practice is directly related to the capacity of that policy or practice to increase student involvement" (p. 298).

Astin's theory (1984) highlights the importance of an educator presenting an opportunity for the student to get involved in classroom and out-of-classroom experiences to encourage student learning. A study of "involving colleges" (Kuh, Schuh, Whitt, & Associates, 1991) documented the value of offering varied experiences and activities that encourage the student to assume new responsibilities and learn new skills. Involvement may occur in many arenas: academic experience, the residence hall, a student organization, athletics, the work environment, or a service-learning opportunity. The size and setting of the institution, of course, influences the type of experience available to the student.

It seems obvious that academic involvement can influence student learning. However, as Astin (1984) stressed, students must invest psychological as well as physical energy to gain from their academic experience. Astin, as well as later writers (see Chickering & Reisser, 1993; Kuh, Douglas, Lund, & Ramin-Gyurnek, 1994), stressed the importance of faculty-student interaction outside the classroom. Activities such as working with a professor on a research project, serving as a peer tutor, participating in an honors program, completing an internship, or being part of a learning community all allow students to go beyond the minimal level of engagement required to pass a class and, in turn, lead to greater learning. Study-abroad experience has also been demonstrated to have a significant effect on student learning and development (Kuh et al., 1994).

The residence hall can be a place where students sleep and shower, or it can be a vibrant learning community. Making opportunities available for participation in hall government, programming decisions, and determining hall policy are ways to encourage active involvement. Partnership with an academic department in creating living-learning experiences are especially valuable for enhancing student learning (Kuh et al., 1994).

Involvement in student organizations is another obvious way to encourage student development. Participation in student government, Greek life, and other clubs and organizations has been shown to lead to greater student satisfaction as well as increased development in areas such as confidence, purpose, mature interpersonal relationships, and intimacy (Astin, 1984; Hood, Riahinejad, & White, 1986; Hunt & Rentz, 1994; Williams & Winston, 1985). Involvement in athletics at the intercollegiate level, however, seems to have a negative effect on career planning and interpersonal relationships, as well as on cognitive development (Kuh et al., 1994; Sowa & Gressard, 1983).

Student employment is yet another form of involvement. According to one study, 79 percent of all students who were enrolled in college in 1995–96 worked; 37 percent worked thirty-five hours or more per week (National Center for Education Statistics, 1998). Developmental outcomes appear to be better for students who work on campus than for those who work off campus (Astin, 1993b), but in a metropolitan area in particular jobs off campus tend to pay better than those on campus. To overcome this dilemma, an institution might attempt to link off-campus work to specific learning experiences (perhaps through an internship), or make on-campus work more attractive by tying it to the student's academic objectives (such as opportunities to serve as an undergraduate research assistant).

Service learning and volunteerism are other forms of involvement. Here are situations where students can enrich their educational experience by employing in a practical setting what they have learned on campus. In a metropolitan area, such experiences can be found in local neighborhoods. Students attending school in a rural setting, however, may need to travel some distance if they have a specific experience in mind. Colleges outside a major metropolitan area often arrange a spring break trip or service semester that enables students to engage in meaningful volunteer activity. Service learning has been shown to have a significant effect on student development (Serow & Dreyden, 1990).

Marginality and Mattering

Schlossberg (1989) argued that a sense of belonging is an influential factor in whether a student succeeds and develops in college. When individuals assume a new role, especially if they are uncertain about their ability to succeed in the role, they often experience feelings of being marginal. Marginality, a sense of not fitting in, can lead to feelings of depression, irritability, and insecurity. Schlossberg noted that many students from minority groups see themselves as an outsider throughout the college years, while other students (new freshmen, or transfers who are members of a dominant group) might temporarily feel marginalized.

Feelings of marginality, in turn, can lead to a sense of not mattering. Schlossberg defined mattering as "our belief, whether right or wrong, that we matter to someone else" (1989, p. 9). Building on a model introduced by Rosenberg and McCullough (1981), Schlossberg (1989) identified five components of mattering: *attention,* a sense of being noticed by others; *importance,* a feeling of being cared about; *ego extension,* believing that another empathizes with one's successes and failures; *dependence,* feeling needed; and *appreciation,* a sense that one's efforts are valued by others.

Schlossberg, Lynch, and Chickering (1989) stressed that an institution must work to create an environment in which people sense that they "matter to someone else, that they are the object of someone else's attention, and that others care about them and appreciate them" (p. 2). Schlossberg (1989) suggested that a sense of mattering is a necessary prerequisite for students to become involved in campus activities and academic pursuits. Kuh, Schuh, Whitt, and Associates (1991) underscored this need: "The most critical issue regarding campus environments and student involvement is creating a sense of belonging, a feeling on the part of the students that the institution acknowledges the human needs of social and psychological comfort, and that they are full and valued members of the campus community" (p. 321).

According to the Carnegie Foundation for the Advancement of Teaching, "caring is the key" (1990, p. 47) to creating an environment in which students feel that they matter. Students must feel that faculty, administrators, and staff value their contributions to the campus, that students' interests are important, and that students' perspectives and backgrounds contribute meaningfully to enriching the campus climate. Particularly important is enabling diverse subcommunities to define their role and contribution (Kuh, Douglas, Lund, & Ramin-Gyurnek, 1994).

Validation

Validation is one method for assuring students that they belong in college (Rendón, 1994). Defined as "an enabling, confirming and supportive process initiated by in- and out-of-class agents that foster academic and interpersonal development" (p. 46), validation is particularly important for building self-confidence and self-esteem among first-generation students and those from an impoverished background who doubt their academic ability and potential. When students hear that they have the skills to succeed in college and are worthy of being there, self-esteem, self-confidence, and motivation are enhanced. Students are encouraged to take an active role in campus life and become involved in the learning process.

Validation can occur in various environmental arenas: the classroom, a student organization, a residence hall, or a work setting. Teachers, student affairs staff, fellow students, employers, or other people who are significant in the student's life can offer it. Validation is particularly important during the first few weeks of college, when students often feel lost, lonely, and overwhelmed. Small gestures, such as an encouraging remark on a paper or acknowledgment during a residence hall floor meeting, are forms of validation that can have a significant impact.

Components of the Environment

The campus environment is a complex entity made up of many components that affect a student's experience, whether positively or negatively. Strange and Banning (2001) outlined four models that address features of the environment:

1. Physical models focus on the natural and synthetic aspects of the environment and the limits they set on human interaction.
2. Human aggregate approaches examine how an environment is shaped by the collective characteristics of the people who inhabit it.
3. Structural organizational models note the influence of goals and purposes on the organizational structures that evolve and how those structures in turn shape various behavioral outcomes.
4. Perceptual approaches reflect on the important role played by subjective interpretation of environmental factors on a person's response to a setting.

These four components of the campus environment, individually and interactively, influence the outcomes of college for students; they are discussed next.

The Physical Setting

The physical setting of a campus includes natural elements (climate, geographic location, terrain) and synthetic features (architecture, building layout, spatial arrangement, accessibility, amenities). The appearance of the campus can have a positive or negative impact on a student's attitude toward the college. Prospective students often note that the physical features of a college are among the most important factors in creating a first impression of the college (Sturner, 1973; Thelin & Yankovich, 1987).

The natural setting of a campus, including its location and surrounding area, can have a major impact on the activities and attitudes of the students who attend. For instance, a college located in a far-northern state may center its student activities program around outdoor winter activities, while a California college bordering the ocean takes advantage of this physical feature. Tunnels or covered walkways connecting buildings might also be a feature of a northern campus; one located in a warm climate could offer more outdoor gathering places and open spaces.

A campus located in a metropolitan area may feature experiences for students that differ from those of a campus located in a rural area. For example, students at an urban college would have more opportunity for leadership development and service in the community than would students at a rural institution. In addition, a metropolitan institution often relies on local art museums, performing groups, area celebrities, and so on to expose students to the fine arts. A rural college in turn needs to create more on-campus opportunities for such exposure.

The terrain of a campus may be of particular concern to a student who has a mobility impairment and faces difficulty walking up and down hilly sidewalks. Other students, however, find rolling hillsides, trees, and ponds to be an attraction (Griffith, 1994).

The architectural environment also influences student satisfaction and behavior. In addition to its aesthetic impact, architecture on a campus can affect the student's comfort level. Those living in high-rise residence halls report a lower level of satisfaction and exhibit a higher rate of attrition and incidence of vandalism than students living in low-rise buildings (Holahan & Wilcox, 1978).

The layout of a campus can affect student feelings of safety and perception of convenience. The location of parking lots, pathways to classroom buildings, and adequacy of lighting are important considerations for commuter students who attend classes at night (Strange, 1996). Students who transfer from a small community college to a large university report difficulty negotiating the distance between buildings and a sense of being overwhelmed by the size of the campus (Hagley, 1999).

The arrangement of rooms, offices, and other locations on campus can affect student interaction. Michelson (1970) noted that the physical characteristics of a setting decree broad limits on the behaviors or transactions that can occur within it, a concept he labeled "intersystems congruence" (p. 25). For instance, a theater-style classroom in which chairs are bolted to the floor retards an attempt at small-group discussion and limits the teaching strategies that an instructor can use in that setting (Strange, 1996). Likewise, residence hall design—the arrangement and style of rooms (singles, doubles, suites), location of common areas, and length of corridors—affects the extent to which students socialize with one another and their overall satisfaction with their living environment (Baum, Aiello, & Colesnick, 1978; Heilweil, 1973; Moos, 1979).

The accessibility of buildings on campus is an issue to which an institution of higher education must pay attention. The Americans with Disabilities Act (ADA) requires that academic programs be accessible to all students, including those with disabilities (Barr, 1996). Many buildings (and offices, classrooms, or equipment within buildings), especially on older campuses, are not physically accessible and must be brought into compliance within a given time period. Campus administrators must give serious consideration to the educational as well as financial implications of the ADA.

How a physical space is decorated also affects student perception of the environment. Banning (1992, 1994) presented evidence that visual displays can indicate either that an environment is inclusive of various student populations (women, students of color) or that it is hostile. Murals in a library that depict women in a subservient role or pictures of distinguished faculty all of whom are white men send a message that women and people of color are not valued. On the other hand, artwork from diverse cultures and portraits of both the heroines and heroes of an institution indicate that all students are welcome and all cultures are celebrated.

The ability to personalize one's physical environment has a positive influence on how one feels about that environment. Students who are able to paint their rooms, arrange their furniture, create murals on the residence hall floor, and so forth feel more of a sense of ownership of the space. Having such control is associated with a higher retention rate (Vinsel, Brown, Altman, & Foss, 1980) and increased academic achievement (Schroeder, 1976).

In summarizing the impact of the physical environment on students, Strange (1996) reflected that "to the extent that various campus physical features contribute to students' sense of safety and security, their sense of belonging and familiarity with an institution, their ease of access and movement through its spaces, and their experience of membership in an educational community is the ultimate test of their design and purpose" (p. 247).

Human Aggregates

The campus environment viewed from the perspective of the human aggregate is a collection of people (Strange & Banning, 2001). The dominant characteristics of the individuals within any setting determine its qualities and impact (Strange, 1996). Human aggregate models include those that focus on differences in student subculture (Clark & Trow, 1966), personality type (Holland, 1985/1992; Myers, 1980), learning style (Kolb, 1984), and student type (Astin, 1993a) within a setting.

For instance, as noted in the previous chapter, Holland (1985/ 1992) identified six types of vocational personality and six parallel types of environment: realistic, investigative, artistic, social, enterprising, and conventional. In addition to presenting a lens through which to consider career development, Holland's theory also suggests a way to interpret environment. According to Holland, each type of environment reflects the characteristics of the people in it. A conventional environment (meaning, one made up of individuals having Holland's conventional personality type) is one in which practicality and efficiency would be valued. One might expect a business school to have a high number of conventional people and to be a place in which a sense of order prevails. By contrast, an artistic environment, one in which many people have artistic personalities (as at a college of fine arts), would be characterized by creativity, expressiveness, and impulsiveness.

In addition, students can be aggregated on the basis of demographic categories such as age, racial or ethnic classification, gender, academic performance, and so forth, with the environment defined by the percentage of each category found therein (Strange, 1996). A disproportionately low number of female students in a college of engineering might make the environment less

welcoming for women. As noted in a previous chapter, the culturally sensitive environment of a tribal college, historically black college, or Hispanic-serving institution is created to a large extent by
the human aggregates that attend the institution. The environment of an Ivy League college, made up of students who all have
outstanding high school academic records, would encourage an
academically challenging curriculum, whereas an open-admission
community college, where students exhibit a range of previous academic performance, would likely have coursework anywhere from
remedial to an honors program.

According to Holland (1985/1992), the power of an environment to influence the people within it is determined by two factors: differentiation and consistency. A differentiated environment
includes a large number of one type (all women, all honors students, all investigatives in Holland's terms, and so on), while an
undifferentiated environment includes many types of people. The
differentiated environment exerts a strong influence on individuals to behave similarly to the dominant type. For example, a fraternity pledge who is undecided about his major would be likely to
decide on business if all the members of his organization are
majoring in business. The undifferentiated environment is more
diffuse and allows greater variety of behavior.

Consistency refers to similarity of type (Holland, 1985/1992).
In a consistent environment, individuals, though not exactly alike,
have much in common. A learning community made up of students majoring in the social sciences, for example, includes people who have similar values related to service to others and interest
in working with people. An inconsistent environment is made up
of dissimilar types of people with few common interests. Students
in such an environment would probably exhibit less interaction
and cohesion than would those in a consistent environment.

The degree of congruence between a person and his or her environment has a significant impact on the person's satisfaction and
success in the environment (Holland, 1985/1992). Congruence
exists when the person and the environment are the same type, as
when an enterprising student (one who enjoys leadership and politics) finds himself in an enterprising environment (such as student government). An incongruent situation exists when the
person and the environment differ, as when a student from an all-

black, inner-city neighborhood finds herself the only African American on a residence hall floor made up of white students from rural Iowa. Students in a congruent environment are more likely to remain in the environment and to be happy and successful. Evans, Forney, and Guido-DiBrito (1998) noted that "congruent environments provide opportunities for individuals to use their skills and interests and reward them for doing so. Incongruent environments seem like 'foreign territory'" (p. 232).

Organizational Structure and Dynamics

An institution of higher education is a complex organization that exhibits characteristics similar to other goal-directed systems. Likewise, a unit that makes up a college or university, such as an academic department, student services area, student organization, residence hall floor, and so forth, is also organized in a way that allows it to accomplish specific goals (Strange, 1996). How an institution or unit is structured influences the behaviors and attitudes of individuals within it.

Hage and Aiken
Hage and Aiken (1970) introduced a model of the complex organization that can be helpful in examining the organizational structures of higher education environments. They proposed that any organization could be placed along a continuum from static to dynamic depending on the extent to which it is open to change. Those that are dynamic (where change is likely to occur) exhibit a high degree of complexity; low levels of centralization, formalization, stratification, and efficiency; and an emphasis on quality over quantity. A static organization (one in which change is unlikely) presents exactly the opposite profile.

Complexity in a higher education institution is determined by the number of specialties or units on a campus, the extent to which high levels of expertise and knowledge are needed to perform in each area, and the emphasis placed on ongoing learning and professional development (Hage & Aiken, 1970). Given the comprehensive nature of higher education, even its smallest institutions are considered complex. However, a small two-year technical institution that relies on part-time instructors and has few support personnel would be considered less complex than a large research university.

Centralization refers to the decision-making process used in an organization (Hage & Aiken, 1970). In a centralized system, power rests in the hands of a few key individuals; in a decentralized organization, many people are involved in decision making. A high degree of centralization is evident if the president of an institution needs to approve all expenditures in all units and interview all candidates for a position. In a decentralized organization, the units affected would make such decisions.

Formalization is defined as the extent to which an organization adheres to explicit or implicit policies and procedures (Hage & Aiken, 1970). For example, because of government policies that it must follow, the financial aid office is almost always more formalized than the office of, say, multicultural affairs. An institution that has many rules and regulations presented in numerous handbooks and manuals, administrative procedures that must be followed to the letter, and detailed job descriptions is considered formalized. Inflexibility and arduous change processes characterize such an environment (Strange, 1996).

Stratification has to do with the distribution of rewards and status in an organization and the degree of mobility enjoyed by those in the system (Hage & Aiken, 1970). In a highly stratified organization, there are many levels of bureaucracy; those at the top of the hierarchy clearly have greater status, higher salaries, and more perks than individuals at the bottom. In addition, it is difficult to advance in such a system. Strange (1996) noted that "stratification tends to be . . . divisive, since reward structures are cast in a competitive framework, and those who share disproportionately in the rewards are vested in the status quo" (p. 251).

Efficiency refers to the cost effectiveness of production (Hage & Aiken, 1970). Especially at a time when resources are limited, making the most of those resources by reducing costs is stressed. However, as Strange (1996) pointed out, it is difficult to assess the efficiency of academic and student services programs. We can never really determine all the factors that contribute to learning outcomes, let alone their costs.

Either quantity or quality of production can be emphasized in an organization (Hage & Aiken, 1970). Many institutions of higher education stress quantity over quality. Some admissions offices (especially if at a struggling college) are constantly pressured to produce a large number of students without regard to their academic potential. Unfortunately, increased emphasis on quantity often leads to decreased quality. As more students are admitted into an academic program, less attention can be given to each one since classes are larger and less time is available for teachers to spend individually with each student. Learning outcomes can be affected when such choices are made.

Strange (1983) argued that a dynamic institution (one with a high level of complexity and low levels of centralization, formalization, stratification, efficiency, and emphasis on quality) fosters learning and development. In such an environment, difference is valued, involvement is encouraged, personal interactions are stressed, and students are encouraged to try new things. Morale is also better in a dynamic environment (Strange, 1996).

Strange (1996) did caution, however, that personality type and cognitive developmental level affect individual perception of and satisfaction with the environment of an organization. For example, a person exhibiting conventional qualities according to Holland's theory of vocational personality (1985/1992)—a preference for order, efficiency, and stability—might prefer a static environment in which change is not likely. In summary, Hage and Aiken's model (1970) is an excellent tool for analyzing organizational dynamics and the likelihood of change in an environment, which in turn can influence student learning.

Berger

Berger (2000) identified five dimensions of organizational behavior and explored how they combine to create a unique college environment. He then examined the impact of the environment on student outcomes. These are the five types of organizational behavior Berger discussed:

1. Bureaucratic, characterized by emphasis on rules, structures, and agreed-upon procedures
2. Collegial, reflected in a collaborative orientation, concern for people, and use of consensus in decision making
3. Political, in which competition for resources and conflict over priorities are apparent

4. Symbolic, evidenced by use of symbols to reflect agreed-upon meaning within the organization
5. Systemic, which underscores the open-system nature of institutions of higher education

Berger (2000) noted that the organization of each college or university exhibits some degree of each behavioral dimension and that the relative mix creates a distinct environment. In his study of nine private colleges, Berger identified three environmental types:

1. Competitive, characterized by a high level of political behavior, low collegiality, and a moderate level of the other behavioral dimensions
2. Casual, which exhibited a low level of bureaucratic behavior and moderate level of the other behaviors
3. Cohesive, found to have a low level of political and systemic behaviors and a high level of bureaucratic, collegial, and symbolic behaviors

The environment varies with the type of institution. For instance, in Berger's study two historically black colleges were both categorized as cohesive institutions, whereas of the six predominantly white institutions three were found to be competitive and the other three casual.

Berger (2000) found relationships between the organizational environment and both psychological and behavioral student outcomes. A cohesive environment had the greatest positive effect on development of humanistic values (his psychological variable) and involvement in community service (his behavioral outcome). A casual environment had a slight negative impact on these outcomes, and a competitive environment had a stronger negative impact on both outcomes.

Berger (2000) suggested that the strength of the five organizational dimensions affects the degree of influence that the environment has on student outcomes. An environment in which all five behavioral dimensions are low has an overall weak effect on student attitude and behavior. If all dimensions are moderate, students are exposed to many forces, with no one being very strong. Overall, then, the influence of such an environment tends to be diverse, with students affected differently. Berger noted that "medium levels of the organizational dimensions are more likely to promote a wider range of student types, experiences, perceptions, behaviors, and outcomes within a college" (pp. 190–191).

An organizational environment in which the level of the behavioral dimensions is high has a strong, uniform impact on student outcomes. Such an environment tends to be homogeneous in nature, with clear expectations for students to engage in certain behavior and hold particular values. Berger (2000) suggested that "involving colleges" (Kuh et al., 1991) are an example of institutions that exhibit a high level of certain behavioral dimensions. At such a college, students are highly involved in activities congruent with the mission, purpose, and values of the institution. Berger also hypothesized that the high level of the behavioral dimensions associated with the cohesive environment found at an HBCU (at least those in his study) may help to explain the higher graduation rate of African American students in these environments as compared to predominantly white institutions (Allen, 1992).

Finally, Berger (2000) noted that an environment dominated by a particular behavioral dimension exhibits outcomes that are reflective of that dimension. For instance, in a competitive environment, which is dominated by political behavior, students exhibited lower humanistic values and were less likely to engage in community service than were students in the other types of environment, despite having entered college scoring higher on these variables. Berger attributed this outcome to the development of a "me first" (p. 193) attitude among the students in the competitive environment. In summary, Berger's approach holds great promise for determining the differential impact of organizational environment on a variety of student outcomes.

Perceptual Approaches

Unlike the three models examined previously, in which the environment is viewed objectively by independent outside evaluators, perceptual approaches rely on the collective assessment of individuals within the environment being examined (Strange, 1991). As such, the description of the environment is subjective rather than objective. Individual impressions are influenced by many factors:

background, past experience, expectation, and personality. In turn, people's behavior and feelings are strongly influenced by their perception of the environment in which they find themselves (Strange, 1996). Several perceptual models have been used to define college environments; the environmental press model (Pace & Stern, 1958; Stern, 1970) and the social climate model (Moos, 1976) are the most familiar. In addition, analyses of the campus culture (Kuh, 1993; Kuh & Whitt, 1988), which are based on the collective perception of individuals within the environment, are considered here.

Environmental Press

Basing their work on that of Murray (1938), Pace and Stern (1958) were among the first to look at the impact of the college environment on the individuals within it. They examined the interaction of environmental press (the characteristics, qualities, and pressures exerted by the environment) and the individual's needs (what the individual seeks in the environment to fulfill her or his goals). These variables were assessed using two self-report instruments. The College Characteristics Index (CCI, measuring press) identified student impressions of the college, including topics such as student-faculty interaction, policies and procedures, teaching methods, and so forth. The Activities Index (AI, measuring needs) asked students about activities in which they engaged.

Press was determined by aggregating individual scores on the CCI. For example, if a high percentage of students reported that intellectual discussion took place in their residence hall after dinner every evening, the intellectual climate press would be inferred to be high. Eleven environmental presses were identified by Saunders (1969): aspiration level, intellectual climate, student dignity, academic climate, academic achievement, self-expression, group life, academic organization, social form, play-work, and vocational climate. Environments in which needs and press were similar were determined to be growth-enhancing, whereas environments in which needs and press differed contributed to unhappiness and retarded personal development (Stern, 1970).

Social Climate

Moos's social climate model (1976, 1979) is based on the idea that environments, like people, have personalities. He suggested that there are three broad categories of dimensions found in every environment, regardless of type:

1. Relationship, focusing on how people interact with each other
2. Personal development, relating to aspects of personal growth and self-development
3. System maintenance and system change, having to do with how an environment functions and the likelihood of change occurring

Moos (1976) developed a number of instruments to assess various environments (residence halls, classrooms, groups, families). Every environment varies somewhat in the specific dimensions found within each of the three main climate variables. For instance, a residence hall environment is characterized by these dimensions:

• Relationship: involvement, emotional support
• Personal development: independence, traditional social orientation, competition, academic achievement, intellectuality
• System maintenance and system change: order and organization, student influence, innovation

The University Residence Hall Environment Scale (URES; Gerst & Moos, 1972) measures how students perceive their residence hall along each of these dimensions. From this aggregated data, a profile of the hall can be developed to indicate which dimensions are perceived as high and which as low.

Various types of residence halls have been found to have unique "personalities" (Moos, 1976). Students living in a coed house with an international relations theme perceived the climate as much higher in the areas of involvement and emotional support than did students living in an all-male house made up of medical students. By contrast, the medical students saw their house as lacking in support, competitive, and achievement-oriented.

Moos (1976) reported that students attending a college where relationship dimensions were perceived to be high were significantly involved in campus activities and had positive feelings about their school. Attrition was also lower at such institutions. In the classroom setting, students were more satisfied and more interested in course material when relationship dimensions were high. However, learning was most likely to occur in a classroom where personal development dimensions, especially competition and intellectual challenge, were high. Moos (1976) summarized these findings by saying "the evidence that high emphasis on Relationship and Personal Growth dimensions fosters student aspiration and achievement is relatively persuasive" (p. 345).

Campus Culture

Kuh and his colleagues (Kuh, 1993; Kuh & Whitt, 1988) have examined campus culture, the factors that influence its development, and its impact. *Campus culture* refers to the "confluence of institutional history, campus traditions, and the values and assumptions that shape the character of a given college or university" (Kuh & Hall, 1993, pp. 1–2). According to Strange (1996), four levels of culture can be found in the campus environment: artifacts, perspectives, values, and assumptions.

Artifacts include physical, verbal, and behavioral aspects of an environment that have agreed-upon meaning for members of that environment (Kuh & Hall, 1993). Physical artifacts are landmarks, buildings, or other physical aspects of the setting, linked with a particular institution or sending a message concerning what is important there. (For instance, Beaver Stadium at Penn State University is a huge, impressive structure at the edge of campus that is one of the first buildings seen there as one drives in from the airport to campus. This building certainly symbolizes the important role of football on the Penn State campus.) Verbal artifacts are the history, stories, and unique language associated with a school. Kuh, Schuh, Whitt, and Associates (1991, p. 84) noted the "terms of endearment" used to describe certain universities, as in referring to Stanford University as "the Farm" because it was built on farmland owned by its founder. Behavioral artifacts are the special activities and events that occur on a campus, such as founder's day or commencement. Artifacts are a way for a student to connect with the campus and to become an insider.

Perspectives define "the way things are done" on a campus (Kuh & Hall, 1993, p. 6). Appropriate etiquette when speaking to a professor, how students dress, and even the espoused values are part of this aspect of the campus culture. For instance, students at Grinnell College are noted for their liberal belief systems and counterculture appearance. A student who is uncomfortable with the perspectives of a campus is not likely to become involved in the campus or to persist to graduation.

Values reflect "what the members of a culture assert to be most important" (Kuh et al., 1991, p. 96). Values underlie decisions that are made on campus and how actions are judged. Core values are often reflected in the mission statement of a college and appear in such official institutional documents as the college catalogue, student handbook, or staff manual (Strange, 1996). Values convey a powerful message to students. For example, the student of color who hears regularly about the commitment of the college to diversity but sees very few faculty members of color is hearing an espoused value that is more like an aspiration or rationalization, according to Kuh and Whitt (1997).

The final level of institutional culture, upon which the other components of culture are based, is that of assumptions, or "tacit beliefs that members use to define their role, their relationship to others, and the nature of the organization in which they live" (Kuh & Hall, 1993, p. 7). Assumptions are the least apparent part of the culture because they seem to exist implicitly and are rarely mentioned. An example pointed out by Kuh, Schuh, Whitt, and Associates (1991) is the assumption at Xavier University that anyone can overcome any type of challenge and succeed academically.

The culture of an institution has a strong impact on the students enrolled. The cultures of the involving colleges identified by Kuh and associates (1991), for example, served to promote student involvement and to encourage feelings of institutional pride. Strange (1996) noted that "campus culture is a critical lens through which institutional members view and evaluate their experiences" (p. 260).

Creating a Positive Learning Environment

Theories of person-environment interaction and models of campus environment yield information on factors that influence student outcomes. Those responsible for creating and managing the campus environment can use these principles to help ensure that the environment has a positive effect on student growth and achievement. Some end goals that an educator should strive for are an intentionally designed environment, a human-scale environment, one that encourages human interaction, and an environment with a strong sense of community.

Intentional Design

Person-environment interaction theory afforded a rationale for a short monograph published by the Western Interstate Commission for Higher Education (WICHE, 1973) that stressed the importance of intentional campus design. This concept was the basis for the campus ecology model (Aulepp & Delworth, 1976; Banning, 1978; Banning & Kaiser, 1974). A basic premise of the campus ecology model is that a transactional relationship exists between students and their campus. Grounded by the idea that "the students shape the environment and are shaped by it" (WICHE, 1973, p. 6), WICHE suggested that the nature of the campus environment and the opportunities it presents can either facilitate or inhibit student behavior: "Campus design is, therefore, an attempt to create campus environments that will foster student growth and development" (p. 5). Those responsible for campus design need to be cognizant of the factors, such as those noted in the section on components of the environment, that produce student experiences that result in the learning desired by the campus. Several assumptions support the process of designing a campus to foster student learning (WICHE, 1973, p. 6):

- The campus environment consists of all the stimuli that impinge upon the students' sensory modalities.
- A transactional relationship exists between college students and their environment.
- For the purposes of environmental design, the shaping properties of the campus environment are focused upon.
- Every student possesses the capacity for a wide spectrum of possible behaviors.
- Students will attempt to cope with any educational environment in which they are placed.

- Fitting the campus environment to the students requires the creation of a variety of campus subenvironments.
- Every campus has a design, whether it has been planned or not.

Designing a campus can result in features that encourage or discourage certain behaviors. With regard to the physical environment, for example, are benches and other seating areas placed in grassy areas to encourage people to converse with each other? Are numerous bulletin boards and kiosks available to advertise campus events?

If students do not have the opportunity to communicate with other students or do not know about campus events, potential growth-producing experiences are lost. Campus design often takes into account features related to the physical development of the campus, meaning ease of access in getting from one building to another or the efficiency with which a building can be cleaned and repaired. But the other feature of campus design, often overlooked, has to do with the learning that the design allows, which has obvious implications for what students take away from their experience. As those responsible for campus planning pay attention to the potential student learning resulting from the design of the campus, the consequence is a value-added experience for students.

Human Scale Environment

Another significant aspect of the environment that affects students is the extent to which it is on a human scale: "Human scale properties permit students to become familiar with and feel competent in their environment" (Kuh et al., 1991, p. 110). Similarly, "human scale environments are not overcrowded, blend in with the natural surroundings, and accommodate small numbers of people in structures usually no more than three stories above the ground" (Hall, 1966, as cited in Kuh et al., 1991, p. 110).

In a human-scale environment, students are not allowed to get lost and experience anonymity. As a consequence, they identify with each other, the institution, and their place of residence, and they know members of the faculty. All of these factors are seen as positively influencing learning and persistence to graduation

(Astin, 1993b; Kuh et al, 1994; Tinto, 1987). The actual size of the campus really has little to with the feeling of anonymity because, as Kuh and associates (1991) reported, a large institution can take specific steps to develop an environment that is human in scale.

Human Interaction

A human-scale environment allows and encourages students to interact with each other and with faculty and other members of the institution, factors that are crucial to the learning process. As Astin (1993b) pointed out, students' cognitive and affective development, two important outcomes of the educational experience, are positively affected when students interact with faculty.

Pascarella and Terenzini (1991) have an additional perspective on this issue. They asserted that "there can be little doubt about the need for faculty members' acceptance of their roles and responsibilities for student learning and their active involvement in students' lives" (p. 655). As a consequence, they urged faculty to be engaged with students in an ongoing sense. Terenzini, Pascarella, and Blimling (1996) added that "student-faculty contact and student learning are positively related, and it would seem that finding ways to promote such contact is in the best educational interests of both students and institutions" (p. 155). They identified several studies indicating that students' interpersonal interactions with peers and faculty shape a number of dimensions of cognitive growth.

The relationship a student has with peers also affects student learning and values development. Astin (1993b) asserted that "the peer group is the single most potent source of influence on growth and development during the undergraduate years" (p. 398). He added that "students' values, beliefs, and aspirations tend to change in the direction of the dominant values, beliefs, and aspirations of the peer group" (p. 398). This being the case, it is clear that to the extent the values of peer groups are consistent with the values of the institution, the group either facilitates or inhibits the desired development of students.

The work of Kuh and Arnold (1993) is instructive on this point. They concluded that fraternity membership has a negative relationship with gains in knowledge acquisition and application. This finding may well be due to the values espoused by these organizations. The task, then, of those responsible for the campus environment is to encourage development of an organization whose values are consistent with those of the institution and discourage those with values that are not. This may be easier to assert than to accomplish. As Sanford (1967) concluded, for example, "often, however, academic ambition is vitiated by the peer culture" (p. 150). Still, he indicated that with perseverance the peer culture could be changed.

Developing Community

In their book on student learning, Kuh, Douglas, Lund, and Ramin-Gyurnek (1994) cited the observations of Lee Upcraft on what matters most in the lives of students, especially as they enter their college or university. Upcraft suggested that at the heart of student concerns is the desire to enjoy academic success, fit in, and make friends. The matter of fitting in and making friends is a fairly basic way of asserting that students want to be members of a community. Community development, then, can be an important element in student success. Kuh and his colleagues (1991) concluded that developing community is an important ingredient in helping students "become full participating members of organizations and activities" (p. 352), which in turn is linked with student persistence and educational attainment (Kuh et al., 1994). The implications of this involvement are obvious. College graduates, as is asserted in other chapters of this book, experience a variety of benefits as a consequence of their education. Since community seems to engender experiences that then result in persistence and educational attainment, developing community becomes an essential building block in the education process. Fostering opportunity for student-faculty interaction, developing meaningful venues for student involvement, and affirming the value of community development are steps that an institution can take that have educationally purposeful results. Strange and Banning (2001) enumerate many examples of community-building interventions.

Implications

Systematic examination and intentional design of the campus environment are important steps that educators can take to enhance student learning. The physical environment, the human aggregate, the organizational environment, and student perceptions all influence student satisfaction and success in college. The outcomes of higher education are shaped as much by the environment as they are by the characteristics of entering students.

Strange and Banning (2001) introduced a campus design matrix to guide assessment and environmental intervention. They encouraged educators to ask three questions in evaluating a specific environment on a campus (such as the impact of a residence hall learning community, the success of a multicultural center in meeting the needs of underrepresented students, or the effectiveness of a sexual assault prevention program):

1. What aspects of the environment are involved (physical, aggregate, organizational, perceptual)?
2. What is the impact of the environment as it is presently designed (on a continuum from active and positive to negative and stressful)?
3. What is the intended purpose of the environmental design (perhaps safety, inclusion, involvement, community)?

These questions can help an administrator determine how well the current environment is meeting student needs and point to areas for future intervention.

Strange and Banning (2001) noted that identifying the impact and purpose of the campus environment has implications for campus policy and practices. Through assessment, information about the campus becomes available that can be shared with constituents, such as potential students and their parents, members of the board of regents, legislators, and others. Such information is a powerful tool in demonstrating the benefits of college. It can also guide strategic planning and quality enhancement efforts. Ongoing assessment is important for evaluating the impact of initiated changes and should be built into any redesign efforts.

Strange and Banning (2001, citing Moos, 1979) also pointed out the importance of "teaching students how to create, select, and transcend environments, how to maximize person-environment congruence when support is the goal, or how to seek an appropriate amount of incongruence and challenge when the goal is personal growth" (p. 216). They contended that "enhancing environmental competence is a goal that encompasses the basic purposes and outcomes of higher education" (p. 216).

Certainly, understanding the college or university environment and its impact on students is necessary to be an effective educator. To ensure that students achieve the outcomes of higher education identified in this book, faculty and student affairs administrators, and other institutional agents, must work to intentionally create, sustain, and enhance a positive campus environment.

References

Allen, W. R. (1992). The color of success: African-American college student outcomes at predominantly White and historically Black public colleges and universities. *Harvard Educational Review, 62*(1), 26–44.

Astin, A. W. (1984). Student involvement: A developmental theory for higher education. *Journal of College Student Personnel, 25*, 297–308.

Astin, A. W. (1993a). An empirical typology of college students. *Journal of College Student Development, 34*, 36–46.

Astin, A. W. (1993b). *What matters in college?* San Francisco: Jossey-Bass.

Aulepp, L., & Delworth, U. (1976). *Training manual for an ecosystem model: Assessing and designing campus environments.* Boulder, CO: Western Interstate Commission for Higher Education.

Banning, J. H. (1978). *Campus ecology: A perspective for student affairs.* Cincinnati: National Association of Student Personnel Administrators.

Banning, J. H. (1992). Visual anthropology: Viewing the campus ecology for messages of sexism. *Campus Ecologist, 10*(1), 1–4.

Banning, J. H. (1994). Use of nonverbal cues of the physical environment in campus consultation. *Campus Ecologist, 12*(4), 1–4.

Banning, J. H., & Kaiser, L. (1974). An ecological perspective and model for campus design. *Personnel and Guidance Journal, 52*, 370–375.

Barr, M. J. (1996). Legal foundations of student affairs practice. In S. R. Komives, D. B. Woodard, Jr., & Associates, *Student services: A handbook for the profession* (3rd ed., pp. 126–144). San Francisco: Jossey-Bass.

Baum, A., Aiello, J., & Colesnick, L. (1978). Crowding and personal control: Social density and the development of learned helplessness. *Journal of Personality and Social Psychology, 36,* 1000–1011.

Berger, J. B. (2000). Organizational behavior at college and student outcomes: A new perspective on college impact. *Review of Higher Education, 23,* 177–198.

Carnegie Foundation for the Advancement of Teaching. (1990). *Campus life: In search of community.* Lawrenceville, NJ: Princeton University Press.

Chickering, A. W., & Reisser, L. (1993). *Education and identity* (2nd ed.). San Francisco: Jossey-Bass.

Clark, B. R., & Trow, M. (1966). The organizational context. In T. M. Newcomb & E. K. Wilson (Eds.), *College peer groups: Problems and prospects for research* (pp. 17–70). Chicago: Aldine.

Evans, N. J., Forney, D. S., & Guido-DiBrito, F. (1998). *Student development in college: Theory, research, and practice.* San Francisco: Jossey-Bass.

Gerst, M., & Moos, R. H. (1972). The social ecology of university student residences. *Journal of Educational Psychology, 63,* 513–522.

Griffith, J. C. (1994). Open space preservation: An imperative for quality campus environments. *Journal of Higher Education, 65,* 645–669.

Hage, J., & Aiken, M. (1970). *Social change in complex organizations.* New York: Random House.

Hagley, M. (1999, December). *Interview paper for HgEd 577 Campus Environments and Cultures.* Unpublished manuscript, Iowa State University.

Heilweil, M. (1973). The influence of dormitory architecture on resident behavior. *Environment and Behavior, 5,* 377–412.

Holahan, C., & Wilcox, B. (1978). Residential satisfaction and friendship formation in high and low-rise housing: An interactional analysis. *Journal of Educational Psychology, 70,* 237–241.

Holland, J. L. (1992). *Making vocational choices: A theory of vocational personalities and work environments* (2nd. ed.). Odessa, FL: Psychological Assessment Resources. (Original work published 1985)

Hood, A. B., Riahinejad, A. R., & White, D. B. (1986). Changes in ego identity during the college years. *Journal of College Student Personnel, 27,* 107–113.

Hunt, S., & Rentz, A. L. (1994). Greek-letter social group members' involvement and psychosocial development. *Journal of College Student Development, 35,* 289–295.

Kolb, D. (1984). *Experiential learning: Experience as a source of learning and development.* Englewood Cliffs, NJ: Prentice Hall.

Kuh, G. D. (Ed.). (1993). *Cultural perspectives in student affairs work.* Lanham, MD: American College Personnel Association.

Kuh, G. D., & Arnold, J. C. (1993). Liquid bonding: A cultural analysis of the role of alcohol in fraternity pledgeship. *Journal of College Student Development, 34,* 327–334.

Kuh, G. D., Douglas, K. B., Lund, J. P., & Ramin-Gyurnek, J. (1994). *Student learning outside the classroom: Transcending artificial boundaries.* (ASHE-ERIC Higher Education Report no. 8). Washington, DC: George Washington University, School of Education and Human Development.

Kuh, G. D., & Hall, J. E. (1993). Using cultural perspectives in student affairs. In G. D. Kuh (Ed.), *Cultural perspectives in student affairs work* (pp. 1–20). Lanham, MD: American College Personnel Association.

Kuh, G. D., & Schuh, J. H. (1983). Perceptions of the RA role: Does a year make a difference? *Journal of College and University Student Housing, 13*(2), 3–7.

Kuh, G. D., Schuh, J. H., Whitt, E. J., & Associates. (1991). *Involving colleges.* San Francisco: Jossey-Bass.

Kuh, G. D., & Whitt, E. J. (1988). *The invisible tapestry: Cultures in American colleges and universities* (ASHE-ERIC Higher Education Report no. 1). Washington, DC: Association for the Study of Higher Education.

Kuh, G. D., & Whitt, E. J. (1997). The invisible tapestry: Culture in American colleges and universities. In E. J. Whitt (Ed.), *College student affairs administration* (ASHE Reader Series, pp. 125–135). Needham Heights, MA: Simon & Schuster.

Lewin, K. (1936). *Principles of topological psychology.* New York: McGraw-Hill.

Michelson, W. (1970). *Man and his urban environment: A sociological approach.* Reading, MA: Addison-Wesley.

Moos, R. H. (1976). *The human context: Environmental determinants of behavior.* New York: Wiley.

Moos, R. H. (1979). *Evaluating educational environments: Procedures, measures, findings, and policy implementations.* San Francisco: Jossey-Bass.

Murray, H. (1938). *Explorations in personality.* New York: Oxford University Press.

Myers, I. B. (1980). *Gifts differing.* Palo Alto, CA: Consulting Psychologists Press.

National Center for Education Statistics. (1998). *Profile of undergraduates in U.S. postsecondary education institutions: 1995–96.* Washington, DC: U.S. Department of Education, Office of Educational Research and Improvement.

Pace, C. R., & Stern, G. G. (1958). An approach to the measurement of psychological characteristics of college environments. *Journal of Educational Psychology, 49,* 269–277.

Pascarella, E. T., & Terenzini, P. T. (1991). *How college affects students.* San Francisco: Jossey-Bass.

Rendón, L. (1994). Validating culturally diverse students: Toward a new model of learning and student development. *Innovative Higher Education, 19,* 33–51.

Rosenberg, M., & McCullough, B. C. (1981). Mattering: Inferred significance to parents and mental health among adolescents. In R. Simmons (Ed.), *Research in community and mental health* (vol. 2, pp. 163–182). Greenwich, CT: JAI Press.

Sanford, N. (1966). *Self and society.* New York: Atherton.

Sanford, N. (1967). *Where colleges fail: A study of the student as a person.* San Francisco: Jossey-Bass.

Saunders, D. R. (1969). A factor analytic study of the AI and CCI. *Multivariate Behavioral Research, 4,* 329–346.

Schlossberg, N. K. (1989). Marginality and mattering: Key issues in building community. In D. C. Roberts (Ed.), *Designing campus activities to foster a sense of community* (New Directions for Student Services, no. 48, pp. 5–15). San Francisco: Jossey-Bass.

Schlossberg, N. K, Lynch, A. Q., & Chickering, A. W. (1989). *Improving higher education environments for adults: Responsive programs and services from entry to departure.* San Francisco: Jossey-Bass.

Schroeder, C. C. (1976). New strategies for structuring residential environments. *Journal of College Student Personnel, 17,* 386–390.

Serow, R. C., & Dreyden, J. J. (1990). Community service among college and university students: Individual and institutional relationships. *Adolescence, 25,* 555–566.

Sowa, C. J., & Gressard, C. E. (1983). Athletic participation: Its relationship to student development. *Journal of College Student Development, 24,* 236–239.

Stern, G. (1970). *People in context: Measuring person-environment congruence in education and industry.* New York: Wiley.

Strange, C. C. (1983). Human development theory and administrative practice in student affairs: Ships passing in the daylight? *NASPA Journal, 21*(1), 2–8.

Strange, C. C. (1991). Managing college environments: Theory and practice. In T. K. Miller, R. B. Winston, & Associates. *Administration and leadership in student affairs* (2nd ed., pp. 159–199). Muncie, IN: Accelerated Development.

Strange, C. C. (1996). Dynamics of campus environments. In S. R. Komives, D. B. Woodard, Jr., & Associates, *Student services: A handbook for the profession* (3rd ed., pp. 244–268). San Francisco: Jossey-Bass.

Strange, C. C., & Banning, J. H. (2001). *Educating by design: Creating campus learning environments that work.* San Francisco: Jossey-Bass.

Sturner, W. E. (1973). The college environment. In D. W. Vermilye (Ed.), *The future in the making* (pp. 71–86). San Francisco: Jossey-Bass.

Terenzini, P. T., Pascarella, E. T., & Blimling, G. S. (1996). Students' out-of-class experiences and their influence on learning and cognitive development: A literature review. *Journal of College Student Development, 37,* 149–162.

Thelin, J. R., & Yankovich, J. (1987). Bricks and mortar: Architecture and the study of higher education. In J. C. Smart (Ed.), *Higher education: Vol. 3. Handbook of theory and research* (pp. 57–83). New York: Agathon.

Tinto, V. (1987). *Leaving college.* Chicago: University of Chicago Press.

Vinsel, A., Brown, B., Altman, I., & Foss, C. (1980). Privacy regulation, territorial displays, and effectiveness of individual functioning. *Journal of Personality and Social Psychology, 39,* 1104–1115.

Western Interstate Commission for Higher Education. (1973). *The ecosystem model: Designing campus environments.* Boulder, CO: Author.

Williams, M. E., & Winston, R. B., Jr. (1985). Participation in organized student activities and work: Differences in developmental task achievement of traditional-aged college students. *NASPA Journal, 22*(3), 52–59.

Chapter Four

The Role of Student Affairs in the Learning Process

Learning is the heart of the undergraduate experience. One can debate where learning occurs, how it occurs, and how it can best be facilitated, but learning is what a college education is about. Learning has cognitive dimensions, such as critical thinking or communication skills; affective dimensions, such as managing one's emotions or dealing with newfound autonomy; and psychomotor dimensions, such as developing and sustaining a regimen of exercise for physical fitness or operating sophisticated electronic equipment.

Description of how to facilitate student learning has gone through a number of iterations over the years. This is especially true for the role of student affairs and its practitioners in promoting student learning. In fact, until the landmark publication *Student Learning Imperative* (American College Personnel Association, 1996), student affairs staff primarily were seen as providing services that may have complemented or facilitated the learning process, but they were not seen as individuals who contributed directly to it. In this chapter, we take a historical look at several salient publications that address promotion of learning as a result of the student's total experience while enrolled in college. We trace through these documents the notion of student learning outside the classroom as it has evolved from a peripheral experience to a central part of the educational experience. We also trace the role of student affairs in the learning process. The chapter does not address learning theory, nor does it focus specifically on learning that occurs through classroom processes.

A Historical Look at the Role of Student Affairs in Student Learning

As student affairs units emerged as a campus entity, the deans or directors of these units tended to come from an academic background other than student affairs or higher education. The reason for this was obvious: "student affairs" or "higher education" as a field of study did not then exist (McEwen & Talbot, 1998). As these fields began to emerge, content was borrowed heavily from the discipline of psychology—especially counseling psychology. This discipline is significantly oriented toward individuals and small groups. For example, persons who consult counseling psychologists often have a "presenting problem"; the client addresses this problem with the assistance of the counselor to make satisfactory progress.

The 1937 document *The Student Personnel Point of View* (or SPPV) (*Points of View*, 1989) prescribed a role for student affairs practitioners that emphasized the counseling and guidance function and complemented the college or university's instructional mission. Student affairs staff were to offer information to instructors so as to enhance instruction, that is, "assembling and making available information to be used in improvement of instruction and in making the curriculum more flexible" (*Points of View*, 1989, p. 53).

The document did not suggest a role for student affairs that is equivalent to that of faculty in the learning process. Clearly, the partnerships that are increasingly common on today's campus and that require collaboration between student and academic affairs were not considered, such as developing service-learning experiences or a learning community. The closest the 1937 document got to identifying a direct role in student learning for student affairs staff was this recommendation: "Assisting the student to reach his [sic] maximum effectiveness through clarification of his purposes, improvement of study methods, speech habits, personal appearance, manners, etc., and through progression in religious, emotional, and social development, and other nonacademic personal and group relationships" (*Points of View*, 1989, p. 52).

Many of the traditional units of student affairs emerged to provide such services and resources to students as housing accommodations, financial aid, or recreation facilities. Although these services helped free up the student to concentrate on academic goals and classroom learning, student affairs units and programs were not considered a site for learning per se. This service orientation is consistent with the SPPV in that the student affairs unit was appropriately positioned to be supportive of the academic mission of the institution. Student affairs staff thus participated peripherally in the learning enterprise of the institution by playing an enabling role, by making accommodations convenient, and by meeting student needs and requests for services. Student affairs units primarily "smoothed the path" and minimized distraction from students' attention to their academic work. On campuses where the various tenets of SPPV were implemented, student affairs staff members would thus have played a supportive though somewhat ancillary role in the student learning process.

The next formal chance to examine appropriate roles for student affairs staff in the learning process occurred when the SPPV was updated and reissued in 1949. The second version of the SPPV expanded on the ideas of 1937 and included more detail about student affairs practice. The role of student affairs with respect to the student learning process, however, was again largely unaddressed. As the 1949 document observed, "in order that each student may develop effective work habits and thereby achieve at his [sic] optimum potential, the college or university should provide services through which the student may acquire the skills and techniques for effective utilization of his ability" (*Points of View,* 1989, p. 28). In a later section of this document, colleges were urged to provide "remedial services in the areas of speech, reading, and study habits recognizing that the presence of defects in these areas may seriously impede the functioning of many able students and also restrict the contributions which may be made by otherwise adequate personalities" (*Points of View,* 1989, p. 36).

Recommendations for a partnership between student affairs and academic affairs to promote student learning were not found. Student affairs was clearly regarded as providing important services and experiences for students, but student affairs practitioners will find precious little in this document that identified for them a central role in the student learning process. Hosting a range of services from student housing to health was regarded as an important responsibility, but it was also framed as supportive of what occurred in the classroom—as in the 1937 statement.

An opportunity to examine this role again occurred in 1987. The fiftieth anniversary of the original document was celebrated in part by publication of a new statement articulating assumptions, beliefs, and the role of student affairs. The document that resulted, "A Perspective on Student Affairs," was "not intended to be a revision of either the 1937 or the 1949 statements," according to Judith Chambers, who was then the NASPA president (*Points of View,* 1989, p. 2). It was, however, an attempt to describe contemporary student affairs practice. As with the first two statements, a primary role for student affairs professionals in student learning was not a central focus of the document.

The 1987 statement asserted the preeminence of an institution's academic mission, with the student affairs unit as a partner in the educational enterprise: "Student affairs enhances and supports the academic mission" (*Points of View,* 1989, p. 12). A number of assertions were articulated with regard to student learning (such as how student involvement, physical circumstances, and the out-of-class environment each affect student learning), and these suggested a more central role for student affairs in the learning process. However, this document does not produce a principled foundation for the kind of partnership identified earlier in this chapter (developing a learning community with faculty, advancing service learning, or working with faculty to develop undergraduate research assistantship or similar campus work experience tied to the learning process).

Substantial progress was made in advancing student affairs between the 1949 statement and the 1987 perspective; for example, the evolution of student development theory as a basis for practice was a major step toward professionalization of the field. However, in most cases, any legitimate place for student affairs in the student learning process remained subordinate to that of faculty. During the latter part of this time frame, however, some statements asserted more forcefully the legitimate role of student affairs in the learning process. In particular, Robert D. Brown's 1972 monograph recommended that student affairs initiate development of more meaningful linkages with academic affairs to advance student learning. Specifically, Brown took issue with the term *extracurricular,* concluding that it could be taken to mean "peripheral and unnecessary." He urged that student development functions become curricular "with no prefix added" (p. 42), thus expanding the scope of "learning" to include out-of-class experience. Brown also made a series of recommendations aimed at integrating student affairs with academic affairs, being certain to underscore that "the purpose of these ties with the academic arena is not just to play at being academicians but actually be academicians and ultimately to expand the typical concerns of the academician to include process as well as content, affective development as well as cognitive development, competency attainment as well as knowledge learned" (p. 42).

Instead of dealing with how services to students could be improved or made more effective, Brown's ideas (1972) about integrating student affairs into the total learning experience of students situated student affairs as a central and essential part of student educational experiences. His argument concluded that the appropriate role of the student affairs practitioner was far from peripheral and that partnership in equal status with teaching faculty was warranted. This concept did not take hold at the time, but the essence of Brown's discussion contributed a far different notion of the student affairs professional as an educator and facilitator of student learning in full partnership with faculty. In these ways, Brown's work foreshadowed more recent conceptions of student learning and the role of student affairs in promoting learning.

Resources That Directly Address Student Learning

One of the most important documents to be released in the recent past was *Involvement in Learning,* prepared by the Study Group on the Conditions of Excellence in American Higher Education (1984). This report questioned not only the extent to which students were engaged in their educational experience but also the ability of four-year colleges, community colleges, and universities to offer a high-quality education given the myriad constraints placed on the educational institution. One recommendation was for students to devote more time, energy, and effort to their undergraduate education. However, the study group members conceded that simply having students put more effort into their education would not suffice; recommendations included developing a learning community "organized around specific intellectual themes or tasks" (p. 33). The learning community was valued by group members because it "can strengthen opportunities for intellectual dialogue and other forms of active learning" (p. 33).

A variety of benefits would accrue to students and faculty participating in this experience: encouraging a feeling of community, building a sense of group cohesion and identity, and encouraging faculty to relate to one another. To support the value of these interpersonally oriented outcomes, the report also pointed out that working and learning in groups was a key predictor of success in many professions. One member of the study group, Alexander Astin, subsequently built upon the ideas of the report and made additional suggestions about involvement (1985). The learning community was highlighted as well as development of more active modes of teaching, fostering more student-faculty contact, and using student life activities to encourage students to engage meaningfully while in college.

On most campuses, existing relationships between student affairs and academic affairs (separate and unequal) inadequately addressed the new way of thinking about learning as student-centered, relational, and encompassing a range of learning experiences. For example, developing a learning community almost inevitably requires cooperation between academic affairs personnel and student affairs staff. Student learning has traditionally been the province of academic affairs, but one obvious site for a learning community is within the residence hall, which is typically the province of student affairs. As learning communities were developed, academic and student affairs professionals would work together to create them and administer them. *Involvement in Learning* stimulated further discussion at the time about student learning and student affairs' place in student learning, but development of true partnerships would begin to be reported in the literature a few years hence.

Ernest Pascarella and Patrick Terenzini (1991) compiled perhaps the finest summary and synthesis of research studies relating to college student outcomes. Their analysis of more than two thousand studies to examine the effects of college attendance on the undergraduate student included particularly noteworthy findings on student learning. Pascarella and Terenzini concluded that students made gains from the first to senior years of college in a variety of areas that are part of the general category of learning and cognitive development. Included in this category are communications skills, quantitative skills, and critical thinking. They also concluded that "the individual becomes a better learner" (p. 559) and added that the effects "cannot be explained away by maturation of differences between those who attend and those who do not attend college in intelligence, academic ability or other precollege characteristics" (p. 567).

Surveys of college graduates indicated that the college experience had a "major positive influence both on their specific and general knowledge bases and on their ability to think critically, analytically, and clearly" (1991, p. 577). According to Pascarella and Terenzini, part of the explanation for the gain in learning is that college graduates are likely to engage "in intellectually challenging activities (serious reading, attending cultural events, participating in continuing education and the like)" (p. 577). As a consequence, they lead adult lives, where acquisition of knowledge is integrated more fully into their activities than is the case for individuals who have not graduated from college.

One of the many recommendations Pascarella and Terenzini (1991) proposed is that systematic and purposeful efforts be undertaken to integrate the student's academic and social lives so as to extend and reinforce one another. In their view, such integration would enhance student learning. This recommendation, stemming from their exhaustive meta-analysis, is a powerful impetus for the partnership that could be formed by academic and student affairs, each of which brings specialized expertise to the table. If the partnership is crafted carefully, Pascarella and Terenzini argued, student learning can be maximized.

The release of the Pascarella and Terenzini book (1991) triggered a number of publications on the effects of college on students. Virtually every study affirmed that partnership between academic and student affairs resulted in an enhanced learning experience for college students. Astin (1993), for example, concluded that specific learning experiences could be tied directly to student learning outcomes. In two of the cases, direct involvement in the experiences by student affairs was clear.

First, participation in internship programs, which often involves interaction with both student affairs and academic affairs, resulted in gains such as self-reported growth in job skills, a rise in college GPA, graduating with honors, completing a bachelor's degree, and increased satisfaction (Astin, 1993). In addition, Astin found that attending a racial or cultural awareness workshop "produces a number of correlations with outcomes having to do with student activism and 'diversity'" (p. 380). Included in these results are such affective learning outcomes as commitment to promoting racial understanding, participating in campus demonstrations, self-reported growth in cultural awareness, and a number of self-reported growth measures. Typically, such workshops are organized and presented by members of the student affairs staff. In the case of these two interventions, then, a direct relationship between student affairs involvement and student learning outcomes can be drawn.

Although Astin's research (1993) included numerous recommendations for improving the experience of the undergraduate student, one related to student and academic affairs partnership stands out. He suggested, as did Pascarella and Terenzini (1991), a more potent residential experience that would include faculty participation, such as teaching a class or holding office hours in a residence hall. Developing such a learning experience, from his point of view, would elicit an enriched educational experience for students.

Kuh, Douglas, Lund, and Ramin-Gyurnek (1994) made an excellent summary of ways in which student classroom learning was enhanced by student learning that took place outside of the classroom. For example, they reported that persistence and educational attainment—outcomes generally associated with learning—were related to living on campus, being a member of a Greek letter organization, working part-time on campus, interacting with faculty and fellow students, and participating in orientation and extracurricular activities. They concluded that "in general, many out-of-class experiences are positively related to student persistence and, therefore, attainment of students' educational objectives" (p. 13).

The next set of experiences Kuh and colleagues (1994) examined had to do with cognitive complexity, or an educated person's ability to "think critically and to evaluate logically or assess the quality of one's own thinking and experience by exercising independent judgment" (p. 25). These experiences included interacting with faculty, living in a house with an academic theme, and having balanced engagement in academic and social activities. Kuh and coauthors concluded that these experiences "tend to be related to the amount of effort students expend in educationally purposeful activities, such as studying or talking with peers and faculty" (p. 25), thus supporting the student effort recommended in *Involvement in Learning.*

An additional area germane to this discussion of student learning is the relationship of out-of-class activity to gain in knowledge acquisition and application (Kuh et al., 1994). One conclusion they draw is the importance of time on task—that is, "the more one studies, the more one learns" (p. 31, citing Pace, 1979, 1990). Among the factors that seemed to enhance knowledge acquisition and application were amount of time spent studying, student-faculty interaction (especially when focused on a substantive topic), devoting time to community service, peer interaction when focused on course content or discussing racial or ethnic issues, holding a leadership position, living in an academic theme house, and tutoring other students.

Included with their analysis is a series of recommendations for practice. For academic administrators, they suggest appointing faculty members to student life committees and student affairs practitioners to academic committees. They also recommend establishing a strong communications link between academic affairs and student affairs. For student affairs administrators, they recommend establishing strong communication links with faculty and academic administrators and developing an early-warning system for all students who face circumstances that may jeopardize their academic success (Kuh et al., 1994, citing Kuh & Schuh, 1991; Kuh, Schuh, & Whitt, 1991).

The work of Kuh and his colleagues is particularly useful since their summary of research examined student learning in general and identified a number of possibilities for collaboration between student affairs and academic affairs. The research they cited is unequivocal for many of the outcomes. Using the recommendations just noted and others, Kuh, Douglas, Lund, and Ramin-Gyurnek (1994) developed a map for enhancing student learning,

with a focus on the total experience of the student. The American
College Personnel Association also has endorsed this direction with
its adoption of "The Student Learning Imperative" and subsequent
initiatives.

"The Student Learning Imperative" and Subsequent Documents

The "Wingspread Report" (Wingspread Group on Higher Education, 1993) asserted that putting student learning at the top of the
institutional agenda was desperately needed to stop what it characterized as "the decline of undergraduate education" (p. 13). As
a response to this report, the American College Personnel Association, under then-president Charles C. Schroeder, outlined how
the student affairs unit can adopt renewed emphasis on student
learning (Blimling, 1996). One response to the Wingspread Report
was a commissioned document titled "The Student Learning
Imperative" (Blimling, 1996). Another was an issue of the *Journal
of College Student Development* that was dedicated to discussing "The
Student Learning Imperative" in detail.

The student affairs division, according to "The Student Learning Imperative," should exhibit certain characteristics:

1. The student affairs division mission complements the institution's mission, with the enhancement of student learning
   and personal development being the primary goal of student
   affairs programs and services.
2. Resources are allocated to encourage student learning and
   personal development.
3. Student affairs professionals collaborate with other institutional agents and agencies to promote student learning and
   personal development.

"The Student Learning Imperative" lays out for the student affairs
practitioner an important series of principles focused on student
learning to guide daily practice. In determining priorities for funding, for example, one criterion can be, To what extent will this
expenditure advance student learning? If the initiative to be supported by the expenditure does not advance student learning, then
perhaps the resources should be targeted elsewhere.

Since the demise of the doctrine and practice of *in loco parentis,* student development theory has been proposed as the primary justification underlying student affairs work (Upcraft, 1998). The student affairs profession also resembles an emerging profession that continues to struggle for guiding principles and a coherent identity (Carpenter, 1998; Upcraft & Schuh, 1996). A significant function of "The Student Learning Imperative," then, was its articulation of a critical role for student affairs in developing students, often equal to the role played by faculty. To be sure, the most important aspect of "The Student Learning Imperative" was advancement of student learning, but the role suggested for student affairs was a crucial by-product. The justification for this student affairs role is simple: faculty members have neither the time nor the know-how to develop a total range of experiences to advance student learning, and since out-of-class experiences have been clearly demonstrated to work, duplication of effort is unnecessary.

Included in the special issue of the *Journal of College Student Development* is an article by Kuh (1996), concluding that a seamless learning environment is characteristic of an institution that fosters student learning and personal development. According to Kuh, "the word *seamless* suggests that what was once believed to be separate, distinct parts (e.g., in-class and out-of-class, academic and non-academic, curricular and cocurricular, or on-campus and off-campus experiences) are now of one piece, bound together so as to appear whole or continuous" (1996, p. 136, emphasis in original). Kuh went on to conclude that "collaboration between students, faculty, and student affairs professionals is essential" (p. 145). Kuh's advocacy of a seamless learning environment also supplants Clyde Parker's 1970 notion (cited in Chickering & Reisser, 1993, p. 435) of a desired "permeable membrane" between in-class and out-of-class experiences to maximize the student's experience, since such a membrane, although permeable, remains a separator between the two realms for learning. Undergirded by a powerful research and literature base, *student learning* had come to the forefront as a purpose of the student affairs professional's work on campus. Additionally, useful advice has become available in the past several years to guide the student affairs professional in efforts to enhance student learning.

The "Principles of Good Practice for Student Affairs" document (ACPA/NASPA, 1997) gave a series of inventories for student affairs practice that also can be used for self-study or internal audit. This document emphasized the role of student affairs in developing student learning experiences with its very first principle: "student affairs engages students in active learning" (n.p.). Inventory items related to student learning include this: "Collaboration with faculty is promoted to integrate civic responsibility and service into the curriculum" (inventory 1, item no. 4, n.p.). This document took student affairs practice as it relates to student learning a step further by advocating for integration of student learning directly into the work of the student affairs practitioner. At this point, then, student learning is no longer a peripheral concern for the practitioner; it has instead become absolutely central to successful accomplishment of this work.

Finally, in a document that broadened the concept of forming partnerships to advance student learning even further, ACPA and NASPA joined the American Association of Higher Education (AAHE) to produce "Powerful Partnerships: A Shared Responsibility for Learning" (1998). This document identified ten principles about learning and how student learning can be strengthened. The collaboration of AAHE with the two student affairs organizations underscored that student learning is now recognized as an important responsibility not just of the teaching faculty but of others in the institution, including student affairs. The document concluded by suggesting a role for student affairs: "Student affairs professionals and other staff take the initiative to connect to each other and to academic units; develop programs that purposefully incorporate and identify learning contributions, and help students to view their education holistically and to participate fully in the life of the institution and the community" (n.p.).

Although to this point this chapter has outlined a relatively linear progression from a service-oriented student affairs field to its current focus on student learning, it is important to note that this development—like most development—has been more complex than that. For example, as early as 1961, Shaffer noted the difficulties posed by the "artificial lines" (p. 60) among the student affairs, academic, and business units and recommended organizing the entire campus environment toward a goal of intellectual growth. On the one hand, greater cooperation in a common undertaking was emphasized, suggesting a campuswide partnership. On the other hand, the partnership would be undertaken to support students' intellectual pursuits, and so the proverbial learning net cast in 1961 was narrower than the current student learning net that includes affective learning as well as other dimensions. Shaffer (1961) did assert the centrality of the academic mission (which was consistent with guiding assumptions at that time) but also advanced creation of a campus environment with greater student-centered "coherence" (p. 60).

Also in 1961, Hardee attempted to broaden the definition of learning as well as promote the student affairs professional's participation in student learning by raising self-audit questions: "Who shapes the context of education on your campus? Are you included in the 'shapers'? What do educators—including you or not including you—want students to learn? . . . Who are the alumni to whom you point with pride? What did you, through your specialty, contribute to their growth and accomplishment?" (p. 123).

In this case, Hardee (1961) challenged student affairs professionals to participate not only in defining what kinds of learning are emphasized but also in articulating the contributions made to this learning by student affairs professionals, units, and programs. She added that student personnel efforts on the so-called periphery of higher education have had "resulting ineffectiveness for the main business of the campus, which is *learning*" (p. 125, italics in original). Hardee concluded that initiating closer coordination with other campus units would not be "the brash intrusions of a second-class educational citizenry but rather a major and totally warranted move toward the integration of the constituent parts of the campus" (p. 126).

In many ways, Shaffer (1961) and Hardee (1961) presaged the current emphasis on learning and the student affairs professional's participation in student learning. However compelling their ideas more than forty years ago, current developments (including the Wingspread Group's report and *Involvement in Learning*) were the impetus for a wider audience to engage these ideas and helped bring them into fruition as the current primary rationale for student affairs work and its importance.

In summary, the role of student affairs has relatively recently moved from being a supporter or enabler of learning to being a partner in the collegiate learning process. Student affairs staff members are infrequently academicians of the kind that Brown (1972) articulated as a counterpoint to a service orientation, but their role in constructing a learning environment and learning opportunities that result in desired student growth are evident. In many ways, this new student affairs role is one of increased proximity to the central work of a higher education institution: fostering student learning. Although a service orientation is complementary to fostering student learning and perhaps highly desirable as well, services were not "confused with" the main work of learning.

Now, as learning is increasingly defined as more than classroom knowledge acquisition, student affairs units can claim a role in student learning that is neither peripheral nor optional. As learning constitutes the heart of the undergraduate experience, student affairs plays an essential role by creating and maintaining a learning environment that fosters and maximizes student learning. This new role also has implications for restructuring student affairs practice and for preparing student affairs professionals.

Implications of Student Learning for Practice and Graduate Education

Partnership and collaboration should increasingly characterize the student learning environment on campus in order to create seamless learning experiences. One area where partnership has been formed between student affairs and academic affairs in the past decade is service learning. Service learning is both curricular and co-curricular "because all learning does not occur in the classroom" (Jacoby & Associates, 1996, p. 4). Service learning builds on higher education's recent history of commitment to service; the learning outcomes deriving from service activities are remarkable. Astin and Sax (1998) concluded that participation in service activities as an undergraduate substantially enhanced the student's academic development, life skill development, and sense of civic responsibility. The research findings "are striking: each of the 35 outcome measures was favorably influenced by engagement in some form of service work" (p. 262). Jacoby's book offered many suggestions for enhancing student learning through service-learning partnership.

A second example relates to African American students, who tend to be underrepresented on college campuses and graduate at a lower rate than their white counterparts do, especially at traditionally white institutions. Nevertheless, the learning experiences of these students can be enhanced through academic and student affairs partnership. In her article on improving academic experiences for African American men, Dawson-Threat (1997) recommended that partnerships be formed between student affairs practitioners and faculty in the specific areas of transition experience to college, role modeling, integration of students into departmental and student organizations, and understanding developmental theory as it applies to these students. In her view, these undertakings will improve student learning.

Although a variety of curricular approaches are taken toward preparing student affairs practitioners, many graduate programs have retained their roots in psychology and counseling (McEwen & Talbot, 1998). Others have borrowed heavily from administrative theory, management, or organizational development (often rooted in organizational psychology). However, students from a number of undergraduate academic backgrounds including psychology and related disciplines (but also all other disciplines) seek a master's degree in higher education or student affairs. The professional standards for graduate education (Miller, 1997) permit broad latitude in preparing student affairs practitioners. Consequently, a graduate program with modest requirements can meet minimum standards, and some individuals may enter the profession with little or no appreciation for how students learn and how student affairs can contribute to student learning.

This observation about less formal background in student learning would be particularly true for those who enter the profession with little or no academic training in student affairs practice; a similar claim can be made as to faculty members who are prepared in traditional academic disciplines. Although the faculty member who moves to a student affairs position has heretofore been evaluated—at least in part—on her or his teaching, advising, and related activities working with students, it is more likely that the primary focus has been in teaching content rather than promoting student learning.

A Final Word

The path leading to student learning as a central function and concern of student affairs has taken quite a few twists and turns, as revealed in the documents briefly highlighted in this chapter, starting with "The Student Personnel Point of View" from 1937. The early role of student affairs could be described as essential but not central to higher education's purposes. With the passage of time and refinement of thinking, the role of student affairs has progressed incrementally toward a central role in fostering student learning. Such recognition of this centrality, however, has definitely been a recent development. With the new emphasis on an integrated approach to developing opportunities to foster student learning, student affairs has assumed a position of centrality and expertise in the educational process. Still, this position is accompanied by increased accountability for advancing learning and demonstrating that such learning occurs in the interventions that are undertaken. The accountability and demonstration of learning in several realms of student-level outcomes is the subject of Part Two of this book.

References

American Association for Higher Education (AAHE), American College Personnel Association (ACPA), National Association of Student Personnel Administrators (NASPA). (1998). "Powerful partnerships: A shared responsibility for learning." Washington, DC: Authors.

American College Personnel Association. (1996). The student learning imperative: Implications for student affairs. *Journal of College Student Development*, 37(2), 118–122.

American College Personnel Association (ACPA), National Association of Student Personnel Administrators (NASPA). (1997). "Principles of good practice for student affairs." Washington, DC: Authors.

Astin, A. W. (1985). *Achieving educational excellence.* San Francisco: Jossey-Bass.

Astin, A. W. (1993). *What matters in college.* San Francisco: Jossey-Bass.

Astin, A. W., & Sax, L. J. (1998). How undergraduates are affected by service participation. *Journal of College Student Development, 39,* 251–263.

Blimling, G. S. (Ed.). (1996). The student learning imperative. (Special issue). *Journal of College Student Development, 37*(2).

Brown, R. D. (1972). *Student development in tomorrow's higher education—A return to the academy.* (Student Personnel Series no. 16). Washington, DC: American Personnel and Guidance Association.

Carpenter, D. S. (1998). Continuing professional education in student affairs. In N. J. Evans & C. E. Phelps Tobin (Eds.), *The state of the art of preparation and practice in student affairs: Another look* (pp. 159–175). Lanham, MD: American College Personnel Association.

Chickering, A. W., & Reisser, L. (1993). *Education and identity* (2nd ed.). San Francisco: Jossey-Bass.

Dawson-Threat, J. (1997). Enhancing in-class experiences for African American men. In M. J. Cuyjet (Ed.), *Helping African American men succeed in college* (New Directions for Student Services, no. 80, pp. 31–41). San Francisco: Jossey-Bass.

Hardee, M. D. (1961). Personnel services for improving the campus climate of learning. *Journal of the National Association of Women Deans and Counselors, 24,* 122–127.

Jacoby, B., & Associates. (1996). *Service-learning in higher education: Concepts and practices.* San Francisco: Jossey-Bass.

Kuh, G. D. (1996). Guiding principles for creating seamless learning environments for undergraduates. *Journal of College Student Development, 37,* 135–148.

Kuh, G. D., Douglas, K. B., Lund, J. P., & Ramin-Gyurnek, J. (1994). *Student learning outside the classroom: Transcending artificial boundaries.* (ASHE-ERIC Higher Education Report no. 8). Washington, DC: George Washington University, School of Education and Human Development.

Kuh, G. D., Schuh, J. H., Whitt, E. J., & Associates. (1991). *Involving colleges.* San Francisco: Jossey-Bass.

McEwen, M. K., & Talbot, D. M. (1998). Designing the student affairs curriculum. In N. J. Evans & C. E. Phelps Tobin (Eds.), *The state of the art of preparation and practice in student affairs: Another look* (pp. 125–156). Lanham, MD: American College Personnel Association.

Miller, T. K. (Ed.). (1997). *The book of professional standards for higher education, 1997.* Washington, DC: Council for the Advancement of Standards.

Pascarella, E. T., & Terenzini, P. T. (1991). *How college affects students.* San Francisco: Jossey-Bass.

Points of View. (1989). Washington, DC: National Association of Student Personnel Administrators.

Shaffer, R. H. (1961). Student personnel problems requiring a campus-wide approach. *Journal of College Student Personnel, 3,* 60–65.

Study Group on the Conditions of Excellence in American Higher Education. (1984). *Involvement in learning: Realizing the potential of American higher education.* Washington, DC: National Institute of Education.

Upcraft, M. L. (1998). Do graduate preparation programs really prepare practitioners? In N. J. Evans & C. E. Phelps Tobin (Eds.), *The state of the art of preparation and practice in student affairs: Another look* (pp. 225–237). Lanham, MD: American College Personnel Association.

Upcraft, M. L., & Schuh, J. H. (1996). *Assessment in student affairs.* San Francisco: Jossey-Bass.

Wingspread Group on Higher Education. (1993). *An American imperative: Higher expectations for higher education.* Racine, WI: Johnson Foundation.

Part Two

Understanding Key Student Outcomes

In this part (Chapters Five through Nine), we identify and discuss each of the five student-level outcomes introduced in the Preface. We further discuss how student development theories inform our knowledge of these outcomes and summarize selected student learning opportunities and strategies that are linked respectively with each outcome.

Chapter Five discusses the outcome of students becoming self-aware and interpersonally sensitive individuals. As greater diversity is acknowledged with respect to (for example) racial and ethnic heritage, social class and status, gender roles, or sexual orientation, it is commensurably more important that students gain an understanding of themselves and others in the context of an increasingly diverse and complex society of individuals. We also trace the development of relevant theories that describe processes by which aspects of individual identity are achieved or affirmed. Through programs including multicultural and international initiatives, an institution of higher education can help its students explore factors related to history, cultural heritage, and social and economic justice and examine how these factors influence identity, affiliation, and allegiances.

In Chapter Six, the outcome of democratic citizen is discussed. The democratic citizen participates with fellow citizens in the political and social workings of the larger society or targeted collective. Citizens also involve themselves in public life through, for example, neighborhood, government, and service organizations. We discuss how colleges and universities are particularly well positioned to offer students the opportunity to understand deeply the rights and responsibilities of citizens, to host occasions for meaningful exercise of collective self-determination, and to affirm the citizenship aspects of students' principled dissent. We also summarize a variety of curricular and co-curricular strategies to promote disposition to citizenship and the strengthening of skills that help the student be an effective citizen within a democracy.

In Chapter Seven, we discuss the outcome of becoming an educated person, which is perhaps the most commonly agreed-upon outcome for students. Mastery of a selected body of knowledge may be a foundation for one's career, but it also generates learning opportunities that, upon reflection, can result in great insight into oneself and one's world. Colleges and universities often pursue this outcome by maintaining a campus community, or set of communities, with an intentional focus on learning, applying knowledge, and extending the learning into other aspects of one's life. Higher education can thus foster the pursuit of lifelong learning among its students by demonstrating the centrality of education to life.

The outcome of skilled worker is the subject of Chapter Eight. The relative emphasis on this outcome is often tied to institutional mission, but higher education in general has increasingly been regarded as desirable workforce preparation. Colleges and universities often complement the development of skilled workers by offering career counseling or mandating an experiential component within an academic degree program. Internship also assists students in evaluating their career choices and prospective employment settings. Such a program offers a ready opportunity for academic affairs and student affairs collaboration, since internship program goals often include students' maturing along a number of developmental lines.

The final outcome, life skills manager, is discussed in Chapter Nine. This outcome involves developing skills to facilitate, if not improve, one's quality of life—such as literacy in personal finance, health and wellness maintenance, and leisure priorities. Although these areas are well within an individual's personal, private sphere of choice, colleges and universities are increasingly becoming involved in these areas through programming such as wellness residences or financial counseling services, as needs and requests for such services emerge. Decisions in these areas can be the foundation, in terms of time, health, and finances, for living a purposeful and satisfying life.

Chapter Five

Self-Aware and Interpersonally Sensitive Individual

One consistently articulated outcome associated with college attendance is that students will graduate with better knowledge of themselves and of others with whom they will work and associate. Bair, Klepper, and Phelps Tobin (1998) went so far as to claim that a current version of the classic admonition to "know thyself" would to a great extent be embodied by Chickering and Reisser's tasks of identity development (1993), which include individual as well as interindividual components. Developing greater human understanding also is an underlying theme of the commonly held core professional value of respect for the worth of all individuals. As the American College Personnel Association's "Statement of Ethical Principles and Standards" (1989) asserted, "Student affairs professionals . . . respect individuality and recognize that worth is not diminished by characteristics such as age, culture, ethnicity, gender, disabling condition, race, religion, or sexual/affectional orientation" (p. 9).

The college experience is widely regarded as offering many opportunities for students to develop, among other things, personal and professional identity; knowledge of their learning, working, and interaction styles and capacities; knowledge of and about other people; and a sense of self as an integral part of such collectives as the work group, family, community, or network. In this chapter, we discuss the emergence and primacy of this student-level outcome of becoming a self-aware and interpersonally sensitive individual, relevant theoretical underpinnings, and a range of collegiate experiences that promote achievement of this outcome.

Historically, the outcome of self-awareness can be seen in several statements about student affairs work. Yet the goal of understanding others can be construed as supportive of or supplementary to the primary task of individual development. For example, the work leading up to the 1937 *Student Personnel Point of View* included a survey of institutions to determine how colleges and universities were fostering the individual development of their students (*Points of View*, 1989). Subsequently, the primary focus of the 1937 document was articulating and affirming the guidance and personal development functions performed by those in student personnel administrative positions. Attending to students holistically was perceived as the appropriate perspective for student affairs, as articulated in a passage from the 1937 statement that emphasized the professional's "obligation to consider the student as a whole— his [sic] intellectual capacity and achievement, his emotional make up, his physical condition, his social relationships, his vocational aptitudes and skills, his moral and religious values, his economic resources, and his aesthetic appreciations" (1989, p. 49).

The writers of the 1937 statement went on to conclude that this philosophical perspective of student affairs "is as old as education itself" (1989, p. 51) and emphasized religious, emotional, and social aspects of college life along with academic pursuits. Student affairs professionals were portrayed as providing service functions related to guidance, counseling, health, placement, and extracurricular activities—all of which combined to help students reach their maximum potential.

The 1949 statement also centered on individual development but focused on others as well, particularly with respect to the assertions that "the student develops individuality and responsibility. . . . The student learns to live with others" (*Points of View*, 1989, pp. 32–34). Important developmental aspects of understanding self and others rest with relationship formation and maintenance and one's sexual identity. One element of the 1949 statement contains a pointed reference to students' sexuality that seems more prescriptive than developmental: "The student progresses toward satisfying and socially acceptable sexual adjustments. During the years when young people are in college, they are normally deeply, although perhaps covertly, concerned with finding congenial marriage partners. This concern may produce anxieties which eventuate in behavior that may be either acceptable or unacceptable to society, and satisfying or unsatisfying to the individuals. Since marriage adjustment is basic to family stability, and since the family is our most important social institution, colleges should help students to effect satisfying, socially acceptable, and ethically sound sexual adjustments" (1989, p. 34).

Such a categorical position seems curious until one considers the historical context surrounding the statement itself. The 1949 statement came on the heels of the post–World War II boom that included older military veterans with their more worldly experience enrolling in colleges and universities. Additionally, the statement was published just one year after the first volume of Kinsey's famous, and at the time, highly controversial, work on adult sexuality, sexual identity, and variety of sexual expression (Kinsey, Pomeroy, & Martin, 1948).

Finally, the 1987 statement on student affairs work retains the focus on individual understanding while developing more fully principles related to other-directedness. For example, student affairs professionals were seen as responsible for creating a rich and diverse campus environment. The environment would be the context for many of the profession's responsibilities to students:

- Help students explore and clarify values.
- Encourage development of friendships among students and a sense of community within the institution.
- Teach students how to resolve individual and group conflicts.
- Help students understand and appreciate racial, ethnic, gender, and other differences (*Points of View,* 1989, p. 17).

As acknowledged in the 1937 statement, however, the interest in students' understanding of themselves and others is not limited solely to the province of student affairs, or even higher education. In his writings on education and democracy, John Dewey (1908/1980) characterized individuals and groups as necessarily interconnected: "Selfhood is not something which exists apart from association" (p. 163). As he concluded, "the fact [is] that regard for self and regard for others are both of them secondary phases of a more normal and complete interest: regard for the welfare and integrity of the social groups of which we form a part" (p. 164). He thus positioned understanding of self and others not as goals in and of themselves but as precursors for achieving and comprehending human interconnectedness and the interdependent nature of individuals within various groups and associations.

In some ways foreshadowing Carol Gilligan's work (1982) many years later, Dewey (1908/1980) described these relationships and implications for individuals who are engaged in relationship: "Since each one of us is a member of social groups and since the latter have no existence apart from the selves who compose them, there can be no effective social interest unless there is at the same time an intelligent regard for our own well-being and development. Indeed, there is a certain *primary* responsibility placed upon each individual with respect to his [sic] own power and growth" (p. 165).

In Dewey's philosophy of education, understanding of self and of others is clearly and inexorably linked, and development of this understanding lies just as clearly within the educational province. In others' frameworks, however, the focus on self-understanding is primary, which is consistent with the discussion in Chapter Two of individual development. As Bowen (1977) wrote: "Personal self-discovery is in a sense a by-product of the instructional process, but it is nevertheless one of the most far-reaching purposes of higher education. . . . The goal of self-discovery justifies and makes intelligible the floundering that is characteristic of many college students who are trying to choose courses, major fields, careers, philosophies of life, and even marriage partners" (p. 42).

In addition to the primary focus on the student's self-understanding, the role that an educator may play in facilitating these processes is not necessarily described or acknowledged. In this case, the student's understanding of self may appear more a happy accident of college attendance than an intended outcome accompanied by theoretically informed and educationally relevant experience. Nonetheless, there are many instances where the goals of self-understanding and other-directedness are regarded as a legitimate institutional undertaking. For example, Michael (cited in Bowen, 1977) enumerated outcomes with particular relevance to relationships and consideration of others: "We must educate for empathy, compassion, trust, non-exploitativeness, [and] non-manipulativeness" (p. 34).

As colleges and universities pursue this outcome of promoting self-awareness and interpersonal sensitivity, the holistic approach has been recommended consistently. Almost thirty years ago, at a time coinciding with the emergence of "new" theories of student development, the study group convened by the Hazen Foundation determined that "by the very fact that it presumes to inform the minds of the young, the college becomes involved in the development of the whole person, of which the intellectual faculties are but a part. The time has come for the college to realize the extent of its power to influence personality development and to take full responsibility for the way this power is executed" ("The Student in Higher Education," 1968, p. 6).

The then-recent developments in behavioral science research of the late 1960s were recommended as a guide for developing the whole person as well as a potential resource for directing students' idealism—which was being expressed on campuses in troubling ways ("The Student in Higher Education," 1968). In a sense, as a response to the growing and visible number of students who declined to regard their college experience as an intellectual journey during which they suspended attention to other aspects of their lives, acknowledgment of the holistic nature of students and the educational experience was reaffirmed. As the 1968 study group noted: "To split 'intellectual' from 'other' development seems highly analytic, for in practice, when dealing with an individual, it becomes virtually impossible to separate intellectual from moral and emotional growth. . . . Thus that form of intellectual development which has no visible impact on the individual's life, his [sic] values, feelings, goals, and deeds, is relatively sterile and undesirable" (p. 9).

Another way in which the notion of self-understanding has become more complex and sophisticated in recent times is how self-understanding—or self-identity—must be predicated on separation from family and extended family. As this excerpt demonstrates, this separation has traditionally been portrayed rather categorically:

> Even those who do not live away from home anticipate that college
> will provide the environment necessary for them to acquire the
> independence, initiative, and sense of responsibility that are
> expected of adults. The final breaking of family ties, especially
> when postponed as in American society, is bound to be a painful
> and ambivalent experience. . . . Since the break only becomes
> possible when a sufficient sense of selfhood has evolved, many
> students enter college ill-prepared to depart from the confines
> of their family, however eager to do so they may be ["The Student
> in Higher Education," 1968, p. 25].

The stark nature of this description seems, in hindsight, unnecessarily narrow if not unreasonable, in light of recent understanding
of self-identity that includes enduring and meaningful connection
with family members and larger cultural traditions (for instance,
Diaz-Guerrero, 1987; McEwen, Roper, Bryant, & Langa, 1990).

How one achieves this understanding of self and others, the
degree to which the educational experience overtly focuses on developing such understanding, and to what end this understanding
should be directed have differed among writers and through
recent years. Nonetheless, achieving a deeper understanding of
oneself and of other people is consistently regarded as a desirable
student-level outcome. For some, self-understanding has appeared
as the primary concern, with understanding of others regarded as
an extension of self-understanding. For others, relationships may
serve as the educational context within which a greater understanding of self can be achieved. These positions stand in contrast
to Dewey's conception of human understanding that, consistent
with his work on democracy, makes the group or collective the
overriding focus. Potentially mitigating against Dewey's conception, however, is May's perspective (1990) on the university as an
increasingly specialized, future-oriented, and diffuse organization
that is consequently ill-prepared to create an integrated and holistic learning environment for students:

> The university has increasingly restricted the scope of its responsi-
> bility to the university's educational mission alone. It has largely
> shed responsibility for the student's personal and social life,
> renouncing the role of *in loco parentis*. This renunciation fits into
> its general orientation to the future rather than the past. It orients

itself less than the college to the community of birth and more to the economic and organizational identities that students will assume on graduation. . . . It is less a community than an organization. It often provides no more than a site, a campus, on which many kinds of educational and research enterprises happen to intersect [p. 237].

Following May's description (1990) of this emerging character of the university, a small college or community college may give more focused and routine attention to the affective as well as educational needs of its students thanks to the relative size of the campus, the more focused mission, and the relatively personalized setting. Professionals at a large, multidimensional university may find that special attention is required to create and sustain a learning environment that hosts opportunities for undergraduate students to increase their understanding of themselves and others.

In the next section, relevant student development theories are presented and discussed. The discussion is followed by examples of collegiate experience that are designed to maximize student's achievement of self-awareness as well as interpersonal sensitivity.

Related Student Development Theories

As noted earlier in this chapter, understanding self and others is at the core of human development. Psychosocial theories focus specifically on the process by which individuals come to know themselves and learn to relate effectively with those around them. Erikson (1959, 1968) was the first theorist to examine development of the self across the life span. Marcia (1966) built on Erikson's work related to identity development. Later, Josselson (1987) studied the applicability of Marcia's ideas for women. Chickering chose to concentrate on the developmental process students experienced in college (Chickering & Reisser, 1993). Understanding self and others is also a key concept in Levinson's adult development theory (1978).

Other theorists have focused on specific aspects of identity. It is particularly important to consider those related to racial and ethnic identity development (Atkinson, Morten, & Sue, 1993; Cross, 1991; Helms & Cook, 1999; Isajiw, 1990; Phinney, 1990; Rowe, Bennett, & Atkinson, 1994; Sodowsky, Kwan, & Pannu, 1995) and development of sexual and gender identity (Cass, 1979; D'Augelli, 1994; Downing & Roush, 1985; Levine & Evans, 1991; McCarn & Fassinger, 1996; O'Neil, Egan, Owen, & Murry, 1993; Ossana, Helms, & Leonard, 1992).

Cognitive development theories are also useful in explaining changes in how people understand themselves and their interpersonal experience. The process of moral reasoning described by Kohlberg (1972, 1976) and Gilligan (1977, 1982) is a critical factor in how individuals view themselves in relation to others. Faith development (Fowler, 1986; Parks, 1986, 2000), ego development (Loevinger, 1976), Kegan's orders of consciousness (1982, 1994), and maturity theories (Heath, 1968, 1977) also present information about how people interpret interpersonal interaction and their own way of being.

Psychosocial Theories

Understanding oneself is the basic process associated with identity development. But because individuals do not live in isolation, part of the process of development is of necessity social; individuals must learn how to relate to those around them and to understand the differences that exist among people. Psychosocial theories explore these issues.

Erikson

Although stressing that self-understanding is a lifelong process, Erikson (1959, 1968) viewed adolescence, the time in which an individual is traditionally in college, as the focal point for development of identity. He also saw learning about oneself as intertwined with learning how to relate to others. Erikson did not directly address the experience of the college student, but his ideas have implications for the college setting.

The campus environment certainly presents challenges and opportunities that have a powerful impact on the development of self-understanding and awareness of others. For instance, being exposed to individuals with different value systems and beliefs can cause one to reflect on one's own worldviews, resulting in recommitment to existing beliefs or else modification of them. Living in a residence hall and attending classes with a diverse population requires a student to consider differing viewpoints. Programs specifically designed to address diversity on campus also enable discussion of differences.

Experiences in college also often require the student to revisit earlier developmental tasks. For example, a student who has not completely worked through the developmental task that Erikson (1959) labeled *industry* will be challenged by the demands of college-level academic work. To complete course assignments, the student must develop effective study habits and time management skills. Academic support programs, tutoring, and developmental education can assist in developing such skills.

Sanford (1967) stressed that development occurs when an appropriate balance between challenge and support is created on a college campus. Erikson's theory (1959, 1968) suggests that educators need to examine the challenges to identity and other developmental tasks facing students and work to create environmental conditions that support them as they address these issues. For example, programming and academic course work focused on values and ethics may help students examine their beliefs in a comfortable and nonthreatening setting. Having the opportunity to consider what is important in their lives and how they wish to relate to others is critical in developing self-awareness.

Marcia

Building on Erikson's work (1959, 1968), James Marcia (1966) focused specifically on the process of identity development in young adulthood, identifying four identity statuses determined by whether or not crisis and commitment has been experienced. The extent to which individuals understand themselves is influenced by the identity status they hold. Individuals in identity diffusion have not considered their values, goals, or future direction (Marcia, 1966); they tend to be drifters. Those in foreclosure have also thought little about the decisions they have made or how they present themselves to others. Instead, they have accepted the values and goals that others think are important. In moratorium, students are struggling with who they want to be; this is a time of much soul searching and anxiety. Identity achievement requires confronting the crises in one's life and active decision making about who one will be and what is important in life.

Understanding that students may be experiencing any of these identity statuses helps the educator work more effectively with students. Opportunities for self-exploration and values clarification in many aspects of life assist students in resolving crises they face and in making life commitments. Marcia (1989) stressed that educators need to ensure safety, structure, and guidance while students experiment. Programming related to vocational decision making, the role of religion and spirituality in a person's life, sexual values and behavior, and political ideologies assists students with the self-examination necessary to know themselves well. Academic advisers might also recommend coursework in the liberal arts that encourages self-reflection and examination of various ideologies and views of critical dimensions of life.

Josselson

Using the work of Marcia (1966) and Schenkel and Marcia (1972) as a starting point, Josselson (1987) studied the process of identity development in women during and after college. Although her study was conducted in a historical time in which women were likely to have been more influenced by traditional gender roles and values than they are currently, Josselson's work does suggest that how women come to understand themselves differs from the same process in men. Women tend to be more influenced than men by relationships with parents and significant others and to see themselves in relation to others more than men.

It is important to consider these differences in counseling, advising, and programming for women. For example, women are more likely than men to be influenced by others in the process of major choice, career decision making, and determination of lifestyle. The desires and plans of parents and significant others are likely to play a role in the choices that women make. Women might also look to advisers and faculty for more assistance in decision making than would men.

Chickering

Chickering also examined the identity development process for college students, breaking down Erikson's stage of identity versus role confusion (1959, 1968) into seven vectors of development (Chickering & Reisser, 1993). All of his vectors are relevant for understanding self and others. Understanding of self includes knowledge of one's skills and a sense that one is intellectually, physically, and interpersonally competent (vector one). Being able to recognize, accept, and appropriately manage one's emotions (vector two) is also part of self-awareness. Increasing emotional and instrumental independence, problem-solving ability, and recognition of the importance of interdependence are all part of moving through autonomy toward interdependence (vector three). These skills are necessary both to understand oneself and to relate effectively with others. Understanding of others requires acceptance and appreciation of differences as well as the capacity to relate in a caring and sensitive way to significant people in one's life (vector four).

Understanding of self is dependent on all the components of establishing identity (vector five) mentioned by Chickering and Reisser (1993): comfort with body and appearance, comfort with gender and sexual orientation, knowledge and pride in one's culture and heritage, comfort with the lifestyle one has chosen, the ability to accept and process feedback from significant others, self-acceptance and self-esteem, and a stable and integrated personality. Having a purpose in life with regard to vocation and personal commitments (vector six) is also a part of knowing oneself. Finally, a sense of integrity based on a humanized and personalized value system (vector seven) is needed if one is to truly conduct oneself in a clear and consistent manner that is indicative of those who understand themselves and others well.

Chickering and Reisser (1993) noted that the college environment can enhance a student's understanding of self and others. To do so, the institution must have a clear mission and vision, communicate its goals and values to students, and develop programs to achieve the goals it has set. In this way, students know what their college is about and receive clear guidance and direction as they explore their own values. Even if students find that the college's mission is not compatible with their personal value system, this cognitive dissonance encourages them to think deeply about the choices they have made, what they will do to resolve the disparity, and what the implications are for how they will address them.

Second, a small college, or a large college that has created the opportunity for students to find a smaller subcommunity, is likely to have an impact on identity since students have more opportunity to assume a meaningful role and test out their self-understanding and their understanding of others. Institutions need to develop and support compatible communities for all their students. These might be learning communities for students in specific majors, student organizations with differing purposes and philosophies, or living options for students from various backgrounds.

Third, faculty can have a powerful impact on students by encouraging self-exploration, serving as a role model, and making leadership opportunities available. Being available to students for one-on-one conversation, sharing decision-making processes and examples from their own life experience, and giving students a chance to work with them on a research project are ways that faculty can assist students in learning more about themselves and others.

Fourth, curriculum and teaching practices that allow students to reflect, interact with others, and engage in meaningful projects are all opportunities for students to examine values, interests, and goals and to learn more about those of others. Examples of such strategies are a self-reflection paper, journaling, a small-group discussion on an assigned topic, an out-of-class assignment that requires teamwork, and a group presentation.

Fifth, student interaction with a diverse community both inside and outside the classroom enables learning about those who are different from oneself and expands one's own thinking. A residence hall program that brings people together for meaningful discussion of current issues, a film critique, or a forum on hot topics facing college students is one option. A community forum on issues salient to the campus is another vehicle for sharing different perspectives. Interassociation programming is yet another way to bring together people with differing backgrounds. For example, a multicultural summit cosponsored and attended by representatives from all the major organizations on campus has been successful at Iowa State.

Finally, seamless educational experiences in which classroom and extracurricular activities complement each other reinforce new ideas and opportunities to try out different ways of acting and relating to others in various settings. Service learning that includes both action and classroom reflection components is one possibility. A leadership development program that includes coursework on leadership theory is another.

Chickering's model (Chickering & Reisser, 1993) has been used as a basis for programming (Hurst, 1978; Klepper & Kovacs, 1978; Lemons & Richmond, 1987; Lott, 1986), needs assessment (Evans, 1982), evaluation (Chickering, 1977), counseling intervention (McBride, 1990), and intervention for students with disabilities (Huss, 1983; Perreira & Dezago, 1989). All of these interventions are designed to assist students in learning more about themselves and others.

Adult Development

Understanding of self and others is a constantly evolving process at the core of adult development theories. In particular, psychologically based approaches, such as that of Levinson (1978; Levinson & Levinson, 1996), explore the increasing complexity of self-awareness and relationships with others that occur over time. Given the increasing number of adult students attending college, it is important to consider theories such as this that cover the life span.

Understanding where students are in Levinson's model (1978) can assist the educator in working more effectively with them. For instance, people often initiate changes in their lives during a transition period. Many adult students make the decision to enter or return to college as a result of the reflection that occurs during a time of transition. Change in family structure (marriage, divorce) can also occur; helping students successfully negotiate such a change and learn more about themselves and others should be a goal for the professional working with this population. Support groups, counseling, and programming on managing transition can be helpful.

Identity Development Theories

Determining the role that race, ethnicity, sexual orientation, and gender play in one's life is an important developmental task that individuals, particularly those belonging to a nondominant population, must address to fully understand themselves and those around them. These processes are often particularly salient during the college years, when students move into young adulthood and are faced with new challenges in the college environment.

Racial and Ethnic Identity Development

Both theories that focus on the identity development process (Atkinson et al., 1993; Cross, 1991; Helms & Cook, 1999; Phinney, 1990) and those exploring acculturation and its impact on development (Isajiw, 1990; Rowe et al., 1994; Sodowsky et al., 1995) help to inform educational practice with regard to developing a self-aware and interpersonally sensitive individual since each of these constructs plays a role in how people come to understand themselves and others.

Atkinson, Morten, and Sue's model of minority identity development (1993), Phinney's ethnic identity model (1990), and other models specific to particular racial and ethnic groups, such as that of Cross (1991), depict how members of various populations view themselves, their racial and ethnic reference groups, and members of other racial and ethnic groups. These models offer useful information for the student affairs professional and other educators working with students from various racial and ethnic groups. Knowing how students makes sense of their racial or ethnic identity and how they view individuals in other racial or ethnic groups can be informative in advising and counseling students, as well as in helping students understand each other, work through conflict, and work effectively together in a group setting. Knowing the needs of the individual at each level of development can also assist in developing programs, educational initiatives, and support services.

Atkinson, Morten, and Sue (1993) viewed development as a continuous process influenced by the type of experience that individuals have with their own cultural group, the dominant cultural group, and other cultural groups. Experience in college and opportunity (or lack thereof) for students to learn about and interact with individuals from their own racial and ethnic group can have a powerful impact on the development of identity. Colleges and universities have a responsibility to create opportunities for students from various racial and ethnic groups to learn about their heritage and to interact with members of their own and other racial or ethnic groups in a positive context. Establishing and supporting multicultural centers, promoting multicultural student organizations, hiring faculty and staff from diverse backgrounds, and including racial and ethnic studies classes in the curriculum are important steps that a college can take to encourage development of racial and ethnic identity.

Educators should also be aware of the impact of acculturation on students from various ethnic backgrounds. Understanding the extent to which individuals have developed a white identity and the degree to which they have retained the identity associated with their ethnic heritage (Sodowsky et al., 1995) can be important in assisting students with the transition to college, career and lifestyle decisions, and conflict with parents and other significant others. Sodowsky and colleagues also stressed that individuals can move from one orientation to another over time and depending on the situation. For example, students moving to school from a cohesive ethnic community may come to campus with a strong ethnic identity. However, the pressures and demands of a predominantly white campus may challenge students to become bicultural in orientation. If they choose to return to the home community upon graduation, they may shift back to a strong ethnic identity.

Educators also have to be sensitive to the impact of the environment on identity and not assume that how students ordinarily present themselves to individuals from the dominant culture is necessarily their true self. Isajiw (1990) pointed out that ethnic identity has both external and internal components, many of which are not readily apparent through observation or superficial exchange yet may be extremely important to the student. Getting to know students at a personal level through meaningful interaction in various settings is necessary to truly understand their cultural values.

Working with majority students as they come to understand their identity as white people and how to relate effectively to people of other racial and ethnic backgrounds can be challenging. Helms and Cook's latest version (1999) of Helms's evolving model of white identity development can be informative. This model focuses on overcoming internalized racism. Acknowledging and overcoming it is an important component of the identity development process for the white student. To effectively interact with others in our increasingly diverse society, an appreciation of difference is necessary. White faculty and staff must first examine their own beliefs and values and work to educate themselves and their students about racism. Clayton and Jones (1993) recommended workshops designed to assist educators in unlearning racism. White identity theory can be used as a framework in counseling and advising, as well as in teaching and programming, to assist students in understanding their attitudes and behaviors as well as those of others with whom they interact (Helms & Cook). Helms's *A Race is a Nice Thing to Have: A Guide to Being a White Person or Understanding the White Persons in Your Life* (1992) is an excellent resource for use in awareness building.

Rowe, Bennett, and Atkinson's model (1994) focuses on attitudes held by individuals regarding the significance of being white and the implications of individual attitude for relationship with nonwhite people. It is useful in examining one's own attitude and actions and in helping students consider their beliefs as well. Since the types presented are based on attitude rather than racial identity ego status as in Helms's model (Helms & Cook, 1999), students often have an easier time understanding and accepting this model as valid. Rowe, Bennett, and Atkinson (1994) suggested that attitudes can be changed through direct and indirect experience, including classroom interaction, extracurricular activity, volunteer work, and other meaningful engagement with individuals from different racial and ethnic backgrounds.

Racial and ethnic identity theories have been used in a number of settings to aid students in becoming more aware of themselves as racial and ethnic people and to learn more about individuals whose backgrounds differ from their own. Improving interaction and understanding among diverse groups is another important goal of such intervention. Howard-Hamilton (2000) suggested ways of creating a positive classroom environment on the basis of understanding minority and white identity development models. Tatum (1992) also used racial identity theories to explain classroom interactions and suggested strategies to assist faculty in improving the classroom climate. Helms and her colleagues (Helms, 1993) have explored use of these theories in counseling situations, while Hardiman and Jackson (1992) have used them as a basis for conflict resolution. Evans and Anderson (1993) also developed programming suggestions for students at various levels of racial and ethnic identity development.

Gay, Lesbian, and Bisexual Identity Development

Determining one's sexual identity is a major aspect of development for all students. For those who are not heterosexual, this aspect of identity is particularly significant in how they view themselves and how they relate to others. Theories of gay, lesbian, and bisexual identity development (Cass, 1979; D'Augelli, 1994; Levine & Evans, 1991; McCarn & Fassinger, 1996) present alternative views of this developmental process. Some models focus more on the internal process of coming to know oneself, but all of them also acknowledge the important role that others play in this endeavor.

Stage theories (for instance, that of Cass, 1979) suggest that individuals progress from nonacceptance of their potential non-heterosexual identity to full acceptance and pride in that identity. It is important for advisers and counselors to understand where a student is in this process as they assist him or her in moving along in development and in determining how sexual identity intersects with other aspects of the student's life and interaction with others.

Cass suggested that sexual identity development builds upon the interaction of psychological and environmental factors. Internally, students experience and interpret their same-sex attraction. A supportive counselor can assist students in the self-exploration necessary to understand their feelings. Externally, development is encouraged when students have contact with positive gay, lesbian, and bisexual role models; have an opportunity to interact with other gay, lesbian, and bisexual people; and receive positive support from others. Specific support services for gay, lesbian, and bisexual students; social outlets for them; and nonheterosexual staff and faculty who are open about their sexual identity help students see that exploration of sexual orientation issues is legitimate and that the college values them as people (Evans & D'Augelli, 1996).

McCarn and Fassinger (1996) saw development as occurring in two arenas: individual sexual identity and group membership identity. Their model is unique in that they separate the psychological and social processes of identity development and acknowledge that individuals can be at different stages in each one, depending on circumstances. For instance, a woman may have fully internalized her individual sexual identity but, because of family circumstances or concerns about being open in her profession, still be in the exploration stage with regard to group membership. Educators are cautioned to recognize that there may be wholly legitimate reasons for gay, lesbian, or bisexual students to choose not to identify their sexual orientation to others or to choose not to join a gay, lesbian, or bisexual student organization. Such a choice does not necessarily mean that students do not accept their sexual identity.

D'Augelli's life span model of gay, lesbian, and bisexual identity development (1994) underscores the important role of the environment in development. He saw three sets of variables influencing development: (1) the individual's actions and interpretations of experience, (2) his or her interaction with significant others, and (3) societal norms influenced by historical time and geographical setting. Opportunities and challenges in college have a great impact on the development of all aspects of gay, lesbian, and bisexual student identity (Evans & D'Augelli, 1996). For instance, the policies of the institution and the extent to which students experience a hostile or supportive environment in the residence hall (Evans & Broido, 1999) and classroom (Connolly, 2000) are the sociohistorical context in which development occurs. The level of support and acceptance extended by significant others—peers, instructors, and staff—is also a major influence.

Increasing the visibility of lesbian, gay, and bisexual people and issues by integrating relevant content into the curriculum (Evans, 2000), hosting student organizations and support groups for gay, lesbian, and bisexual students (Scott, 1991), and developing "safe zone" programs that offer a way for supportive faculty and staff to display stickers or other visible signs of support (Evans, in press) help to create a positive environment in which a student can explore various aspects of identity, come to understand oneself better, and learn to relate to others effectively. Other suggestions for working with gay, lesbian, and bisexual students can be found in Wall and Evans (2000) and Evans and Wall (1991).

Gender Identity

Because gender plays such an important role in determining how one lives life, having a clear understanding of oneself with regard to gender is an important component of identity development in college. O'Neil, Egan, Owen, and Murry's "gender role journey" (1993) can be used to design a program to help male and female students examine the role of gender in their lives. Regarding work with women, Downing and Roush's feminist identity model (1985) and Ossana, Helms, and Leonard's womanist identity model (1992) are frameworks through which to examine what it means to be a woman in today's society. Courses in gender studies, classes related to gender in psychology and human development, programming about gender roles in residence halls and fraternities and sororities, and examination in leadership development programs of the impact of gender on leadership are all ways that students can be encouraged to examine who they are as gendered people. Role modeling of nonsexist behavior is another important component of education about gender.

Cognitive Structural Theories

Cognitive structural theories emphasize how individuals make meaning of their experience and how such interpretation changes over time, moving from a simplistic view to complex understanding. Many aspects of development are largely cognitive in nature, among them moral development, faith development, ego development, consciousness, and maturity. All involve how people view themselves and others.

Moral Development

Moral dilemmas are those in which values are in conflict. Generally, a dilemma of this sort has implications for both the individual experiencing it and for others who are affected. Moral reasoning is the process individuals use in making a decision about how to resolve such a situation. The moral development theories of Kohlberg (1976) and Gilligan (1982) have implications for how an individual justifies action in relation to others.

Kohlberg. Kohlberg (1976) saw justice as the basis for moral decision making. How justice is interpreted is the basis for each of his stages. At the preconventional level, an individual's decisions are self-focused; she or he does not yet have awareness of societal expectations. The conventional level of reasoning is characterized by adherence to the rules and expectations set by others. An individual using postconventional thinking is able to separate self from the expectations of others and make decisions on the basis of self-chosen principles. Understanding the motivation behind an individual's decision making can be useful in explaining rules and policies and in working with a student in a disciplinary or counseling situation.

Two conditions are necessary for movement through these stages: the ability to reason logically and the ability to see the point of view of another (Kohlberg, 1976). Development occurs when the individual's current way of thinking is challenged or no longer seems adequate, and when opportunity is presented to the individual to confront a situation that has moral overtones (Kohlberg, 1972). Moral dilemmas are common on the college campus. Students are confronted with lifestyles different from their own, cheating in the classroom, violation of university policy by their friends, and the opportunity to engage in such illegal behavior as underage drinking or drug use. Programs, course content, and other experiences that intentionally expose the student to alternative points of view and pose an opportunity to engage in moral decision making encourage development of higher-level thinking on the basis of sensitive and respectful consideration of others (Rest, 1986).

Gilligan. In contrast to Kohlberg (1976), Gilligan (1977, 1982) believed that, for women, morality was based on concern for others rather than justice and rights. In her first level of morality, the basis for decision making is what is best for the self; one's own needs and desires take precedent. Decision making in the second level has as its base pleasing others; one's own needs are deferred to ensure that the needs of others are addressed. In the final level, the prohibition against hurt is seen as applying to oneself as well as to others. The individual now understands that self and others must be equally considered in decision making. Along with Kohlberg's theory, Gilligan's is useful to the professional trying to understand the reasons underlying students' moral decisions and to talk with students concerning possible actions they might take in a specific situation.

In working with students, particularly women, an educator has to keep in mind that connection and responsibility, in addition to justice and rights, are important considerations in decision making. As Evans, Forney, and Guido-DiBrito (1998) pointed out, the educator "should understand how care and justice, connection and autonomy, interdependence and independence, relationship and individuality are fostered or hindered by organizational culture" (p. 202). Gilligan's ideas (1977, 1982) have been applied to counseling intervention (Enns, 1991; Hotelling & Forrest, 1985), residence life

(Picard & Guido-DiBrito, 1993; Porterfield & Pressprich, 1988), career planning (Stonewater, 1989), and leadership development (Fried, 1994; Picard & Guido-DiBrito, 1993).

Faith Development

Love and Talbot (1999) argued that everyone searches for meaning in life. They viewed spiritual development as an ongoing process and an important component of understanding oneself. According to these authors, it involves a quest for self-understanding and wholeness that imparts direction and purpose to one's life. Exploring one's spiritual side requires openness to self-exploration, great connectedness with others, and exploration of a relationship with "an intangible and pervasive power or essence that exists beyond human existence and rational human knowing" (p. 367).

Fowler. Fowler's theory of faith development (1981, 1986) helps the educator understand how an individual finds direction and meaning with regard to the various factors and relationships that are a part of life. Some students, at stage two of Fowler's model, adopt without reflection the beliefs of the faith community in which they were raised; their interpretation of faith is literal. By contrast, students at Fowler's third stage are strongly influenced by the group with which they most identify. This could be parents, friends, or romantic partners; reflection still plays no role. Only at stage four do individuals begin to develop their own views, which may be different from those of their friends and family. At this stage, they seek out a community with compatible beliefs to help them resolve conflict that may occur. Understanding the role played by faith in a student's life and how that faith is defined is important for educators as they work with students to determine life goals and in counseling students struggling with faith issues.

As in other cognitive structural theories, movement through these stages is influenced by internal maturational processes and by environmental factors. Certainly, exposure to different people and ideas in the college setting presents students with challenges that can propel them into a more advanced stage of faith development. Intentional examination of faith is easier in a religiously affiliated institution, but a program about spirituality can be incorporated into a holistic wellness approach in any institution. Knowledge of and referral to resources and individuals who can assist the student with faith-based concerns are also important (Temkin & Evans, 1998).

Parks. Unlike Fowler (1981), who wrote about faith development over the life span, Parks (1986, 2000) specifically focused on the young adult years. As a result, her work is particularly helpful to college educators working with traditional-aged students. According to Parks (2000), most students begin to make a tentative faith-based commitment during college, independently from others. To accomplish this task, they need a compatible mentoring community in which to explore. Older students may have already solidified their beliefs and may be seeking a community of individuals with compatible values. In either case, a faith-based student organization, on-campus or off-campus religious group, or chaplain or other religious personnel can assist the student in finding such a community. Educators can extend support for the exploration process by legitimizing the student's self-reflection and questioning and ensuring a safe setting in which discussion of faith and spirituality can occur.

Parks (2000) viewed the college campus as a community of imagination that could affect faith development positively or negatively. By creating opportunities for a student to be exposed to new ideas, reflect on them, and try out positions, a college can positively influence faith development. This process can occur in the classroom, in the living environment, and even in a work setting.

Ego Development

Loevinger (1976) defined ego as the core aspect of the self that "provides the frame of reference within which one perceives the world" (p. 9). Development, according to Loevinger, is facilitated by the interaction of the individual and the environment as one seeks equilibrium in the face of environmental challenges that demand complex response. Loevinger did not elaborate on elements of the environment that facilitate development, but an educator can learn much from studying the progression in ego development that she proposed. Understanding how students view themselves and their world can help the educator create opportunity for students to consider alternative perspectives. For instance, Knelfelkamp, Parker, and Widick (1978) suggested that the self-aware level is the model for adults in U.S. society. Thus, most college students would likely be at this level, or perhaps the previous (conformist) stage.

At the conformist stage, students are likely to be much influenced by their peers and need support to think for themselves. This goal can be addressed through leadership opportunities, a class assignment that requires independent research, or a values exploration workshop. A student who has moved into self-awareness would need support for this new, more autonomous way of relating to the world. Reinforcing the student's independent decisions and praising reflective thought demonstrated in class discussion or student organization decision making are examples of appropriate support.

Kegan's Orders of Consciousness

In considering how self and interpersonal awareness develop over time, Kegan's theory (1982, 1994) is informative. It focuses on how individuals make meaning of themselves in relation to others and how the demands of adult life affect a person's views. His five orders of consciousness determine how people think, feel, and relate to self and others at each level.

Drawing on Sanford's concepts of challenge and support (1966), Kegan (1994) argued that society presents many challenges to the individual. Supports must be introduced to maintain proper balance if development is to take place. Kegan urged educators to serve as "sympathetic coaches" (p. 43), supporting students as they currently are while introducing dissonance to move them to a more complex way of being. Love and Guthrie (1999) noted that "Kegan's theory underscores the value of creating programs that are highly acknowledging of, and sensible to, students' current ways of meaning making while at the same time promoting the development of the next higher order of consciousness" (p. 76).

Most college students are in either the second or third order of consciousness. At the second level, individuals are concerned primarily with satisfying their own interests and with looking good in the eyes of others. Resolution of roommate conflict, acceptance of group living norms, and a collaborative learning situation all challenge second-order consciousness. Initiatives that involve cooperating with others or being part of a community can best be promoted by demonstrating how the student will personally benefit from such an endeavor. Love and Guthrie (1999) also pointed out the importance of offering opportunities for an individual at this level of consciousness to explore values, beliefs, and social roles to develop skills of self-reflection.

At the third order of consciousness, individuals are aware of the needs and perspectives of others as well as their own. Love and Guthrie (1999) suggested that, at the third level, relationships are preeminent for students. They need the opportunity to think independently and take action on their own, rather than relying on the opinions of others. A leadership workshop can assist in developing such skills, but it must be followed up with experiences that allow the student to test out those skills in real-life decision making. A student government position, activities board, or other student-led initiative represents such an opportunity, along with those that are academically focused, such as independent research or study abroad.

Maturity Theory

Douglas Heath's self systems (1968)—intellect, values, self-concept, and interpersonal relationships—are all a part of individuals' knowing themselves and others. In his longitudinal study of Haverford College students (all male), Heath found that students mature from their first year to their senior year and that the first half of the first year was particularly instrumental in this process. Major effects were found with regard to increased self-awareness and the ability to be close and open with others. In particular, he found that intellectual growth was a necessary precursor for growth in self-awareness. This research supports the belief that understanding self and others is a major outcome of college.

In his exploration of maturity, Heath (1968, 1977) suggested that an individual moves from immaturity toward maturity whenever an environmental challenge creates disequilibrium within a self system and the individual attempts to restore balance by trying a new response. If supportive conditions exist in the environment, increasingly mature behavior results; if not, the individual may handle the challenge by regressing to less mature behavior. Heath

(1968) noted that development was influenced by interaction with close same-sex friends and roommates as well as by "the ethos of the college, courses which explicitly focused on values, faculty who were models of maturity, and an honor system" (Widick et al., 1978, p. 88). Heath's work (1968, 1977) underscores the importance of ensuring that both the academic and the out-of-classroom environments of college offer challenges requiring the student to try out new behaviors and also supply necessary supports that encourage increasingly mature response demonstrating self-understanding and sensitivity to others.

College Experiences Related to Becoming a Self-Aware and Interpersonally Sensitive Individual

Psychosocial development, as was stated earlier, is an important outcome desired in college. Gardiner (1994) suggested that a number of affective outcomes are sought from the college experience, notably self-confidence, acceptance of others, moral principles, and acceptance of self (citing Bowen, 1977).

In general, according to Pascarella and Terenzini (1991), the evidence is persuasive that "college attendance is reliably and positively related to increases in students' academic and social self-concepts, as well as their self-esteem" (p. 572). Students also experience a gain in self-esteem, including the extent to which they see themselves as capable, worthy, or of value, according to Pascarella and Terenzini.

Kuh, Douglas, Lund, and Ramin-Gyurnek (1994) defined self-esteem as "one's self-assessment of what one wishes to be contrasted with what one is in the present. Satisfaction with this self-assessment leads to a generally positive or negative conceptualization of self" (pp. 35–36). They added that "a student's feelings of social and academic competence can lead to a greater self-satisfaction and increased confidence. Taken together, these factors contribute to the foundation of a person's identity and self-understanding" (p. 36).

This section of this chapter focuses on research related to development of interpersonal and intrapersonal self-awareness in college. The overall effect of college is examined, as are specific experiences that have an influence on college student development.

Research on Development of Self-Awareness and Interpersonal Sensitivity

Numerous researchers have examined how the college experience contributes to developing various aspects of self-awareness and interpersonal sensitivity. This research has considered development of autonomy, self-efficacy, other psychosocial outcomes, moral reasoning, and religiosity.

Autonomy Development

Autonomy development is a key component in Chickering's theory (Chickering & Reisser, 1993). Mather and Winston (1998) concluded that developing autonomy is related to self-confidence or self-efficacy. They also saw creation of community as an important aspect of student growth and development. In their view, student affairs practitioners are not well served by planning programs or making decisions. Rather, they recommended that student affairs staff articulate values and principles and encourage the student's active participation in creating and sustaining community. In short, their position is that student affairs staff should serve as agents who stimulate learning.

Taub (1995) indicated that three factors make significant, independent contributions to autonomy: the quality of a student's relationships, the role of parents in providing emotional support, and other-group orientation. She concluded that interpersonal relationships offer a context for developing autonomy for women. She observed that women's autonomy development can be promoted through active efforts to build community and relationships on campus by employing strategies that include cooperative learning, cluster scheduling of classes, encouraging study groups, and fostering community in campus organizations and residence halls. Taub also concluded that a carefully crafted community service program or service learning program can promote development of interdependence, which also addresses development of autonomy in women.

Students' relationships with their parents can have an effect on autonomy development. At one time it may have been thought that establishing autonomy meant that students would separate themselves psychologically and emotionally from their parents, but several studies suggest that such is not the case. Taub (1997) studied the extent to which autonomy and parental attachment varied by class year. Seniors, in fact, were more autonomous than juniors and freshmen. They were better managers of their time and their money and were more independent in an emotional sense from their peers than were first-year students. But they were no more emotionally independent from their parents than other participants in the study. This finding suggests that women may make gains in emotional independence from their peers, without being emotionally independent from their parents. Of particular importance to those who work with college women is that attachment to parents does not necessarily indicate that a woman lacks autonomy. Moreover, continued attachment to parents in later college years should not be interpreted as a delay or regression of development.

Kenny and Donaldson (1992) would agree with Taub's conclusions (1997). They observed that most women describe themselves as being close affectively to their parents, and that parents also help to foster a woman's autonomy and give her support. Kenny and Donaldson suggested that students need to be helped to resolve conflict with their family and develop their own values and ideas, but educators should also help students preserve their feeling of connection to their parents. The authors recommended that seminars for students and their parents be considered and that through this process students can develop their own attitudes without damaging their attachment to their parents.

Heyer and Nelson (1993) studied the effect of parents' marital status on the development of identity and emotional autonomy in college students. They found that children whose parents were divorced scored higher on sexual identity and confidence scores but about the same on autonomy development as those from families that were intact or in which the parents had remarried. They concluded that "children with only one parent may have to rely more on themselves because of the many demands of the single parent. The single parent may also be less available to the children" (pp. 434–435). An institution could design various interventions building on this research: group counseling activity, workshops for students whose parents have divorced, or a peer mentoring program that uses upperclass students whose parents have divorced to work with first-year and transfer students to help in the transition to their new environment.

Taub and McEwen (1991) investigated the effect of class standing on autonomy development and found that seniors scored higher on autonomy and academic autonomy scales. They also scored higher on the mature interpersonal relationships scale. Freshmen, sophomores, and juniors did not score significantly different on these scales from one another, which led the authors to conclude that focusing concern on underclass students in the general area of developing autonomy may be misplaced. They suggested that the timing of interventions focusing on autonomy development in underclass women should be reexamined. This study also compared the score of African American women with whites. A significant difference emerged on one scale, intimacy, where white women scored higher. The explanation offered by the authors was that since the study was conducted at a large, predominantly white university, opportunities for African American women to engage in intimate relationships may have been quite limited because they had so few peers.

Self-Efficacy

A study of the sense of self-efficacy of resident assistants was conducted by Denzine and Anderson (1999). Self-efficacy is characterized as "an individual's belief system about their competencies and abilities in a given situation" (p. 247). The authors found that "the majority of RAs in this sample had a positive sense of self-efficacy regarding their ability to positively influence the development of students" (p. 254). Denzine and Anderson suggested that self-efficacy can be enhanced by making good mentors available, or through social persuasion, or giving individuals the opportunity to learn vicariously from the experience of others.

Other Psychosocial Outcomes

Martin (2000) examined the effect of certain college experiences on psychosocial outcomes. She found "a clear relationship between student-faculty interaction and the development of purpose as well as a sense of competence. Sense of competence and purpose were also influenced heavily by student community factors such as clubs and organizations, student acquaintances, topics of conversation and information in conversation" (p. 299).

Bauer's study (1992) of academic and social skills included nearly one thousand students from a mid-Atlantic university. Both women and men indicated gains from their college experience in such areas as understanding themselves, understanding others, and developing values and ethics; in a statistical sense, women had greater gains than did men. Bauer also found that students who indicated that they had higher grades reported greater gains in these areas.

Springer, Terenzini, Pascarella, and Nora (1995) examined the concept of learning for self-understanding in a study of six hundred students. They viewed this form of learning as, "explicitly or implicitly, part of the educational mission of most American colleges and universities" (p. 5). They found that in-class and out-of-class experiences contribute to learning for self-understanding. They concluded that "this study offers *further* evidence supporting the long-held theory that college's effects on student learning are holistic" (pp. 15–16, italics in original). They added that "these findings suggest the importance of a more comprehensive perspective in educational program planning and development, and close collaboration among academic and student affairs divisions in the delivery of educational programs and services" (p. 16).

Moral Reasoning

Pascarella and Terenzini (1991) also concluded that moral reasoning is affected by the college experience. They indicated that when compared to people who do not progress beyond high school, gains in the use of principled reasoning widen in the years after college.

Sanders (1990) compared the moral reasoning of men living in a campus residence with those who chose to live in a fraternity house. Both groups scored lower on a posttest than the pretest administered to them. The residential students scored higher on both administrations of the instrument. Given the results of her study, Sanders recommended that "special programming with the purpose of introducing students to higher moral reasoning principles could be implemented in college environments" (p. 8).

Religiosity

The college experience appears to have a mitigating effect on development of religiosity on the part of students. Pascarella and Terenzini (1991) observed the following: "We conclude that maturation alone cannot explain all the declines observed to occur in students' conventional religious preferences, religiosity and religious behaviors" (p. 293). On the other hand, as is cited later in this chapter, service learning was an opportunity to fulfill a religious commitment (Eyler & Giles, 1999).

The College Environment and Intrapersonal and Interpersonal Development

Researchers have examined the impact of specific aspects of the college environment on self-awareness and interpersonal sensitivity. Studies have focused on participation in college athletics, service learning, student employment, residence hall living, and involvement in a Greek letter organization. Others have examined the overall impact of institutional initiatives on development, including that of students of color.

Athletic Participation

Several studies have examined the effect of participating in college athletics on student growth and development. In the studies cited here, the institutions participated at a level lower than NCAA Division I, the level of athletics that gains the most public notoriety and attention.

Taylor (1995) studied athletes at a Division II institution and found no statistically significant differences between athletes and nonathletes using a measure of self-esteem, although the athletes scored more positively than nonathletes. As Taylor concluded, "These findings suggest that athletic participation has a positive effect on self-esteem, but it is not strong enough to have a statistically significant effect by itself" (p. 449).

Richards and Aries (1999) conducted a similar study of Division III athletes at a single institution. They concluded that "participation in athletics at this Division III school was associated with growth and did not impede academic achievement or campus involvement" (p. 217). These findings differ from those of Terenzini, Pascarella, and Blimling (1999), who questioned the participation of freshmen in intercollegiate athletics, especially at the Division I level. Perhaps the most important conclusion is that students who compete at different NCAA levels may well have differing experiences and require institutional support in varying degrees to be successful as athletes as well as students, in and out of the classroom.

Service Learning

Service learning appears to have a number of important influences on personal development. Astin and Sax (1998) reported on several outcomes of service learning participation and found that participants, when compared with nonparticipants, had a greater increase in social self-confidence and leadership ability. Service learning also enhanced interpersonal skills and knowledge of people from various races and cultures in this study.

Eyler and Giles (1999) found similar results. Participants in service learning experiences in their study reported growth in the following areas: self-knowledge, finding reward in helping others, learning how to work with others, and leadership skills. Students also reported strengthening self-efficacy; "some saw service as a definite opportunity to fulfill their religious commitment" (p. 37).

Myers-Lipton (1996) also examined the effect of service learning, focusing on international understanding. Students who participated in service learning had a greater increase in global understanding than those who were nonparticipants. Service learning participation is something that an institution should encourage of virtually all its students. The power of service learning is extraordinary; enhanced international understanding is an important outcome of this experience.

Student Employment

Work on campus seems to have an effect on self-reported affective growth, according to Terenzini, Pascarella, and Blimling (1999). They cited Kuh (1995) in affirming that "to the extent that part-time employment opportunities can be linked to students' academic experiences, however, they constitute additional opportunities to share students' academic and cognitive development as well as their interpersonal and practical skills" (p. 615).

The obvious implication here is that a college or university would be well advised to develop on-campus work opportunity for students even beyond what exists currently if fostering affective growth is an institutional objective.

Residence Hall Living

Residential living can have an effect on self-esteem, as pointed out by Kuh, Douglas, Lund, and Ramin-Gyurnek (1994). They concluded that "exposure to people with diverse views is often developmentally challenging and contributes to the formation of personal identity—or the integration of such attributes as integrity, civic responsibility, aesthetic appreciation, confidence and self-esteem" (p. 38). Pascarella, Terenzini, and Blimling (1994) also identified benefits of residence hall living on student development. They concluded "the evidence shows that living in college residence halls (versus commuting to college) has its strongest and most consistent positive influence in the areas of social/extracurricular involvement, satisfaction with college, persistence in college, and degree attainment" (p. 27). They added that students living in a traditional residence hall tend to make gains in a number of psychosocial areas, and that the net effect of living in a residence hall tends to be cumulative and may increase in magnitude during a student's career in college.

Involvement in Greek Letter Organizations

The relationship between Greek letter involvement and development of moral reasoning and psychosocial development also has been reported in the literature. Kuh and his colleagues (1994) saw membership in a fraternity or sorority as having a mixed impact on the gain in interpersonal or intrapersonal competence. Hunt and Rentz (1994) studied 321 fraternity and sorority members at a Midwestern university. They concluded that membership "was significantly related to: establishing and clarifying purposes, developing mature interpersonal relationships and establishing an intimate relationship with another based on trust, reciprocal caring and honesty" (p. 293). They added "it may be concluded that involvement, outside or in conjunction with involvement in a Greek-letter social group, is related to increases in specific measures of psychosocial development" (p. 294).

Institutional Initiatives

Love and Love (1995) recommended that an institution develop strategies to ensure that experiences inside and outside of class are complementary and contribute to student growth. In summarizing the work of Kuh and others (1991), Love and Love concluded that "the involving colleges studied by Kuh et al. are most noted for their attention to the connections between academic and social experiences of students. They found that by creating connections between the intellectual and the social and encouraging students to do the same, these institutions avoid putting students in the position of having to choose one over the other" (1995, p. 80). A seamless approach to student learning, then, should be used to conceptualize this aspect of the student experience since, as Schroeder (1999) concluded, "seamless learning environments comprise a network of components that work together to accomplish a common end" (p. 6).

Baxter Magolda (2000) reported on her study of individuals' experiences in the eight years immediately after college, with a specific focus on mutuality, defined in the service learning literature as "the intended relationships between students and those served" (p. 154). The author extended this concept to other experiences for college students, including leadership development, educational programming in the interpersonal arena, career services, residential life, and diversity programming. She concluded with this observation: "The primary implication of the 39 journeys I have witnessed is that intentional development of an internal foundation should be a goal of a college education" (p. 155).

Picklesimer and Miller (1998) posited similar recommendations. They advocated that "student development professionals can redesign programs to maximize the healthy growth-integration of emotional, social, and intellectual aspects of the students—a healthy system of higher education to foster mental health" (p. 107).

Experiences of Students of Color

A comparison of the sociocognitive growth of white and Chicano students was conducted by Durham, Hays, and Martinez (1994) in southern Colorado and northern New Mexico. Using the Perry scheme, they found that students developed at about the same level, but white students received a combination of peer, sibling, and parental encouragement for academic achievement. Chicanos received parental encouragement, but peers were not as supportive. The authors concluded that for the Chicano students, "success in college probably comes from perseverance and motivation rather than the usual sources of support enjoyed by Anglo American students" (p. 181). There are obvious implications for practice in this study, not the least of which is to help students develop social support groups and provide more information for parents and others so that support for these students can begin to approximate what their white colleagues experience. African American students in general (and African American men in particular) face significant challenges in adjusting to the collegiate environment. The interventions already described help address their lack of preparedness for the collegiate experience "resulting from poorer schooling; financial hardships; and other social, cultural and economic disadvantages" (Cuyjet, 1997, p. 14).

Pope (1998) studied the relationship between racial identity formation and psychosocial development for 250 African American students. She found that "the results of this study do suggest a significant relationship between the broader constructs of Psychosocial Development and Racial Identity" (p. 279). She went on to observe that "Although this study does offer support for the notion that racial identity influences psychosocial development, the nature of that influence is not yet fully understood" (p. 279). There are obvious implications for the student affairs practitioner and others to remember these differences in working with students as they develop potential experiences to help students learn and grow.

Implications for Practice

Whereas the implications for practice for the other outcomes discussed in this book included a variety of suggestions applicable to many areas of the college, the implications for practice for this section focus primarily on student affairs. This section discusses those implications, with a few for faculty to follow.

Implications for Student Affairs

Development of community appears to have a positive influence on how well students understand themselves and relate to others. Among the various strategies that can be employed in this area of endeavor are development of mutual values, goals, and assumptions by students for their education. Self-governance is one way this can be manifested. Use of an honor code, a student judicial board, or a student board that allocates student activity fees is a mechanism for helping to establish community (See Kuh et al., 1991).

Using paraprofessionals to deliver services is another valuable approach in development of understanding self and others, especially for the student paraprofessionals themselves. Service as a resident assistant enhances understanding of self and others, according to one study cited earlier in this chapter. A variety of benefits accrue to those who serve as resident assistants (Lillis & Schuh, 1982), and this kind of activity should be encouraged for undergraduates.

Living on campus appears to have a direct relationship in helping students understand themselves and others better than if the students did not live on campus. On-campus living ought to be encouraged, even if students do so for just a semester or a year. If necessary, scholarship programs might be developed by the college so that students who ordinarily would live at home for financial reasons could live on campus and have the full benefit of residence hall living.

Work on campus seems to have a positive relationship with this dimension of student growth. It is suggested elsewhere in this book that as meaningful work experiences on campus are developed for students, they are likely to grow and develop. Moreover, students should be encouraged not to work long hours off campus in circumstances that have no relationship to their course of study. This might mean generating more funding for campus work opportunity, or more funding so that the hourly wage is commensurate with what students might earn off campus. In either event, students will benefit from their on-campus work experience, especially if it relates to their course of study.

Greek letter organizations, as is the case for other dimensions, entail positive and negative experiences for students. In the case of understanding self and others, the results are mixed. In some studies, the Greek letter experience has been seen as facilitating development, while in others it has been an inhibiting factor. Thus careful work with Greek advisers, chapter advisers, student leaders, and the collegians themselves is warranted. Structured inputs could be helpful in the membership intake process, as well as in leadership development programs to make sure that students who are members of a Greek letter organization develop at approximately the same rate as their independent counterparts.

Participation in a student club or other organization has been found to be an excellent experience in terms of promoting student growth. On some campuses, forming a club and securing funding can be easy, while in other situations it is quite difficult (Kuh et al., 1991). Making sure that students can form a club or other organization easily, and secure funding without excessive delay, is an important strategy in this area of student life. Student affairs staff can work to develop user-friendly policies and procedures that facilitate formation of a student organization.

Students often come to campus having experienced difficulty in their lives before enrollment. Especially poignant can be the stories of students whose parents have divorced. Counseling centers can make sure that students are aware of programs available for children of divorce. Be it a group counseling intervention or an individual session, such an experience can be important for a student. Making sure that opportunities are widely publicized helps make the experience available to students who need it.

Finally, students of color as well as gay, lesbian, and bisexual students, according to the literature, need some additional support so that their experiences are equivalent to those from the majority culture. Student affairs staff can assist these students in forming an organization or club that provides support for students from nonmajority cultures. Additionally, information can be given to the parents of these students so that they can also support their students as needed.

This amounts to a segue to one last intervention for student affairs staff. Parents may not understand the growth and developmental process their children are experiencing while they are enrolled in college. Parents need information so that as the student appears to change or need special support, they are able to respond accordingly. This information can be offered directly by the college or through developing a parent association, which can be especially helpful in organizing events for parents, getting information to them through the mail, or being available to take telephone calls when parents have questions about their students.

Implications for Faculty and Student Affairs

Several implications emerge for faculty and student affairs staff to work collaboratively in this area of student growth. Among the most important are development of cooperative learning experience and service learning experience.

Cooperative learning experiences place students in the field where they are able to field-test what they have learned in class in practical work situations. This can be done either by having the student take a class for a semester and then participate in a cooperative experience off campus for another semester, or through a situation where the student studies and works simultaneously. Student affairs staff can help identify work sites and provide support to the student who is engaged in cooperative learning; faculty can assist students in processing their experiences and linking them to what they have been learning in class.

A similar approach can be taken to service learning. Faculty and student affairs staff can make similar contributions to the service learning effort, with the consequence being that students learn and grow from the experience. The literature on service learning experience is quite clear: students benefit substantially from it and the college is well served if it encourages students to participate.

Implications for Faculty

Finally, the research suggests that students benefit when they have routine informal contact with faculty outside the classroom. In spite of the potential drain on their time, faculty serve students well if they are available for serious discussion related to class work outside of class, be it in a faculty office, in the student union, or in the residence hall cafeteria. The experience benefits students and can be quite rewarding for faculty as well.

Creating an opportunity for self-reflection in a class assignment or for discussion of significant issues during class also allows students to develop awareness of their own values and beliefs as well as those of their classmates. Collaborative learning activities (such as outside-of-class group projects) and other interactive experiences also contribute to interpersonal sensitivity.

Finally, class content should reflect the diversity of our society and extend an opportunity for the student to learn about other cultures and populations. The contributions of various racial and ethnic groups as well as of women and gay, lesbian, and bisexual individuals should be included in relevant courses in history, sociology, literature, psychology, and other disciplines.

References

Astin, A. W., & Sax, L. J. (1998). How undergraduates are affected by service participation. *Journal of College Student Development, 39,* 251–263.

Atkinson, D. R., Morten, G., & Sue, D. W. (1993). *Counseling American minorities: A cross-cultural perspective* (4th ed.). Dubuque, IA: Brown and Benchmark.

Bair, C. R., Klepper, W. M., & Phelps Tobin, C. E. (1998). Institutional issues facing student affairs. In N. J. Evans & C. E. Phelps Tobin (Eds.), *The state of the art of preparation and practice in student affairs: Another look* (pp. 21–45). Lanham, MD: American College Personnel Association.

Bauer, K. W. (1992). Self-reported gains in academic and social skills. *Journal of College Student Development, 33,* 492–498.

Baxter Magolda, M. B. (2000). Interpersonal maturity: Integrating agency and communion. *Journal of College Student Development, 41,* 141–156.

Bowen, H. R. (1977). Investment in learning: The individual and social value of American higher education. San Francisco: Jossey-Bass.

Cass, V. C. (1979). Homosexual identity formation: A theoretical model. *Journal of Homosexuality, 4,* 219–235.

Chickering, A. W. (1977). Potential contributions of college unions to student development. *Association of College Unions-International Conference Proceedings,* pp. 23–27.

Chickering, A. W., & Reisser, L. (1993). *Education and identity* (2nd ed.). San Francisco: Jossey-Bass.

Clayton, S. A., & Jones, A. (1993). Multiculturalism: An imperative for change. *Iowa Student Personnel Association Journal, 8,* 35–49.

Connolly, M. (2000). Issues for lesbian, gay, and bisexual students in traditional college classrooms. In V. A. Wall & N. J. Evans (Eds.),

Toward acceptance: Sexual orientation issues on campus (pp. 109–130). Lanham, MD: American College Personnel Association.

Cross, W. E., Jr. (1991). *Shades of Black: Diversity in African-American identity.* Philadelphia: Temple University Press.

Cuyjet, M. J. (1997). African American men on college campuses: Their needs and their perceptions. In M. J. Cuyjet (Ed.), *Helping African American men succeed in college* (New Directions for Student Services, no. 80, pp. 5–16). San Francisco: Jossey-Bass.

D'Augelli, A. R. (1994). Identity development and sexual orientation: Toward a model of lesbian, gay, and bisexual development. In E. J. Trickett, R. J. Watts, & D. Birman (Eds.), *Human diversity: Perspectives on people in context* (pp. 312–333). San Francisco: Jossey-Bass.

Denzine, G. M., & Anderson, C. M. (1999). I can do it: Resident assistants' sense of self-efficacy. *Journal of College Student Development, 40,* 247–256.

Dewey, J. (1980). *Theory of the moral life.* New York: Irvington. (Original work published 1908)

Diaz-Guerrero, R. (1987). Historical sociocultural premises and ethnic socialization. In J. S. Phinney & M. J. Rotheram (Eds.), *Children's ethnic socialization: Pluralism and development* (pp. 239–250). Newbury Park, CA: Sage.

Downing, N. E., & Roush, K. L. (1985). From passive acceptance to active commitment: A model of feminist identity development for women. *Counseling Psychologist, 13,* 695–709.

Durham, R. L., Hays, J., & Martinez, R. (1994). Socio-cognitive development among Chicano and Anglo American college students. *Journal of College Student Development, 35,* 178–182.

Enns, C. Z. (1991). The new relationship models of women's identity: A review and critique for counselors. *Journal of Counseling and Development, 69,* 209–217.

Erikson, E. H. (1959). Identity and the life cycle. *Psychological Issues, 1,* 1–171.

Erikson, E. H. (1968). *Identity: Youth and crisis.* New York: Norton.

Evans, N. J. (1982). Using developmental theory in needs assessment. *Journal of the National Association for Women Deans, Administrators, and Counselors, 45*(3), 34–39.

Evans, N. J. (2000). Creating a positive learning environment for gay, lesbian, and bisexual students. In M. B. Baxter Magolda (Ed.), *Teaching to promote intellectual and personal maturity: Incorporating students' worldviews and identities into the learning process* (New Directions for Teaching and Learning, no. 82, pp. 81–87). San Francisco: Jossey-Bass.

Evans, N. J. (in press). The impact of an LGBT safe zone project on campus climate. *Journal of College Student Development.*

Evans, N. J., & Anderson, D. (1993, February). *Identity development models: A key to effective diversity programming.* Presented at the NASPA-IV East Regional Conference, Des Moines, IA.

Evans, N. J., & Broido, E. M. (1999). Coming out in college residence halls: Negotiation, meaning making, challenges, supports. *Journal of College Student Development, 40,* 658–668.

Evans, N. J., & D'Augelli, A. R. (1996). Lesbians, gay men, and bisexual people in college. In R. C. Savin-Williams & K. M. Cohen (Eds.), *The lives of lesbians, gays, and bisexuals* (pp. 201–226). New York: Harcourt Brace.

Evans, N. J., Forney, D. S., & Guido-DiBrito, F. (1998). *Student development in college: Theory, research, and practice.* San Francisco: Jossey-Bass.

Evans, N. J., & Wall, V. A. (Eds.). (1991). *Beyond tolerance: Gays, lesbians and bisexuals on campus.* Alexandria, VA: American College Personnel Association.

Eyler, J., & Giles, Jr., D. E. (1999). *Where's the learning in service-learning?* San Francisco: Jossey-Bass.

Fowler, J. W. (1981). *Stages of faith: The psychology of human development and the quest for meaning.* San Francisco: HarperCollins.

Fowler, J. W. (1986). Faith and the structure of meaning. In C. Dykstra & S. Parks (Eds.), *Faith development and Fowler* (pp. 15–42). Birmingham, AL: Religious Education Press.

Fried, J. (Ed.). (1994). *Different voices: Gender and perspective in student affairs administration.* Washington, DC: National Association of Student Personnel Administrators.

Gardiner, L. F. (1994). *Redesigning higher education: Producing dramatic gains in student learning.* (ASHE-ERIC Report no. 7). Washington, DC: George Washington University, Graduate School of Education and Human Development.

Gilligan, C. (1977). In a different voice: Women's conceptions of self and morality. *Harvard Educational Review, 47,* 481–517.

Gilligan, C. (1982). *In a different voice: Psychological theory and women's development.* Cambridge, MA: Harvard University Press.

Hardiman, R., & Jackson, B. W. (1992). Racial identity development: Understanding racial dynamics in college classrooms and on college campuses. In M. Adams (Ed.), *Promoting diversity in college classrooms: Innovative responses for the curriculum, faculty, and institutions* (New Directions for Teaching and Learning, no. 52, pp. 21–37). San Francisco: Jossey-Bass.

Heath, D. (1968). *Growing up in college.* San Francisco: Jossey-Bass.

Heath, D. (1977). *Maturity and competence: A transcultural view.* New York: Gardner.

Helms, J. E. (1992). *A race is a nice thing to have: A guide to being a white person or understanding the white persons in your life.* Topeka, KS: Content Communications.

Helms, J. E. (Ed.). (1993). *Black and white racial identity: Theory, research and practice.* Westport, CT: Praeger.

Helms, J. E., & Cook, D. A. (1999). *Using race and culture in counseling and psychotherapy: Theory and process.* Needham Heights, MA: Allyn & Bacon.

Heyer, D. L., & Nelson, E. S. (1993). The relationship between parental marital status and the development of identity and emotional autonomy in college students. *Journal of College Student Development, 34,* 432–436.

Hotelling, K., & Forrest, L. (1985). Gilligan's theory of sex-role development: A perspective for counseling. *Journal of Counseling and Development, 64,* 183–186.

Howard-Hamilton, M. F. (2000). Creating a culturally responsive learning environment for African American students. In M. B. Baxter Magolda (Ed.), *Teaching to promote intellectual and personal maturity: Incorporating students' worldviews and identities into the learning process* (New Directions for Teaching and Learning, no. 82, pp. 45–53). San Francisco: Jossey-Bass.

Hunt, S., & Rentz, A. L. (1994). Greek-letter social group members' involvement and psychosocial development. *Journal of College Student Development, 35,* 289–295.

Hurst, J. C. (1978). Chickering's vectors of development and student affairs programming. In C. A. Parker (Ed.), *Encouraging the development of college students* (pp. 113–126). Minneapolis: University of Minnesota Press.

Huss, J. K. (1983). Developing competence and autonomy for disabled students. *AHSSPPE Bulletin, 1,* 81–92.

Isajiw, W. W. (1990). Ethnic-identity retention. In R. Breton, W. W. Isajiw, W. E. Kalbach, & J. G. Reitz (Eds.), *Ethnic identity and equality* (pp. 34–91). Toronto: University of Toronto Press.

Josselson, R. (1987). *Finding herself: Pathways to identity development in women.* San Francisco: Jossey-Bass.

Kegan, R. (1982). *The evolving self.* Cambridge, MA: Harvard University Press.

Kegan, R. (1994). *In over our heads: The mental demands of modern life.* Cambridge, MA: Harvard University Press.

Kenny, M. E., & Donaldson, G. A. (1992). The relationship of parental attachment and psychological separation to the adjustment of first-year college women. *Journal of College Student Development, 33,* 431–438.

Kinsey, A. C., Pomeroy, W. B., & Martin, C. E. (1948). *Sexual behavior in the human male.* Philadelphia: Saunders.

Klepper, W. M., & Kovacs, E. (1978, December). What is the impact of the college union program on today's students? *Association of College Unions-International Bulletin,* pp. 17–20.

Knefelkamp, L., Parker, C. A., & Widick, C. (1978). Jane Loevinger's milestones of development. In L. Knefelkamp, C. Widick, & C. A. Parker (Eds.), *Applying new developmental findings* (New Directions for Student Services, no. 4, pp. 69–78). San Francisco: Jossey-Bass.

Kohlberg, L. (1972). A cognitive-developmental approach to moral education. *Humanist, 6,* 13–16.

Kohlberg, L. (1976). Moral stages and moralization: The cognitive-developmental approach. In T. Lickona (Ed.), *Moral development and behavior: Theory, research, and social issues* (pp. 31–53). New York: Holt, Rinehart and Winston.

Kuh, G. D., Douglas, K. B., Lund, J. P., & Ramin-Gyurnek, J. (1994). *Student learning outside the classroom: Transcending artificial boundaries.* (ASHE-ERIC Report no. 8). Washington, DC: George Washington University, Graduate School of Education and Human Development.

Kuh, G. D., Schuh, J. H., Whitt, E. J., & Associates. (1991). *Involving colleges.* San Francisco: Jossey-Bass.

Lemons, L. J., & Richmond, D. R. (1987). A developmental perspective of sophomore slump. *NASPA Journal, 24*(3), 15–19.

Levine, H., & Evans, N. J. (1991). The development of gay, lesbian, and bisexual identities. In N. J. Evans & V. A. Wall (Eds.), *Beyond tolerance: Gays, lesbians and bisexuals on campus* (pp. 1–24). Alexandria, VA: American College Personnel Association.

Levinson, D. J. (1978). *The seasons of a man's life.* New York: Knopf.

Levinson, D. J., & Levinson, J. D. (1996). *The season's of a woman's life.* New York: Ballantine.

Lillis, C. J., & Schuh, J. H. (1982). The perceived long-term benefits of holding a resident assistant position. *Journal of College and University Student Housing, 12*(1), 36–39.

Loevinger, J. (1976). *Ego development: Conceptions and theories.* San Francisco: Jossey-Bass.

Lott, J. K. (1986). Freshman home reentry: Attending to a gap in student development. *Journal of Counseling and Development, 64,* 456.

Love, P., & Talbot, D. (1999). Defining spiritual development: A missing consideration for student affairs. *NASPA Journal, 37,* 361–375.

Love, P. G., & Guthrie, V. L. (1999). *Understanding and applying cognitive development theory* (New Directions for Student Services, no. 88). San Francisco: Jossey-Bass.

Love, P. G., & Love, A. G. (1995). *Enhancing student learning: Intellectual, social and emotional integration.* (ASHE-ERIC Report no. 4). Washington, DC: George Washington University, Graduate School of Education and Human Development.

Marcia, J. E. (1966). Development and validation of ego-identity status. *Journal of Personality and Social Psychology, 3,* 551–559.

Marcia, J. E. (1989). Identity and intervention. *Journal of Adolescence, 12,* 401–410.

Martin, L. M. (2000). The relationship of college experiences to psychosocial outcomes in students. *Journal of College Student Development, 41,* 292–300.

Mather, P. C., & Winston, R. B., Jr. (1998). Autonomy development of traditional-aged students: Themes and processes. *Journal of College Student Development, 39,* 33–50.

May, W. F. (1990). Public happiness and higher education. In P. J. Palmer, B. G. Wheeler, & J. W. Fowler (Eds.), *Caring for the commonweal: Education for religious and public life* (pp. 227–247). Macon, GA: Mercer University Press.

McBride, M. C. (1990). Autonomy and the struggle for female identity: Implications for counseling women. *Journal of Counseling and Development, 69,* 22–26.

McCarn, S. R., & Fassinger, R. E. (1996). Revisioning sexual minority identity formation: A new model of lesbian identity and its implications for counseling and research. *Counseling Psychologist, 24,* 508–534.

McEwen, M. K., Roper, L., Bryant, D., & Langa, M. (1990). Incorporating the development of African-American students into psychosocial theories of student development. *Journal of College Student Development, 31,* 429–436.

Myers-Lipton, S. J. (1996). Effect of service-learning on college students' attitudes toward international understanding. *Journal of College Student Development, 37,* 659–668.

O'Neil, J. M., Egan, J., Owen, S. V., & Murry, V. M. (1993). The Gender Role Journey Measure: Scale development and psychometric evaluation. *Sex Roles, 28,* 167–185.

Ossana, S. M., Helms, J. E., & Leonard, M. M. (1992). Do "womanist" identity attitudes influence college women's self-esteem and perceptions of environmental bias? *Journal of Counseling and Development, 70,* 402–408.

Parks, S. D. (1986). *The critical years: Young adults and the search for meaning, faith, and commitment.* New York: HarperCollins.

Parks, S. D. (2000). *Big questions, worthy dreams: Mentoring young adults in their search for meaning, purpose, and faith.* San Francisco: Jossey-Bass.

Pascarella, E. T., & Terenzini, P. T. (1991). *How college affects students.* San Francisco: Jossey-Bass.

Pascarella, E. T., Terenzini, P. T., & Blimling, G. S. (1994). The impact of residential life on students. In C. C. Schroeder, P. Mable, & Associates, *Realizing the educational potential of residence halls* (pp. 22–52). San Francisco: Jossey-Bass.

Perreira, D. C., & Dezago, J. L. (1989). College student development: Is it different for persons with disabilities? *Proceedings of the 1989 AHSSPPE Conference,* pp. 51–54.

Phinney, J. S. (1990). Ethnic identity in adolescence and adulthood: A review of the research. *Psychological Bulletin, 108,* 499–514.

Picard, I. A., & Guido-DiBrito, F. (1993). Listening to the voice of care: Women's moral development and implications for student affairs practitioners. *Iowa Student Personnel Association Journal, 8,* 21–34.

Picklesimer, B. K., & Miller, T. K. (1998). Life-skills development inventory—college form: An assessment measure. *Journal of College Student Development, 39,* 100–110.

Points of View. (1989). Washington, DC: National Association of Student Personnel Administrators.

Pope, R. L. (1998). The relationship between psychosocial development and racial identity of Black college students. *Journal of College Student Development, 39,* 273–282.

Porterfield, W. D., & Pressprich, S. T. (1988). Carol Gilligan's perspectives and staff supervision: Implications for the practitioner. *NASPA Journal, 25,* 244–248.

Rest, J. R. (1986). *Moral development: Advances in research and theory.* New York: Praeger.

Richards, S., & Aries, A. (1999). The Division III athlete: Academic performance, campus involvement, and growth. *Journal of College Student Development, 40,* 211–218.

Rowe, W., Bennett, S. K., & Atkinson, D. R. (1994). White racial identity models: A critique and alternative proposal. *Counseling Psychologist, 22,* 129–146.

Sanders, C. E. (1990). Moral reasoning of male freshmen. *Journal of College Student Development, 31,* 5–8.

Sanford, N. (1966). *Self and society: Social change and individual development.* New York: Atherton.

Sanford, N. (1967). *Where colleges fail: A study of the student as a person.* San Francisco: Jossey-Bass.

Schenkel, S., & Marcia, J. E. (1972). Attitudes toward premarital intercourse in determining ego identity status in college women. *Journal of Personality, 40,* 472–482.

Schroeder, C. C. (1999). Partnerships: An imperative for enhancing student learning and institutional effectiveness. In J. H. Schuh & E. J. Whitt (Eds.), *Creating successful partnerships between academic and student affairs* (New Directions for Student Services, no. 87, pp. 5–18). San Francisco: Jossey-Bass.

Scott, D. (1991). Working with gay and lesbian student organizations. In N. J. Evans & V. A. Wall (Eds.), *Beyond tolerance: Gays, lesbians and bisexuals on campus* (pp. 117–130). Alexandria, VA: American College Personnel Association.

Sodowsky, G. R., Kwan, K. K., & Pannu, R. (1995). Ethnic identity of Asians in the United States. In J. G. Ponterotto, J. M. Casas, L. A. Suzuki, & C. M. Alexander (Eds.), *Handbook of multicultural counseling* (pp. 123–154). Thousand Oaks, CA: Sage.

Springer, L., Terenzini, P. T., Pascarella, E. T., & Nora, A. (1995). Influences on college students' orientations toward learning for self-understanding. *Journal of College Student Development, 36,* 5–18.

A statement of ethical principles and standards. (1989). Washington, DC: American College Personnel Association.

Stonewater, B. B. (1989). Gender differences in career decision making: A theoretical integration. *Initiatives, 52*(1), 27–34.

The student in higher education: Report of the committee on the student in higher education. (1968). New Haven, CT: Hazen Foundation.

Tatum, B. D. (1992). Talking about race, learning about racism: The application of racial identity development theory in the classroom. *Harvard Educational Review, 62,* 1–24.

Taub, D. J. (1995). Relationship of selected factors to traditional-age undergraduate women's development of autonomy. *Journal of College Student Development, 36,* 141–151.

Taub, D. J. (1997). Autonomy and parental attachment in traditional-age undergraduate women. *Journal of College Student Development, 38,* 645–654.

Taub, D. J., & McEwen, M. K. (1991). Patterns of development of autonomy and mature interpersonal relationships in Black and White undergraduates. *Journal of College Student Development, 32,* 502–508.

Taylor, D. L. (1995). A comparison of college athletic participants and non-participants on self-esteem. *Journal of College Student Development, 36,* 444–451.

Temkin, L., & Evans, N. J. (1998). Religion on campus: Suggestions for cooperation between student affairs and campus-based religious organizations. *NASPA Journal, 36,* 61–69.

Terenzini, P. T., Pascarella, E. T., & Blimling, G. S. (1999). Students' out-of-class experiences and their influence on learning and cognitive development: A literature review. *Journal of College Student Development, 40,* 610–623.

Wall, V. A., & Evans, N. J. (Eds.). (2000). *Toward acceptance: Sexual orientation issues on campus.* Lanham, MD: American College Personnel Association.

Widick, C., Parker, C. A., & Knefelkamp, L. (1978). Douglas Heath's model of maturing. In L. Knelfelkamp, C. Widick, & C. A. Parker (Eds.), *Applying new developmental findings* (New Directions for Student Services, no. 4, pp. 79–91). San Francisco: Jossey-Bass.

Chapter Six

Democratic Citizen

On any number of campuses, on any given day, students engage in a variety of acts. One student reviews her agenda for a student government meeting or a campus task force meeting. Another drops off a letter to the editor of the campus newspaper. Another attends a floor meeting to identify possible solutions to a current problem in the residence hall. Another volunteers in the local hospice or in his child's classroom. Another voices opposition to a new campus policy or decision. Another turns away from or challenges an offensive joke told by her fellow student. Another picks up a discarded paper cup on the way to class and drops it into a trash can. Another finishes packing his suitcase for a spring break service trip to an underserved area of the state. These and countless other acts are examples of experiences that can lead to the learning outcome of active citizenship.

In this chapter, we offer a broad definition of citizenship and examine sources that identify citizenship as a desired learning outcome for postsecondary education. We then examine citizenship-related aspects of student development theories and describe opportunities for in-class and out-of-class experience that appear to foster successful development of citizenship. The chapter concludes with principles of citizenship development and implications for educational practice.

We certainly do not assume that active and involved citizenship is the sole property of college-educated individuals, but we do maintain that certain college experiences appear to give students multiple opportunities to exercise citizenship, empower themselves as citizens, and develop their citizenship potential.

Three Perspectives on Citizenship

Democratic perspectives on citizenship emphasize collective social determinism (for example, Barber, 1992; Gutmann, 1987). Emphasis in a democratic framework is placed on direct or representative procedures to assess and reevaluate the will of the majority, conducted with an underlying commitment to principles of nonrepression of ideas and nondiscrimination of participation (Gutmann, 1987). Citizens in this framework participate by voting or participating in a representative body, influencing the deliberative process, consenting to the legitimate will of the majority once it has been determined, and critiquing the decision-making process and decisions reached through it. Vigilance is therefore an essential citizen role in this framework, which is often though not solely undertaken by members of the loyal opposition who disagree with aspects of the current collective vision and seek to change it without subverting democratic values or processes.

By contrast, liberal perspectives on citizenship emphasize individual determinism upon which formal government should not unnecessarily infringe (see, for instance, Rawls, 1971). The citizen's freedom to determine and pursue his or her own visions and goals is the paramount concern, provided that the pursuit does not prevent or unduly restrain others' visions and pursuits. The protection of equal liberty is thus the core value of citizenship in a liberal framework, complemented by pursuit of social justice to benefit the least advantaged or least favored in society since these citizens do not currently have equal liberty and opportunity (Rawls, 1971). Citizens in a liberal society therefore should identify their individual goals, prepare themselves to pursue these goals, and vigilantly protect their rights to pursue their own self-interests. Additionally, citizens work to improve the position of the least-advantaged citizens through pursuing systematic change in society and government or through individual acts of charity and involvement.

Communitarian perspectives on citizenship emphasize support for the moral order of communities and one's responsibility to and for one's communities (Bellah, Madsen, Sullivan, Swidler, & Tipton, 1985, 1991; Etzioni, 1993). Communitarianism has six objectives: essential moral education, development of community without intragroup hostility, increased social responsibility, controlling powerful special interests without limiting the personal rights of lobbying and petitioning those chosen to serve, and affirming the public interest with safeguards of the rights of various constituencies (Ottenritter & Parsons, 1996). In a communitarian framework, the citizen's concerns center on fragmentation of social ties and communities and efforts to revitalize social and moral ties.

A Working Definition of Citizenship

What, then, is citizenship? The overview just given demonstrates that a citizen is caught up in tensions involving the authority of the polity, the authority of the individual, and the authority of the community. Any collective vision that restricts exercise of an individual's pursuit of his or her own goals, for example, is resolved differently in each of the three frameworks outlined in the previous section, and each echoes an enduring tension between individualism and collectivism (Bowen, 1977; Bull, Fruehling, & Chattergy, 1992). Additionally, fundamental differences among core values of the three perspectives make creating an amalgamated framework to merge these three perspectives impossible. For the purposes of this chapter, the definition of citizenship is quite broad. Citizenship means actively attending to the well-being, continuity, and improvement of society through individual action or actions or civic and social collectives; the learning outcome of citizenship is therefore development of a personal commitment to identify and advance social interests.

Proceeding from this definition, evidence of active citizenship includes, but is not limited to, holding elective or appointed office, voting and participating in campaign activity, attending meetings of a civic or social board, organizing a neighborhood advocacy group, writing letters and petitions, planning or participating in a service project such as a community watch patrol or tutoring, sharing chores with a neighbor or extending help to those unable to perform certain tasks, and engaging in acts or organizations to advance principled dissent.

College-educated citizens do, in fact, vote and participate in related civic activities at a higher rate than do citizens with a high school education or less (*The Condition of Education*, 1998), but citizenship also permeates everyday life in the form of routine acts or as an organizing life commitment. For example, Komives, Lucas, and McMahon (1996) proposed that citizenship encompassed reporting a broken parking lot light to the appropriate authorities and attending one's departmental brown-bag lunch series in support of the friends and colleagues who planned the event. Additionally, commitment to community service and social justice is a way of life that individuals can choose, rather than an option in only certain careers such as social work or as a separate activity to be done around the edges of other commitments (Fisher, 1996). However, citizenship is a commitment that must be taught (*Points of View*, 1989), since it does not simply emerge over time.

As we turn to a discussion of postsecondary education and citizenship learning, it is critical to acknowledge that colleges and universities are most often not collectively governed by internal members (Gutmann & Thompson, 1996). Although a college or university encourages public deliberation as part of its educational mission, a public forum is not necessarily a formal part of institutional governance. However, for the purposes of citizenship education, all colleges and universities constitute an integral "middle democracy," or "land of everyday politics" (Gutmann & Thompson, 1996, p. 12), in which students learn about these particular societies and their roles and potential social roles within them. At a college or university, students see institutional representatives making decisions that affect them directly or indirectly. A rationale may or may not be offered for a decision, and the people affected by the decision may or may not have had a voice in the deliberation and decision making. Nonetheless, important elements of vision and goals are determined through administrative process.

A distinction between *institution* and *campus* may be useful here. Although a college or university as an institution is most often not democratically governed, students are nonetheless exposed to decision-making processes, outcomes, and avenues for appeal of an administrative decision. However, certain elements of the campus environment (such as student government, residence hall governance, and group projects for course credit) are deliberately established to cultivate forms of participatory self-governance and directedness. In these ways, citizenship learning persists as an enduring feature within the higher education institution that is itself not a democracy.

Historical and Contemporary Citizenship Education

The importance of citizenship education is clearly apparent in the history of U.S. postsecondary institutions. First, citizenship development was among the purposes of the first colonial colleges, with their sometimes complicated allegiance to the state as well as a sponsoring religious denomination: "a college is a support of the state; it is an instructor in loyalty, in citizenship, in the dictates of conscience and faith" (Rudolph, 1962, p. 13). Although the Virginia legislature rejected Thomas Jefferson's 1779 proposal that William and Mary establish a professorship to help prepare "public servants for positions of responsibility in a democracy" (Rudolph, 1962, p. 41), Jefferson subsequently experimented with such preparation in the University of Virginia's curriculum. Commitment to citizenship as an intended outcome of higher education continues into the present. Citizenship was included in Bowen's taxonomy of intended outcomes of higher education (1977), and as recently as 1995 one national study revealed that more than 90 percent of Americans surveyed believed that a central task of the college or university was to develop contributing citizens (Harvey & Immerwahr, 1995).

Citizenship learning is articulated in many institutional mission statements and assessment strategies. For example, Alverno College, a Catholic women's college, includes preparation for citizenship not only in its mission statement but also in the list of eight abilities that guide institutional assessment of Alverno graduates. According to Alverno College documents, effective citizenship means that students will "be involved and responsible in the community. Act with an informed awareness of contemporary issues and their historical contexts. Develop leadership abilities" (Alverno College Website, 2000). At Alverno, activities are designed to help students obtain an increasing level of sophistication in citizenship preparation as well as the seven others deemed important. Students elect courses both for their content and for the skills they are designed to develop (Chickering & Reisser, 1993).

Colleges and universities serving traditionally underrepresented populations often emphasize outreach and service aspects of citizenship development. For example, Howard University's vision statement articulates a "commitment to educating youth, African Americans and other people of color in particular, for leadership and service to the nation and the global community" (Howard University Website, 2000). The University of Texas at El Paso "aims to extend the greatest possible educational access to a region which has been geographically isolated with limited economic and educational opportunities for many of its people" (University of Texas at El Paso Website, 2000). Occidental College, a highly selective liberal arts college, places strong emphasis on preparing students for citizenship as articulated in its mission statement. In part, the statement asserts that "the distinctive interdisciplinary and multicultural focus of the College's academic program seeks to foster both the fulfillment of individual aspirations and a deeply-rooted commitment to the public good" (Occidental College Website, 2000).

Student Affairs Commitment to Citizenship Education

The commitment to citizenship education articulated by individual colleges and universities has been echoed in a fairly consistent refrain in the professional field of student affairs. Three historical statements that articulated evolving assumptions, values, and purposes of student affairs all contain passages regarding the importance of citizenship development:

> This conference also wishes to emphasize the necessity for conceiving of after-college adjustment as comprehending the total living of college graduates, including not only their occupational success but their active concern with the social, recreational, and cultural interests of the community. Such concern implies their willingness to assume those individual and social responsibilities which are essential to the common good [1937 statement, *Points of View*, 1989, p. 58].

> As a responsible participant in the societal processes of our American democracy, his [sic] full and balanced maturity is viewed as a major end-goal of education and, as well, a necessary means to the

fullest development of his fellow citizens. From the personnel point of view any lesser goals fall short of the desired objectives of democratic educational processes and is [sic] a real drain and strain upon the self-realization of other developing individuals in our society [1949 statement, *Points of View,* 1989, p. 22].

A democracy requires the informed involvement of citizens. Citizenship is complex; thus, students benefit from a practical as well as an academic understanding of civic responsibilities. Active participation in institutional governance, community service, and effective management of their own affairs contributes significantly to students' understanding and appreciation of civic responsibilities [1987 statement, *Points of View,* 1989, p. 14].

The most recent of student affairs purpose and vision statements, the Student Learning Imperative (American College Personnel Association, 1996), included in its preamble a need for college graduates to "deal effectively with such major societal challenges as poverty, illiteracy, crime, and environmental exploitation" (p. 118).

Campus Activism

Clearly, the Student Learning Imperative passage just cited emphasized the citizenship responsibilities of critique, dissent, and reform of the status quo. This citizen vigilance is critical to preserving society and effectively challenging potential tyranny.

Historical accounts of early college life include stories of students' organized protests and collective subversion in response to, for example, the restrictive social life that gave rise to literary societies and eventually fraternities (Rudolph, 1962). Contemporary students, however, are far more critical of politics, politicians, and government than were their predecessors (Levine & Cureton, 1998). Students do not believe that there can be a quick fix or broad-scale solution to society's problems. They do not expect government to come to the rescue; they have instead chosen to focus on their community, neighborhood, or block (Levine & Cureton, 1998). During the 1980s, waves of student activism challenged institutional responses to larger social and political issues. For example, shanty towns appeared on many campuses in protest of trustees' or foundation officers' decisions regarding South African divestment. Most recently, student movements have centered on administrative decisions regarding multicultural initiatives or international concerns—issues related to diversity (Rhoads, 1997).

Traditional student political organizations have declined in importance. There are few right-wing or left-wing groups at colleges. The new breed of organization might be called a support or advocacy group. This type of organization has been with higher education since at least the nineteenth century, when Christian students banded together to support themselves and their religion and women enrolling at coeducational colleges coalesced to seek refuge and reform in a hostile environment (Levine & Cureton, 1998).

Although the actions of student activists can be viewed as divisive and alienating, dissenting students are in fact making an ultimate commitment of citizenship to their home campus. Their principled dissent to a decision or policy reflects their unwillingness to be apathetic when the perceived good of the collective is at stake (Hamrick, 1998).

Commitment to citizenship as a learning outcome for postsecondary education is consistently articulated in historical accounts of the development of higher education, literature examining the purposes and goals of higher education, institutional mission statements, and statements of purpose for the student affairs profession. Student development theories also afford insight into how students develop understanding of citizenship and make decisions about their role in society.

Citizenship and Student Development Theory

Several theorists have alluded to factors that contribute to developing citizenship. Psychosocial theorists see this outcome as related to a number of the developmental tasks of adolescence and adulthood. They also note environmental conditions that contribute to achieving these related tasks. Identity development models help in understanding how individuals who are members of various nondominant populations develop a sense of group identity and how they relate to the dominant culture. These theories can offer guidance concerning what it means to contribute to a society when one's cultural beliefs and values diverge from the norm. Cognitive-structural theorists examine the process of meaning making. They help one understand how people make sense of what it means to be a citizen.

Psychosocial Theory

Psychosocial theories that contribute to our understanding of citizenship development include those of Erikson (1959), Marcia (1980), and Chickering and Reisser (1993).

Erikson

Erik Erikson (1959) would argue that interpretation of the concept of citizenship is contingent on the historical period and social context being examined. What it means to be a citizen in Eastern Europe is quite different from what it means in North America. Likewise, U.S. citizens during the McCarthy era of the early 1950s probably defined this concept differently from citizens in the Vietnam era of the late 1960s.

Of particular significance to citizenship are Erikson's idea about generativity (1959), a midlife stage in which an adult actively considers what his or her contribution to society will be and engages in giving back to society. Erikson viewed generativity as "primarily the interest in establishing and guiding the next generation" (p. 103), but he also recognized that some individuals, "from misfortune or because of special or genuine gifts in other directions" (p. 103), make other forms of altruistic contribution. Erikson believed that if the generativity needs of the individual are not met the person experiences a "sense of stagnation and interpersonal impoverishment" (p. 103). Thus, Erikson saw giving back to society, an integral role of the citizen, as necessary if an adult is to live a happy and fulfilled life.

Marcia

Along with religious and occupational decision making, Marcia (1980) included political decision making as a primary focus of identity formation. He viewed identity achievement, a state arrived at when a crisis has been worked through and commitment has been made, as the healthiest psychological status a person can obtain.

For Marcia, then, considering and making a commitment to a political ideology is necessary for developing a secure ego identity. Certainly, such a commitment is important for any citizen of a society.

Chickering

Several of the vectors proposed by Chickering and Reisser (1993) relate to becoming a contributing citizen of a society. Their first vector, *developing competence,* is a foundation for such activity. Critical thinking and reasoning ability, both aspects of intellectual competence, are certainly important skills for a citizen. Additionally, skills in communication, leadership, and working effectively with others are components of interpersonal competence that contribute to citizenship.

Vector four, *developing mature interpersonal relationships,* builds on the interpersonal skills component of vector one; it includes development of intercultural and interpersonal sensitivity, appreciation of differences, and the ability to see commonality among people. It is particularly important for a citizen of a diverse society to possess these skills.

Part of *developing purpose,* vector six in Chickering and Reisser's scheme (1993), involves making meaningful commitment to a specific interest or activity as well as making any decision thoughtfully and remaining committed to it even in the face of opposition. Having a sense of purpose and staying true to it is an important part of citizenship.

Finally, *developing integrity,* the last of Chickering and Reisser's vectors (1993), focuses on the processes of identifying and affirming values of personal importance and humanizing values so that the perspectives and values of others are acknowledged and respected along with one's own. An additional aspect of this vector is developing congruence between one's values and actions. Self-interest is balanced with a sense of social responsibility. Integrity is a large part of what it means to be a citizen.

Chickering and Reisser (1993) suggested a number of influences in the college environment that contribute to student development. First, they advocated clear and consistent institutional objectives. They noted that the consistency in programs, policies, and practices resulting from such objectives allows a student to agree with or challenge the underlying values. This opportunity leads to developing along each of the vectors identified as contributing to the development of citizenship.

Chickering and Reisser (1993) also noted the relevance of institutional size in student development. They cited Astin's research indicating that students at a small institution achieve a higher level of competence because they are given more challenging tasks and responsibility than students at a larger school. Mature interpersonal relationships are also more likely to occur in a smaller setting if people have to work together to accomplish goals. Stereotypes are broken down as people work cooperatively. Astin (1977) also reported that altruism was more likely to develop among students at a small school, while those at larger schools became more hedonistic. Chickering and Reisser noted that values are clarified when people are forced to make choices and when the effects of their decisions are discernible. Students in a smaller setting are more likely to be faced with such situations.

Of the vectors related to citizenship, Chickering and Reisser (1993) suggested that student-faculty relationships influence development of competence, purpose, and integrity. In particular, faculty interaction positively affected the sense of intellectual competence experienced by women (Astin & Kent, 1983; Komarovsky, 1985) and African American students (Gurin & Epps, 1975). With regard to developing purpose and integrity, faculty members serve as important role models and have been found to be influential in helping students form values and attitudes (Endo & Harpel, 1982; Ory & Braskamp, 1988).

With regard to curriculum, Chickering and Reisser (1993) offered four guidelines for facilitating student development and preparing students to live and work in the twenty-first century. They seem particularly important for encouraging development of citizenship. These suggestions are (1) making "content relevant to students' backgrounds and prior experiences" (p. 362); (2) recognizing "significant dimensions of individual difference between students" (p. 364); (3) creating "encounters with diverse perspectives that challenge preexisting information, assumptions, and values" (p. 365); and (4) providing "activities that help students integrate diverse perspectives, assumptions, values orientations" (p. 367).

Chickering and Reisser (1993) stressed the importance of teaching in enhancing student development. They advocated techniques that actively involve students in the learning process, pointing to research (see Pascarella & Terenzini, 1991) that indicates that such involvement leads to development of the reasoning skills and increased cognitive complexity we see as necessary for effective citizenship. Gamson and her associates (1984) suggested that people learn by working in a community where they are encouraged to take into account the needs of others. They view the learning community as a crucial support for the learning of democracy. Chickering and Reisser (1993) also stressed the importance of experiential learning to encourage students to see the personal and social relevance of what they are studying.

Friendships and student communities present many opportunities for meaningful dialogue leading to student growth along each of Chickering and Reisser's vectors (1993). Being part of a peer support network helps the student see the value of community and making a contribution to a larger group, values necessary for effective citizenship. Significant interaction with peers from differing backgrounds and cultures leads to greater understanding of diversity and development of tolerance and appreciation of difference. Sharing one's ideas with peers and defending them against challenges leads to development of integrity. Powerful interaction with peers occurs in residence halls that enhance a strong sense of community and opportunities for involvement.

An academic program that offers students a high level of responsibility and participation, such as a learning community or honors program, also encourages cognitive and values development (King, 1973; MacGregor, 1991). In addition, it fosters appreciation for the importance of community in the larger society, a value we see as contributing to effective citizenship. The Carnegie Foundation for the Advancement of Teaching (1990) also stressed the importance of creating community in higher education to overcome some of the problems in society today.

Chickering and Reisser (1993) viewed student development programs and services as important for enhancing student development. From the first interaction with admissions counselors and orientation staff, students learn what is expected of them. Academic and personal support services extend assistance in developing competence and purpose. Involvement in student union programming (Chickering, 1997; Klepper & Kovacs, 1978) and student organizations facilitates development of interpersonal competence and mature interpersonal relationships as well as humanitarian concern. Todaro (1993) has also detailed the contributions of recreational sports programs to development along each of Chickering's vectors.

Identity Development Models

Racial identity theories (for example, Atkinson, Morten, & Sue, 1993; Cross, 1991, 1995; Helms, 1993, 1995; Helms & Cook, 1999; Phinney, 1990) grew out of "the tradition of treating race as a sociopolitical and, to a lesser extent, a cultural construction" (Helms, 1995, p. 181). Evans, Forney, and Guido-DiBrito (1998) noted that the notion of race in the United States is based on the assumption that certain racial groups are dominant and others are oppressed. What it means to be a citizen is greatly influenced by one's perceived dominant or subordinate position in society and how one chooses to relate to those who are in the opposite category. Similar dynamics related to the person's sexual orientation would be expected (see Cass, 1979; D'Augelli, 1994; Troiden, 1989).

It seems likely that an individual at an early stage of identity development who views the world through a dominant culture lens would view civic involvement as supporting the values, norms, and goals of that culture. In contrast, an individual who is immersed in a newly found nondominant racial, ethnic, or sexual identity would actively reject and protest against these aspects of dominant culture. An individual with an internalized identity might find many values and actions of the dominant culture to be repressive but advocate for structural change to create a more egalitarian society.

Likewise, members of a dominant population who hold racist or homophobic ideas are unlikely to see these values as problematic, despite the fact that they are in conflict with the democratic ideals espoused in U.S. society. Those individuals who have abandoned an oppressive belief system will, to varying degrees, work in conjunction with members of nondominant groups to create an inclusive society in line with the tenets of a true democracy.

One study (Mitchell & Dell, 1992) supports the notion that participation in a student organization is influenced by racial identity. Students in later stages of identity development were more likely to participate in a cultural activity on campus, but only students who had reached the internalization stage of Cross's model (1995) were involved in both cultural and noncultural student organizations. One could hypothesize that this finding might also apply to civic involvement. Individuals immersed in their own culture might be more likely to be involved in racial, ethnic, or lesbian/ gay/bisexual community organizations, while an individual whose identity was more integrated might also be involved in other civic organizations designed to promote values of inclusion and equality.

Cognitive-Structural Theories

How individuals interpret what it means to be a good citizen and the factors that motivate them to contribute to society vary considerably depending on the stage of cognitive development that constitutes a lens for their activity. Both epistemological and moral development theories yield useful information for considering how students think about citizenship.

Perry

People at each level of Perry's scheme (1968) would view citizenship differently and reason in unique ways about their responsibility to society. For individuals using dualistic reasoning, authority figures offer a definition and understanding of what it means to be a good citizen. If their parents, religious leaders, and teachers consider societal involvement important, they will as well. They base their beliefs and activities on the statements heard from their parents and teachers as they progress through school. For example, if their authority figures are patriotic and loyal to American democratic values, dualistic individuals are quite likely to take seriously duty to country and respect for the principles espoused by this country's "founding fathers." On the other hand, if authority figures have no use for the leaders of the country, see voting as a waste of time, and criticize the laws of the land, dualistic individuals are likely to take a similar position. Independent decision making and action are highly unlikely for a person using dualistic reasoning. Dualistic thinkers also assume that any position other than their own is "bad" or "wrong" and reject it out-of-hand.

Multiplistic thinker, who have difficulty evaluating the merits of an idea or argument, are likely to support civic leaders on the basis of such personal characteristics as charisma, appearance, membership in a particular racial or ethnic group, party membership, and so forth. They consider any idea to be as valid as any other and do not "waste time" trying to determine the most appropriate course to take with regard to a particular issue. They are likely to regard civic involvement as a personal choice rather than a responsibility.

Relativistic thinkers consider the positions taken by particular leaders and evaluate the arguments leader present in support of their views. Varying arguments are weighed against each other. The relativistic individual might have a difficult time coming to a decision about which position to support or which candidate for office to endorse. A decision to become involved in a specific civic activity is carefully considered and involvement is on the basis of belief in its value for the individual, the community, or society. The responsibilities of citizenship are clear to the relativistic thinker and balanced against the individual's other responsibilities, such as family, career, and leisure activities. Relativists might tentatively commit to particular groups to evaluate the fit between the groups' goals and their own.

Committed relativists have a clear sense of their values and identity. They evaluate the views of civic leaders in light of their own beliefs and support candidates to the extent their views are compatible. Occasionally, a persuasive argument might convince committed relativists to alter their thinking. Committed individuals are actively involved in civic organizations and support causes that reflect their belief systems. Depending on their values, they might be activists committed to changing society or they might totally support currently existing policies, organizations, and laws. In either case, committed relativists engage in ongoing evaluation of the value of their involvement.

Certainly, reasoning about citizenship becomes more complex as cognitive development progresses. Encouragement of cognitive development is also likely to enhance the potential for development of more comprehensive views of citizenship. Unfortunately, Perry (1968) had little to offer with regard to means of advancing cognitive development beyond stating that it takes place in response to environmental challenge.

King and Kitchener

King and Kitchener's reflective judgment model (1994) is designed to answer the question of "how people decide what they believe about vexing questions" (p. 2). The vast majority of issues that face a citizen are vexing, ill-structured problems that have no certain solutions. Whom to vote for in an election, what to do about pollution, which educational initiatives to support, how tax money should be spent, and whether to pass a bond issue in favor of building a new jail are some examples. Even the issue of whether or not to get involved in a community organization or political party is an ill-structured question.

Prereflective thinkers do not see such issues as uncertain. As with the dualistic thinker in Perry's scheme (1968), with this person opinions and actions are based on personal experience or what authorities state. No attempt is made to find evidence to support a decision. For instance, a decision on whether to support the jail referendum might be based on the position taken by the mayor supported in the last election or what the union boss advocates.

Quasi-reflective thinkers recognize that some uncertainties exist. They see that some issues present genuine problems, but they have trouble using evidence effectively and consistently to support the position taken. Quasi-reflective thinkers might read up on the jail referendum and be able to quote statistics about current jail overcrowding, but they might also note that the last tax bill was pretty high and be swayed by a desire not to pay more taxes. They are unable to reconcile the two conflicting pieces of evidence. Depending on whom they are talking to, they might favor one position or the other.

Reflective thinkers consider the context in which a decision has to be made and base action on the best evidence available. Any conclusions reached or actions taken are open to reevaluation on the basis of new evidence or changing circumstances. Reflective thinkers might study the jail issue systematically, seeking out statistics on jail overcrowding, the condition of the current jail, the views of local law officials, the cost of the project, and other possible alternatives to a new jail, such as an addition to the old jail. They base their vote on their analysis of all available evidence. If new evidence is presented, they consider reevaluating their position.

This analysis suggests that individuals who reach the level of reflective thinking approach citizenship in a thoughtful and considered manner. King and Kitchener (1994) reported that reflective thinking develops slowly and consistently among individuals engaged in an educational program, particularly when faculty and staff intentionally encourage such thinking. Thus encouragement of reflective thinking in college seems to lead to reasoned understanding of one's obligations to society.

Kohlberg

Kohlberg (1972) stated that "the principle central to the development of moral judgment . . . is that of justice" (p. 14). He defined justice as "regard for the value and equality of all human beings" (p. 14). Certainly concern for justice is a hallmark of citizenship. How individuals think about moral issues and make a decision affecting themselves and others influences the extent and character of their involvement in society. Each level of moral reasoning is defined by its sociomoral perspective (Kohlberg, 1976); people interpret and approach citizenship according to their level of reasoning.

At the preconventional level of thinking, individuals do not understand or take into consideration the rules and expectations of society. Decisions are self-focused and made on the basis of what results in the best personal outcome. The idea of making a contribution to society would be beyond their comprehension. Any involvement they might have is based purely on the possibility of personal gain. For example, involvement in a civic organization might be considered to enhance one's resume.

At the conventional level of reasoning, people identify with the norms and values of significant others and society in general. They are greatly influenced by authorities and the expectations of peers. They work hard to gain the approval of those around them and seek involvement in activities that make them look good in the eyes of others. They are unlikely to question rules and regulations established by anyone they view as an authority. From the perspective of conventional thinkers, citizenship means doing one's best to please individuals whose opinions matter and to obey the laws and maintain the principles that have been established by those in positions of power. This interpretation might mean active involvement in civic organizations, voting regularly, always obeying the laws of the land, and standing up for the values of one's country. It can also mean the opposite, however, if one's reference group is nondominant. In such a case, citizenship might be interpreted as loyalty to one's racial or ethnic group, involvement in a minority organization, and adherence to the values and norms of the reference group rather than the nation as a whole.

Postconventional or principled thinkers comprehend that they have a role in determining the laws and norms of society and do not have to blindly adhere to the established order. Their decisions are based on self-chosen principles. Principled thinkers understand their responsibility as a citizen to actively work to create a just society and to advocate for fair and equitable policies and laws. They are aware that they have a voice in determining those policies and laws through their involvement. Principled thinkers might also choose not to obey a law or regulation they believe to be unfair, fully understanding that they have to accept the consequences of their actions.

Moral reasoning has been found to be related to a number of variables associated with citizenship, including cheating, cooperative behavior, voting preferences, and delinquency (Kohlberg & Candee, 1984; Rest, 1986). Principled reasoning is specifically linked to social activism, adhering to contracts, and helping people in need (Pascarella & Terenzini, 1991). Moral reasoning is also related to liberal versus conservative belief systems, attitudes toward authority, and attitudes toward capital punishment.

As with epistemological theories, a high level of moral reasoning appears to be related to carefully considered citizenship. Research has indicated that two factors are related to development of moral reasoning: exposure to higher-level thinking and cognitive conflict (Walker, 1988). Discussion and analysis of issues presented at a level of thinking beyond that used by the individual challenges the person's current perspective and offers an alternative not previously considered. Such discussion might occur, for example, in a classroom setting, in a residence hall, at a work site, or on a student judicial board.

Cognitive conflict can occur when individuals find that their way of reasoning is different from that of others, or when they face a situation that their moral reasoning structure does not adequately address (Kohlberg, 1976). Conflict resulting from consideration of real-life issues experienced in a residence hall setting was found to be particularly effective in facilitating moral development (Haan, 1985).

Gilligan

In Gilligan's view (1982/1993), moral reasoning, particularly reasoning used by women, centers on relationship and care. Responsibility to and for others, as well as for self, plays a central role in decision making for all citizens. Gilligan (1977) identified three levels of reasoning, determined by the person's understanding of the tension between selfishness and responsibility. As with Kohlberg's theory (1976), each interpretation of morality leads to its own view of citizenship.

People using Gilligan's first level of reasoning, orientation to individual survival (1977), are self-centered and concerned only with personal welfare. They do not consider the needs or concerns of others. Individuals at this level do not actively participate in activities that do not result in personal reward. The idea of participating in society and taking on the responsibilities of citizenship are foreign concepts.

At the second level of moral reasoning proposed by Gilligan (1977), goodness as self-sacrifice, social acceptance is the person's central goal. The goal of being a "good citizen" is based on the desire to win praise and connect with others. The needs of others are placed above those of the individual. People at this level are likely to volunteer for many civic activities, particularly those in which they can be of service to others. Staying in the good graces of significant people is of paramount importance, and conflict is avoided at all costs to achieve this goal.

In the third level of Gilligan's model (1977), morality of nonviolence, avoiding hurt to others and to self becomes the overriding principle upon which decisions are made. Both individual needs and the needs of others are taken into consideration when volunteering for various activities, engaging in political action, or considering the position of a candidate. The principle of nonviolence guides the decision about a position or action the individual will take.

As with the previously discussed cognitive-structural theories, the final level of development in Gilligan's scheme (1977, 1982/ 1993) is the most complex and desirable with regard to interpretation of citizenship. Unlike Kohlberg (1976), Gilligan made no statements concerning how to encourage development of moral reasoning along her model; nor does existing research offer any guidance.

Opportunities for Citizenship Education

To cultivate citizenship development, students benefit from both a practical and an academic understanding of their citizenship responsibility. Community service and collective management of their own affairs contributes greatly to students' understanding and appreciation of their civic responsibility (*Points of View,* 1989). According to Mathias (1996), administrators, faculty, and staff must collaborate to make available experiences designed to help the student become a competent citizen. Moreover, the board of trustees and those who are responsible for college operations must demonstrate civic literacy as a value. This can be done through forming partnerships, using variable technology to develop a collective voice, and making preparation of citizen-workers a priority (Mathias, 1996).

Effects of the College Experience

According to a National Center for Education Statistics report (1998): "There was a positive relationship between the educational attainment of adults and their participation in civic activities: as adults' educational attainment increased, so did their rate of participation in civic activities such as being a member of an organization (for example, a community or church group) and participating in ongoing community service" (p. 110). Those who attained a bachelor's degree were also more likely to have voted, contributed money to candidates, a political party or political cause; worked for pay or volunteered for a candidate, political party or political cause; and attended a public meeting than those who had not received a bachelor's degree (National Center for Education Statistics).

Those who earned a bachelor's degree, according to the same report, were more likely to read a newspaper at least once a week, read about the national news at least once per week, watch national news on television at least once per week, and read books than were individuals who had not graduated from college.

Service Learning

Providing opportunities throughout college for the student to reflect on service experience and its meaning forms the essential base for pregraduation strategies to help the student consider career and life choices (Fisher, 1996). Service learning experience has been demonstrated to have a significant influence on students in both the short and the long run. This unique approach of linking service experience within the framework of academic credit is a method that has significant benefits for the student, the institution, and the community.

A range of student learning and developmental outcomes is attainable through well-designed and carefully implemented intensive service learning programs: civic education or education for citizenship, personal and spiritual development, critical thinking, values clarification, integration of theory and practice, applications enrichment of content-based knowledge, and maintaining a civil society. Although the nature of productive activity in our capitalistic economy might be alienating, service offers a way to enrich our lives, to achieve self-actualization and caring, and thus to minimize alienation. Service experience is a plus for job candidates; pro bono service is a criterion for promotion in some corporations. Service also increases social connection between volunteers and recipients of service (Forte, 1997). Delve, Mintz, and Stewart (1990) added that "reciprocal learning results when the server (the student) is educated and develops a deeper sense of civic responsibility and the served (individual or community) is empowered" (p. 3).

Exley (1996) found that student motivation for service begins with the chance to gain course credit, desire to help others, and opportunity to seek a new experience. Social concerns, in this study, were not a part of student motivation to participate in service learning. The effects of the experience at Miami-Dade Community College were a positive attitude toward community involvement, a sense of personal achievement, a sense of social responsibility, and a positive attitude toward experiential programs.

The effect of college on service and volunteerism seems to be highly positive. O'Brien (1998) reported that 69 percent of recent college graduates have performed some kind of community service. Most (84 percent) volunteer twenty or fewer hours per month, but 9 percent perform more than thirty-five hours of service per month. More than 90 percent of college graduates report that they are registered to vote, compared with 68 percent of the general population. Many recent graduates give back to their alma mater by contributing money, serving as admissions and recruiting volunteers, or even working as an employee.

Astin (1998) reported that there has been a recent increase in engagement in volunteer work at the precollege level. Since 1987, the percentage of students who report spending at least some time in volunteer service the year before entering college increased from 42 percent to 59 percent, an all-time high. Some could argue that this is another sign of students' increasing desire to gain a competitive edge in the college admissions process, but the increase has been accompanied by a parallel rise in students' intentions to volunteer while they are enrolled in college.

What are the outcomes of volunteer service while in college? Preliminary findings of Astin's study (1996) are encouraging. Every one of thirty-four outcome measures appears to be positively affected by participation in service learning or volunteer service. Among the more interesting outcomes affected by service learning are increased persistence in college, interest in graduate study, development of critical thinking skills, increased leadership skills, and commitment to promoting racial understanding. Participation in volunteer service during the undergraduate years has positive effects on enrollment in postgraduate study, engagement in volunteer service after college, and socializing across racial and ethnic lines.

Astin and Sax (1998) reported that "as a consequence of service participation, students become strongly committed to helping others, serving their communities, promoting racial understanding, doing volunteer work, and working for nonprofit organizations. They also become less inclined to feel that individuals have little power to change society" (p. 256). The authors go on to say that "service participants showed greater positive change than did nonparticipants on all eight items, with the largest difference occurring in understanding community problems, knowledge of different races and cultures, acceptance of different races and cultures, and interpersonal skills" (p. 259). Astin and Sax noted that "these findings constitute compelling evidence of the beneficial effects of service participation on life skills during the undergraduate years" (p. 259).

Students believed that service learning had facilitated increased appreciation for diversity, development of additional skills, and greater awareness of self. Civic awareness was displayed by many individuals before they began the service learning experience and was hard to evaluate since change on this dimension was small (Jordan, 1995).

In a study of the effects of a service learning experience, Eklund-Leen (1994) found a relationship between co-curricular involvement in community college student organizations and estimated future behavior in volunteer community service. Kollross (1998) also found that participation in a service learning experience resulted in the participants' indicating a desire to be involved in some sort of community service in the future.

Students have translated their local involvement into community service. Nearly two-thirds (64 percent) are currently involved in volunteer activity. A majority of students at all types of institutions (two-year college, four-year college, university) are participating. This is also true for every region of the country, and it is true for older and younger students, residential and commuter students, and full-time and part-time students (Levine & Cureton, 1998). During the 1980s, three-quarters of all colleges and universities reported an increase in student participation in volunteer activity.

Student Activism

Activism is local in orientation, and there is high turnover in leadership. Protest activities have become more peaceful and rooted in consumer tactics, making them less visible to national reporting.

Students are yearning for and demanding change. Their greatest concerns include issues of multiculturalism, student finances, administrative policies, and creating a campus climate suitable for a diverse population. Conzett (1994) found that involvement in civil rights and antiwar organizations afforded a safe social network, a sense of stability and structure, a moral purpose, and a way of looking at community.

Chambers and Phelps (1993) emphasized the developmental potential of activist behavior and thought for college students. In addition to pointing out the direct connection between principled activism and Astin's theory of student involvement (1977), they identified specific developmental outcomes, notably greater cognitive complexity, psychosocial task mastery, and environmental awareness.

Effects of a Student Leadership Position

Serving as a student leader appears to have a positive effect on developing civic literacy for students. In their study of 4,843 students, Pascarella, Ethington, and Smart (1988) found that a student's involvement in social leadership experience during college had a potentially significant, positive influence on the importance he or she attached to civic and humanitarian activity after college. For white students in particular, involvement in social leadership experience played a central role in transmitting the indirect effects of precollege traits and college characteristics on development of humanitarian and civic involvement values. They also reported that the humanizing of individuals is no more likely at a selective college than a nonselective college; nor does it appear that these changes are much influenced by the institution's racial composition.

Kuh and Lund (1994) concluded that students who are involved in campus governance are involved in civic affairs later in life. They added that "student government had a powerful, enhancing influence on humanitarian attitudes for certain individuals" (p. 11). Moreover, they asserted that "if habits of good citizenship are not cultivated when students are in college—if they are kept at arm's length—it is not surprising that later in life these same people remain detached from civic life" (p. 14).

Kuh, Douglas, Lund, and Ramin-Gyurnek (1994) also reported that social leadership activities such as serving as president of a student organization or being involved in committee work are correlated with development of humanitarian and civic values (citing Astin & Kent, 1983; Kuh, 1995; Kuh & Lund, 1994; and Pascarella, Ethington, & Smart, 1988). Kuh (1995) also found a relationship between leadership activities and gains in interpersonal competence and practical competence reported by students at large and nonresidential institutions, and in humanitarianism by students at public and nonresidential institutions.

Street (1998) also found that student organizations play an important role on the college campus in that they amount to a learning laboratory for students to develop leadership, communication, negotiation, problem solving, and decision-making skills.

Implications for Practice

The higher education experience helps develop citizenship skills in students. The research literature makes that point quite clear. More important, what can a college or university do to enrich the student experience so that it can be as potent as possible? Several implications for practice emerge that can accomplish this objective.

Activism, and student participation in activist experiences, appears to enhance citizenship skills. There may be some temptation to discourage activism, or find a way to marginalize such activity on campus, but the fact is that such experiences are important for students. As a consequence, we urge institutions to ensure the free exchange of ideas within the framework of our national tradition of dissent. This means that the learning experience for students is such that they understand they have a right to dissent as their conscience so dictates, but that they also understand their obligation to allow others to express their ideas, all within the context of allowing still others to conduct their routine business without interference.

In practical terms, this means that places are identified for debate and free expression of ideas; that students understand their obligation as a member of the collegiate community to allow others to express their point of view; and that the institution can regulate the time, place, and manner of dissent.

Moreover, the institution certainly should attend to integration of the nation's tradition of dissent in the curriculum from a variety of perspectives—philosophical, historical, and political, to name a few. Addressing issues of dissent permits natural collaborative activity that cuts across institutional lines of organization and can occur inside the classroom or as part of out-of-class learning experiences, or both.

Recommendations for Faculty

Faculty members are often called upon to advise student clubs and organizations. This work, too frequently in our view, is done as an afterthought and is not perceived as serious work. We think the opposite is or should be the faculty member's perspective. Advising student organizations, working with student officers and members, is a wonderful opportunity to assist in the citizenship development of students. But this also means that faculty advising has to be taken as serious business and that faculty members need to be prepared to assume this role (Dunkel & Schuh, 1998). Training ought to be regularly available for any faculty member who becomes an organization adviser, and consultation should be routinely provided for faculty advisers of student organizations. If students develop from their leadership experiences, then faculty should be well equipped to expedite that development.

Faculty members should also realize they can serve as role models for their students. This means they need to be regular participants in the civic activities of the college as well as the community. They should attend college events, support their colleagues who organize departmental activities, and contribute their time and expertise to the community. It is one thing for faculty to instruct students in the finer points of service; it is even more powerful for them to model this behavior.

It is clear from the research that service learning contributes to citizenship development. As a consequence, integrating service and learning in the curriculum ought to be considered by any institution that has not taken this step, and broadened where service learning exists. Service learning is often regarded as resting most appropriately in the social sciences, but with creativity and commitment the concept can be extended to other disciplines, including engineering, business, and agriculture.

Implications for the Student Affairs Practitioner

Obviously, a place to start for the student affairs administrator is to assist in educating the campus regarding the value of service learning, leadership development, and other experiences shown to contribute to citizenship development. Typically, these outcomes appear in the student affairs literature. As a consequence, a student affairs practitioner can make information available to the rest of the campus.

The student affairs practitioner often creates experiences for students that help them develop their leadership skills through workshops, institutes, and classes for credit. As more students learn of the value of such experience, it is important for the student affairs practitioner to make sure that the experiences are accessible to students. This may mean alternative scheduling formats, such as holding the experience on the weekend or at night for nontraditional learners or those students who work unusual hours; in alternative sites, such as off-campus, in a residence hall, or at a Greek letter house; and in alternative formats. Could a workshop be delivered by television, distance learning, or over the World Wide Web? As students become more diverse, institutions have to respond with creativity to meet their wide-ranging needs. Providing leadership development ought to be a high priority for student affairs staff, and it should be available for all students, not just the traditional ones.

Student affairs officers often have a hand in determining funding for student organizations, and the process by which organizations can be founded. These actions should be as easy as possible, consistent with the institution's mission and regulations. For example, can a student organization be funded at virtually any time of the year, or must students wait for months to be funded? How easy is it to form an organization? The objective should be for the student affairs officer to make student participation in an activity as easy as possible, so that leadership opportunities become redundant.

Implications for Institutional Advancement Staff

Those responsible for institutional advancement and external relations can contribute to developing citizenship by cultivating relationships and partnerships with off-campus agencies and enterprises so that students have a place to engage in service learning and internship. These relationships do not happen overnight; they have to be cultivated over time. This is a special area of expertise for advancement staff. They should get in on the action.

Advancement staff also can be helpful in developing financial support for several areas of endeavor. They can identify funding to support a workshop, retreat, or other leadership development activity. Normally, these activities do not require substantial funding, but lunches, snacks, materials, and so on have to be provided. Advancement staff can support these activities.

Advancement staff also can develop scholarship support for students who serve in a leadership position. Students from a modest economic background often work substantial hours per week to pay their bills. They do not have the luxury of being able to devote long hours to a leadership position. With scholarship support, they may not have to work the lengthy hours required to pay the tuition bills.

Implications for Senior Executive Officers

How can a president or chancellor support these efforts? First, they can affirm the value of these experiences at such public forums as a convocation, orientation activity, commencement, and so on. Senior officers also have the opportunity to use their pulpit to remind the campus community of how valuable leadership development activities and service learning can be to the student's total educational experience. In addition, senior officers can recognize these activities through ceremonies, awards, lunches, and other initiatives designed to express the institution's affirmation for the activity.

Implications for Community College Staff

What has been indicated before for various institutional members is also true for community college staff. But we want to emphasize that community colleges, because of their history, tradition, and mission, have a special obligation to assist in citizenship education. We believe that community colleges, because of the special role they play in their community, should be particularly concerned about preparing the community's leaders, providing services to the community, and integrating learning with service to the community.

References

Alverno College Website. (2000). [On-line]. Available: http://www.alverno.edu/glance/g_glance/g_eightabilities.html.

American College Personnel Association. (1996). The student learning imperative. *Journal of College Student Development, 37,* 118–122.

Astin, A. W. (1977). *Four critical years: Effects of college on beliefs, attitudes, and knowledge.* San Francisco: Jossey-Bass.

Astin, A. W. (1996). The role of service in higher education. *About Campus, 1*(1), 14–19.

Astin, A. W. (1998). The changing American college student: Thirty-year trends, 1966–1996. *Review of Higher Education, 21*(2), 115–135.

Astin, A. W., & Sax, L. J. (1998). How undergraduates are affected by service participation. *Journal of College Student Development, 39,* 251–264.

Astin, H., & Kent, L. (1983). Gender roles in transition: Research and policy implications for higher education. *Journal of Higher Education, 54,* 309–324.

Atkinson, D. R., Morten, G., & Sue, D. W. (1993). *Counseling American minorities: A cross-cultural perspective* (4th ed.). Madison, WI: Brown and Benchmark.

Barber, B. R. (1992). *An aristocracy of everyone: The politics of education and the future of America.* New York: Oxford University Press.

Bellah, R. N., Madsen, R., Sullivan, W. M., Swidler, A., & Tipton, S. M. (1985). *Habits of the heart.* New York: Harper & Row.

Bellah, R. N., Madsen, R., Sullivan, W. M., Swidler, A., & Tipton, S. M. (1991). *The good society.* New York: Harper & Row.

Bowen, H. R. (1977). *Investment in learning: The individual and social value of American higher education.* San Francisco: Jossey-Bass.

Bull, B. L., Fruehling, R. T., & Chattergy, V. (1992*). The ethics of multicultural and bilingual education.* New York: Teachers College Press.

Carnegie Foundation for the Advancement of Teaching. (1990). *Campus life: In search of community.* Lawrenceville, NJ: Princeton University Press.

Cass, V. C. (1979). Homosexual identity formation: A theoretical model. *Journal of Homosexuality, 4,* 219–235.

Chambers, T., & Phelps, C. E. (1993). Student activism as a form of leadership and student development. *NASPA Journal, 31*(1), 19–29.

Chickering, A. W. (1997). Potential contributions of college unions to student development. *Association of College Unions-International Conference Proceedings,* pp. 23–27.

Chickering, A. W., & Reisser, L. (1993). *Education and identity* (2nd ed.). San Francisco: Jossey-Bass.

The Condition of Education. (1998). Washington, DC: U.S. Department of Education, National Center for Education Statistics.

Conzett, K. S. (1994). Female college students' perceptions of their role in the civil rights and antiwar movements of the 1960s. (Doctoral dissertation, University of Iowa, 1994). *Dissertation Abstracts International,* 56/04, 1554.

Cross, W. E., Jr. (1991). *Shades of Black: Diversity in African-American identity.* Philadelphia: Temple University Press.

Cross, W. E., Jr. (1995). The psychology of Nigrescence: Revising the Cross model. In J. G. Ponterotto, J. M. Casas, L. A. Suzuki, & C. M. Alexander (Eds.), *Handbook of multicultural counseling* (pp. 93–122). Thousand Oaks, CA: Sage.

D'Augelli, A. R. (1994). Identity development and sexual orientation: Toward a model of lesbian, gay, and bisexual identity development. In E. J. Trickett, R. J. Watts, & D. Birman (Eds.), *Human diversity: Perspectives on people in context* (pp. 312–333). San Francisco: Jossey-Bass.

Delve, C. I., Mintz, S. D., & Stewart, G. M. (1990). Editors' notes. In C. I. Delve, S. D. Mintz, & G. M. Stewart (Eds.), *Community service as values education* (New Directions for Student Services, no. 50, pp. 1–5). San Francisco: Jossey-Bass.

Dunkel, N. W., & Schuh, J. H. (1998). *Advising student groups and organizations.* San Francisco: Jossey-Bass.

Eklund-Leen, S. J. (1994). A study of the relationship of student cocurricular activity, intensity of involvement and estimated behavior toward community involvement among community college students. (Doctoral dissertation, Kent State University, 1994). *Dissertation Abstracts International,* 56/06, 2089.

Endo, J., & Harpel, R. (1982). The effect of student-faculty interaction on students' educational outcomes. *Research in Higher Education, 16,* 115–138.

Erikson, E. (1959). *Identity and the life cycle.* New York: Norton.

Etzioni, A. (1993). *The spirit of community: Rights, responsibilities, and the Communitarian agenda.* New York: Crown.

Evans, N. J., Forney, D. S., & Guido-DiBrito, F. (1998). *Student development in college: Theory, research, and practice.* San Francisco: Jossey-Bass.

Exley, R. J. (1996). Commitment to community: Service learning at Miami-Dade Community College. In M. H. Parsons & C. D. Lisman

(Eds.), *Promoting community renewal through civic literacy and service learning* (New Directions for Community Colleges, no. 93. pp. 35–42). San Francisco: Jossey-Bass.

Fisher, I. S. (1996). Integrating service-learning experiences into post-college choices. In B. Jacoby & Associates, *Service-learning in higher education* (pp. 208–228). San Francisco: Jossey-Bass.

Forte, J. A. (1997). Calling students to serve the homeless. *Journal of Social Work Education, 33*(1), 151–166.

Gamson, Z. F., & Associates. (1984). *Liberating education.* San Francisco: Jossey-Bass.

Gilligan, C. (1977). In a different voice: Women's conceptions of self and morality. *Harvard Educational Review, 47,* 481–517.

Gilligan, C. (1993). *In a different voice: Psychological theory and women's development.* Cambridge, MA: Harvard University Press. (Original work published 1982)

Gurin, P., & Epps, E. (1975). *Black consciousness, identity, and achievement: A study of students in historically Black colleges.* New York: Wiley.

Gutmann, A. (1987). *Democratic education.* Princeton, NJ: Princeton University Press.

Gutmann, A., & Thompson, D. (1996). *Democracy and disagreement.* Cambridge, MA: Belknap.

Haan, N. (1985). Processes of moral development: Cognitive or social disequilibrium? *Developmental Psychology, 21,* 996–1006.

Hamrick, F. A. (1998). Democratic citizenship and student activism. *Journal of College Student Development, 39,* 449–459.

Harvey, J., & Immerwahr, J. (1995). *Goodwill and growing worry: Public perceptions of American higher education.* Washington, DC: American Council on Education.

Helms, J. E. (1993). Toward a model of white racial identity development. In J. E. Helms (Ed.), *Black and white racial identity: Theory, research, and practice* (pp. 33–47). Westport, CT: Praeger.

Helms, J. E. (1995). An update of Helms's white and people of color racial identity models. In J. G. Ponterotto, J. M. Casas, L. A. Suzuki, & C. M. Alexander (Eds.), *Handbook of multicultural counseling* (pp. 181–198). Thousand Oaks, CA: Sage.

Helms, J. E., & Cook, D. A. (1999). *Using race and culture in counseling and psychotherapy: Theory and process.* Needham Heights, MA: Allyn & Bacon.

Howard University Website. (2000). [On-line]. Available: http://www.howard.edu.

Jordan, K. L. (1995). The relationship of service learning and college student development. (Doctoral dissertation, Virginia Polytechnic

Institute and State University, 1995). *Dissertation Abstracts International,* 55/10, 3053.

King, P. M., & Kitchener, K. S. (1994). *Developing reflective judgment: Understanding and promoting intellectual growth and critical thinking in adolescents and adults.* San Francisco: Jossey-Bass.

King, S. (1973). *Five lives at Harvard: Personality change during college.* Cambridge, MA: Harvard University Press.

Klepper, W. M., & Kovacs, E. (1978, December). What is the impact of the college union program on today's student? *Association of College Unions-International Bulletin,* pp. 17–20.

Kohlberg, L. (1972). A cognitive-developmental approach to moral education. *Humanist, 6,* 13–16.

Kohlberg, L. (1976). Moral stages and moralization: The cognitive-developmental approach. In T. Likona (Ed.), *Moral development and behavior: Theory, research, and social issues* (pp. 31–53). New York: Holt, Rinehart, & Winston.

Kohlberg, L., & Candee, D. (1984). The relationship of moral judgment to moral action. In L. Kohlberg (Ed.), *Essays on moral development: Vol. II. The psychology of moral development* (pp. 498–581). San Francisco: Harper & Row.

Kollross, C. A. (1998). Service-learning and citizenship: Is there a connection? (Master of science thesis, California State University, Long Beach, 1997). *Dissertation Abstracts International,* 35/06, 1580.

Komarovsky, M. (1985). *Women in college: Shaping new feminine identities.* New York: Basic Books.

Komives, S. R., Lucas, N., & McMahon, T. R. (1996). *Exploring leadership.* San Francisco: Jossey-Bass.

Kuh, G. D. (1995). The other curriculum: Out-of-class experiences associated with student learning and personal development. *Journal of Higher Education, 66,* 123–155.

Kuh, G. D., Douglas, K. B., Lund, J. P., & Ramin-Gyurnek, J. (1994). *Student learning outside the classroom.* (ASHE-ERIC Higher Education Report no. 8). Washington, DC: George Washington University, School of Education and Human Development.

Kuh, G. D., & Lund, J. P. (1994). What students gain from participating in student government. In M. C. Terrell & M. J. Cuyjet (Eds.), *Developing student government leadership* (New Directions for Student Services, no. 66, pp. 5–17). San Francisco: Jossey-Bass.

Levine, A., & Cureton, J. (1998). Student politics: The new localism. *Review of Higher Education, 21,* 136–150.

MacGregor, J. (1991). What differences do learning communities make? *Washington Center News, 6*(1), 5–9.

Marcia, J. E. (1980). Identity in adolescence. In J. Adelson (Ed.), *Handbook of adolescent psychology* (pp. 159–187). New York: Wiley.

Mathias, E. A. (1996). Incorporating civic literacy into technical education: Why? How? In M. H. Parsons & C. D. Lisman (Eds.), *Promoting community renewal through civic literacy and service learning* (New Directions for Community Colleges, no. 93, pp. 43–51). San Francisco: Jossey-Bass.

Mitchell, S. L., & Dell, D. M. (1992). The relationship between black students' racial identity attitude and participation in campus organizations. *Journal of College Student Development, 33,* 39–43.

National Center for Education Statistics. (1998). *The condition of education: 1998.* (NCES report no. 98–013). Washington, DC: U. S. Department of Education, Office of Educational Research and Improvement.

O'Brien, C. T. (1998, December). Life after college. *AAHE Bulletin,* pp. 7–10.

Occidental College Website. (2000). [On-line]. Available: http://www.oxy.edu/oxy/welcome/mission.htm.

Ory, J., & Braskamp, L. (1988). Involvement and growth of students in three academic programs. *Research in Higher Education, 28,* 116–129.

Ottenritter, N., & Parsons, M. H. (1996). In good company: A ten-year odyssey. In M. H. Parsons & C. D. Lisman (Eds.), *Promoting community renewal through civic literacy and service learning* (New Directions for Community Colleges, no. 93, pp. 61–70). San Francisco: Jossey-Bass.

Pascarella, E., & Terenzini, P. (1991). *How college affects students: Findings and insights from twenty years of research.* San Francisco: Jossey-Bass.

Pascarella, E. T., Ethington, C. A., & Smart, J. C. (1988). The influence of college on humanitarian/civic involvement values. *Journal of Higher Education, 59,* 412–437.

Perry, W. G., Jr. (1968). *Forms of intellectual and ethical development in the college years: A scheme.* New York: Holt, Rinehart, and Winston.

Phinney, J. S. (1990). Ethnic identity in adolescents and adults: Review of research. *Psychological Bulletin, 108,* 499–514.

Points of view. (1989). Washington, DC: National Association of Student Personnel Administrators.

Rawls, J. (1971). *A theory of justice.* Cambridge, MA: Belknap.

Rest, J. R. (1986). *Moral development: Advances in research and theory.* New York: Praeger.

Rhoads, R. (1997). Interpreting identity politics: The educational challenge of contemporary student activism. *Journal of College Student Development, 38,* 508–519.

Rudolph, F. (1962). *The American college and university: A history.* New York: Random House.

Street, J. L., Jr. (1998). Leadership development: A comparison of strategies for college student organizations. (Doctoral dissertation, University of Georgia, 1997). *Dissertation Abstracts International, 58/06,* 2110.

Todaro, E. (1993). The impact of recreational sports on student development: A theoretical model. *NIRSA Journal, 17*(3), 23–26.

Troiden, R. R. (1989). The formation of homosexual identities. *Journal of Homosexuality, 17*(1–2), 43–74.

University of Texas at El Paso Website. (2000). [On-line]. Available: http://www.utep.edu/register/catalog/catalog.htm.

Walker, L. J. (1988). The development of moral reasoning. *Annals of Child Development, 5,* 33–78.

Chapter Seven

Educated Person

That students should graduate from college knowing more about themselves and the world than they did upon matriculation is perhaps the most long-standing and least controversial outcome of the collegiate experience. Although it is constantly reinterpreted in light of (for example) institutional type, it is almost never refuted. Upon first consideration, the outcome of "educated person" may appear to be the province of faculty and academic departments. With the advent of current thinking such as that articulated in the Student Learning Imperative (ACPA, 1994), however, this outcome need not be the sole concern of the "academic side" of the institutional house. In this chapter, we outline selected aspects of becoming an educated person, highlight the developmental influences that contribute to this outcome, and review major college experiences that facilitate this development.

The outcome of educated person covers issues of competence or mastery of subject matter as well as development of skills that foster this competence. For example, Bowen's catalogue of student level outcomes from higher education (1977) begins with a section on cognitive learning that includes subsets of verbal skills, quantitative skills, substantive knowledge, rationality, and intellectual tolerance (p. 55). In a statement specific to the student affairs field, two of the three purposes of higher education cited in the 1987 Perspective on Student Affairs (*Points of View*, 1989) were preservation and transmittal of knowledge and personal development of students.

There is little dispute that subject area mastery is a highly desirable outcome of college, and Pascarella and Terenzini (1991) found that gains in subject mastery and cognitive skills were clearly demonstrable from first year to senior year. However, the scope and type of content matter appropriate to higher education study remains the subject of debate. Historically, the Yale Report of 1828 reinforced the liberal arts as the course of study that would produce educated persons, while other colleges continued to include the study of science and other more practical courses in the undergraduate curriculum (Rudolph, 1990). A few decades later, the first Morrill Act heralded inclusion of mechanical sciences and agriculture as legitimate areas of study, research, and dissemination. Throughout their development, community colleges have offered a range of curricula that are designed to prepare students for transfer to a four-year college as well as produce skilled, capable workers through highly specific, short-term courses of study. Through their characteristic curricular offerings, a variety of institutions thus offer myriad perspectives on what it means to be an educated person.

With respect to the various outcomes listed by Bowen (1977) and appearing here, an institution's character influences the relative emphasis among the educational goals for its students. According to Bowen, educators at various institutions are to "sort out priorities among the goals, to recognize what can and cannot be achieved with the resources that are likely to be available. . . . However, it is hard to avoid the conclusion that the purpose of higher education is to seek all of them to the degree that time, resources, and human improvability permit" (p. 54).

However, a student's fulfillment of degree, major, or course requirements does not necessarily coincide with becoming an educated person, according to the Association of American Colleges (AAC, 1985). The AAC's "Integrity in the College Curriculum" encouraged faculty members to bring coherence to the undergraduate experience and to institute opportunities for cross-disciplinary issue analysis to foster educational goals. As part of the cross-disciplinary analysis recommendation, the AAC incorporated emphases on international and multicultural experiences as well as values development—opportunities for learning that are often found in co-curricular experiences.

The outcomes of personal development and content mastery have often been regarded as distinct but complementary with respect to student learning. For example, because the student affairs professional focuses on the student's personal maturity, interpersonal skills, sensitivity, and identification of life and career objectives, Shoben (1962) concluded there was "no contradiction" (p. 10) between the goals of student affairs and instructional personnel. Maintained in this view, however, is the notion of separate spheres for academic and student affairs, whatever parallels are drawn. With the more recent call to focus on student learning, however, there are ever more attempts to merge the spheres into a coherent learning environment.

The pursuit of lifelong learning further extends the educational sphere into a person's entire life. Indeed, lifelong learning and continued self-improvement are paramount in the ideal of an educated person. Newman's frequently cited phrase that a college graduate will "fill any post with credit" (p. 135) is from a passage extolling continued learning. He concluded that a university education "prepares [a student] to fill any post with credit, and to master any subject with facility. . . . He [sic] can ask a question pertinently, and gain a lesson seasonably, when he has nothing to impart himself" (1958/1982, p. 135). Dewey reached similar conclusions about the enduring qualities of education: "It is a commonplace to say that education should not cease when one leaves school. . . . The purpose of school education is to insure the continuance of education by organizing the powers that insure growth. . . . Hence education means the enterprise of supplying the conditions that insure growth, or adequacy of life, irrespective of age" (1916/1985, p. 56).

University graduates are then not only holders of certain knowledge; they are lifelong learners. However, the goal of lifelong learning is not to assemble an exhaustive catalogue of information and facts. Brownlee (1993), although acknowledging the growth of information technologies, concluded that these sources are a supplement to—not a substitute for—an education. As she said, "It is important to distinguish the difference between the well-informed and the well-educated graduate!" (p. 63). The intent instead is for students to exercise critical thinking and to make their own decisions. In outlining principal goals for higher education with respect to educating students, a mid-1960s study group concluded that a student should "reach the point of being able to see the structure and interrelations of knowledge so that he [sic] may begin the process of forming judgments on his own" ("The

Student in Higher Education," 1968, p. 10). In short, the outcome of education for the student is to become more critical and evaluative in his or her thinking and a judicious decision maker.

A feminist perspective on education further draws the individual learner more intimately into the world he or she inhabits, since good teaching necessarily leads to realization of interconnectedness. As Pagano (1990) maintained:

> When we talk about education, we talk about a public phenomenon. We talk about the production, confirmation, and distribution of knowledge in the interest of some public good. But when we talk about teaching and learning, we talk about private phenomena as well. The practice of teaching demands that we understand the way in which the private and the particular instantiate the public and the general, and the way in which the public and the general inform the private and particular. Practical wisdom in teaching is the disposition to transform knowledge into experience and experience into knowledge by acknowledging relationship and connection. The person so disposed has distance from the personal and a radical, personal nearness to the public [p. 90].

This perspective also echoes Dewey's fundamental notion of education as reflection on one's experiences, and good teaching as that which helps students adopt habits of reflection. A presentation of developmental perspectives on becoming an educated person, such as development of critical thinking, is followed by a discussion of key campus experiences to promote development of well-informed students who are also capable of critical evaluation and judgment.

Student Development Theory

When theorists such as Sanford (1967) and Heath (1968) turned their attention to the development of young people in college, they did so assuming that the experience of receiving a college education changes people in a unique way. An educated person has many qualities that seem less apparent in individuals who have not attended college. Student development theorists began their investigations to determine what these qualities were and how they were developed in the college environment.

Primary among the characteristics that define a "mature personality," according to Heath (1968), are the ability to evaluate one's thinking, connect thoughts to reality, systematically solve problems, synthesize material, organize thoughts, and use data impartially. These qualities all contribute to cognitive complexity. Being able to think in a complex manner is the end result of the intellectual development that should take place in college.

Psychosocial theorists, particularly Chickering (1969), have included intellectual development as one of many developmental tasks that students must address in college. Cognitive structural theorists, beginning with Perry (1968), have focused their attention on how this development progresses, examining cognitive processes such as analytic reasoning, reflective judgment, and other intellectual skills associated with being an educated person. Other theorists, such as Kolb (1984) and Gardner (1993), have specifically addressed the many styles of learning used by individuals and the manner in which they develop.

Psychosocial Theory

Psychosocial theorists focus on the "what" of development. They examine the tasks that contribute to growth. Important components of this process are the cognitive skills associated with becoming an educated person.

Chickering

Chickering and Reisser (1993) suggested that developing competence is the first developmental skill that the student must master. One of the three areas of competence that they discussed is intellectual competence, which includes "development of intellectual, cultural, and aesthetic sophistication" (Reisser, 1995, p. 506). Being intellectually competent involves acquiring knowledge and skills related to specific content areas, as well as being able to reason and think critically. Having confidence in one's intellectual skills is another necessary component of this vector of development. Pascarella and Terenzini (1991) cited evidence that students' academic self-concepts become increasingly more positive as they progress through college regardless of the type of institution the student attends.

Chickering and Reisser (1993) hypothesized several factors in the college environment that influence development of competence:

- Opportunities for active involvement and assumption of responsibility
- Meaningful interaction with faculty
- A curriculum that is challenging and relevant
- Teaching that encourages active and collaborative learning
- Supportive communities and friendships in which meaningful exchange occurs

Collaborative initiatives involving both academic and student services personnel can increase the likelihood of creating an educationally powerful environment that includes these components.

Loevinger

Loevinger (1976) saw development as a progression through a series of six stages involving both cognitive and affective aspects. In the autonomous stage, the fifth in her model, conceptual complexity is the cornerstone. This concept involves the ability to integrate conflicting ideas and to deal with a high degree of ambiguity. Loevinger believed that deliberate efforts to encourage development were misguided; therefore she did not attempt to identify factors in the environment that might help individuals progress through her stages (Knefelkamp, Parker, & Widick, 1978). Certainly, the complex issues facing students in college are an opportunity for the student to learn to deal with ambiguity and to confront situations involving conflict.

Cognitive Structural Theory

Cognitive structural theorists consider the "how" of development. They examine the manner in which intellectual development and its various components unfold as the person moves toward the end goal of cognitive complexity.

Intellectual Development

Perry's theory of intellectual development (1968) gives educators a picture of how students' reasoning processes develop over time, moving from the rigid either-or thinking of dualism to the complex process used in the commitment stage. Knowing that students make sense of their experience and approach learning in many ways can help a faculty member or student affairs staff person understand the reactions received from students and how to best present information in a way that students at differing stages will understand.

Perry saw development through his nine positions occurring as a result of assimilation and accommodation to environmental challenges. Evans, Forney, and Guido-DiBrito (1998) advocated the use of "plus-one staging" to create a developmental mismatch designed to encourage cognitive growth. In such a situation, an educator provides an appropriate amount of challenge by using reasoning at the level just beyond that of the student. For instance, dualistic students can understand an argument using multiplistic reasoning, although they might not be able to generate such an argument on their own. Over time, exposure to such higher-order thinking contributes to development and use of multiplistic thinking. However, relativistic reasoning would be too much of a challenge for a dualistic student and would be rejected as making no sense.

Knefelkamp and Widick (Knefelkamp, 1984) presented a developmental instruction model consisting of an appropriate balance of challenges and supports that they saw facilitating development; the model consists of structure, diversity, experiential learning, and personalism. For example, students who are dualistic thinkers benefit from a well-organized and predictable classroom environment in which assignments and expectations are clearly spelled out. Students also do better when exposure to diverse ideas is moderate and learning occurs through direct experience rather than presentation of abstract ideas. Personalized attention from the instructor supports students grappling with new ideas and concepts.

Reflective Judgment

King and Kitchener's reflective judgment model (1994), which outlines the "the ways that people understand the process of knowing and the corresponding ways that they justify their beliefs about ill-structured problems" (p. 13), is applicable to almost any setting since most problems individuals face are complex and without easy answers. The three levels of thinking included in the model—pre-reflective, quasi-reflective, and reflective—can be seen in how students respond to issues they face in everyday life as well as to academic problems. *Prereflective thinkers* do not recognize that some problems have no right answer, and they do not use evidence in reasoning toward a conclusion. *Quasi-reflective thinkers* use evidence but have trouble drawing reasoned conclusions and justifying beliefs. Only at the *reflective thinking level* is the individual aware that knowledge must be actively constructed and that conclusions must be viewed in context. Educators also need to remember, as Lamborn and Fischer (1988) pointed out, that individuals use a range of thinking rather than being limited to one stage at a time. Factors such as stress level, amount of support, and feedback provided influence how an individual approaches a problem (Kitchener, Lynch, Fischer, & Wood, 1993).

King and Kitchener (1994) posited that reflective judgment develops as a result of "an interaction between the individual's conceptual skills and environments that promote or inhibit the acquisition of these skills" (p. 18). King (1996) suggested a number of educational strategies for fostering reflective judgment. She wrote that "teaching for reflective thinking requires that educators create and sustain learning environments conducive to the thoughtful consideration of controversial topics, that they help students learn to evaluate others' evidence-based interpretations, and that they provide supportive opportunities for students to practice making and explaining their own judgments about important and complicated problems" (p. 232).

Student affairs professionals have the opportunity to work closely with students in a variety of settings where the student is faced with significant problems—perhaps a leadership position in a club or student government, a judicial board, a service learning experience, or a Greek letter organization. As Love and Guthrie (1999) pointed out, "Our challenge is to stimulate students to ask more complex questions and make more effective judgments on the complex issues they face" (p. 49). They suggested allowing students to struggle with decisions on significant matters of policy and procedure, giving them feedback concerning their arguments, offering guidelines for evaluating the adequacy of an argument, and modeling reflective thinking in interaction with a student.

Suggestions for working with students at each level of reflective judgment and enhancing development of these skills are presented in Evans, Forney, and Guido-DiBrito (1998) and Love and Guthrie (1999).

Women's Ways of Knowing

The research conducted by Belenky, Clinchy, Goldberger, and Tarule (1986) gives the educator information about how women relate to authority and to knowledge itself. Women appear to be much more affected by the interpersonal dynamics of the learning environment than are men. They need confirmation of themselves as learners and work best when given "structure without an accompanying excessive degree of control by others" (Evans et al., 1998, p. 150).

Belenky and her colleagues (1986) recommended experiential and collaborative learning as vehicles for enhancing the intellectual development of women. They also noted the importance of pedagogy that stresses connection, acceptance, and respect for students. Classroom discussions, for example, should allow expression of diverse opinions without criticism or debate that sends the message that the woman's perspective is not valued.

The ideas of Belenky and colleagues (1986) have been used successfully in a learning theory course at a women's college (Ortman, 1993), a group dynamics course (Crowley, 1989), a composition course (Tedesco, 1991), and in art and art history courses (Crawford, 1989). Ursuline College based its core curriculum on the work of Belenky, Clinchy, Goldberger, and Tarule (1986), emphasizing group discussion and collaborative learning approaches in their freshmen seminars (Gose, 1995). These same principles could be used in designing residence hall programming, leadership development programs, and training for student government and student organizations.

Epistemological Reflection

Baxter Magolda's longitudinal study (1992b) of the development of epistemological reflection during college and her resulting theory also gives educators information concerning how students approach learning and how they view their instructors and peers in this process. For example, in Baxter Magolda's first stage, *absolute knowing,* students look to faculty for correct information and do not understand that some questions may not have a right answer. But by the third stage, *independent knowing,* students recognize that most knowledge is uncertain and they take responsibility for their own learning. Instructors teaching students at the first stage need to take a much more active role in structuring the learning process and encouraging students to see alternatives than instructors whose students are at the third stage.

Along with faculty, student affairs professionals can also benefit from knowledge of Baxter Magolda's stages. For instance, Bock (1999) offered an excellent example of the manner in which students at each stage might approach career counseling. Similar differences in relating to authorities and peers would be noticed in a residence hall setting, student organization, or other out-of-class environment.

The gender-related patterns of thinking Baxter Magolda (1992b) discovered are also informative. Many women tended to focus on relational aspects of learning whereas most men approached learning impersonally. These findings parallel those of Belenky, Clinchy, Goldberger, and Tarule (1986) and suggest that a cooperative learning environment in which students are respected for their contribution is particularly important when working with women students.

The progression through Baxter Magolda's stages (1992b) is characterized by three "story lines": "the development and emergence of voice, changing relationships with authority, and evolving relationships with peers" (Evans et al., 1998, p. 157). Students who find themselves in a subordinate role with an authority or peers are less likely to find their own voice than individuals in a more egalitarian relationship (Baxter Magolda, 1992b). Traditional gender-role socialization of women and messages of inferiority given to people of color, for instance, have contributed to the suppression of their voice. Educators need to work to ensure that every student's voice is heard and taken seriously.

Baxter Magolda (1992b) offered a number of suggestions for instructors interested in facilitating development of epistemological reflection: "validating the student as a knower, situating learning in the students' own experience, and defining learning as jointly constructing meaning" (p. 270). She stressed the importance of relational learning strategies to encourage intellectual development, in the classroom and in a co-curricular setting.

Orders of Consciousness

Being an educated person also involves making meaning of one's experience. Kegan's theory (1982, 1994), which suggests that this process evolves in an orderly manner through six orders of consciousness over the course of the person's life, is a helpful lens for understanding how students make sense of their world. Most late adolescents and adults make meaning using order three or four (Kegan, 1994).

A goal of higher education is to help the student progress from the third order of consciousness, fused meaning making, to the fourth order, self-authorship. In order three, the meaning a person makes of an event or situation "is based on a *fusion* of others' expectations, theories, and ideas, and those expectations become integrated into how one thinks" (Ignelzi, 2000, pp. 7–8). Independent thinking and construction of self are absent at this stage. Ignelzi pointed out that students functioning at this level rely on their instructors, peers, and material presented in textbooks to make meaning of a concept or experience.

In contrast, meaning making in order four involves the ability to evaluate and synthesize various positions to arrive at a theory or interpretation separate from that of others; "the individual's meaning-making is influenced by but not determined by external sources" (Ignelzi, 2000, p. 8). Students at the fourth order of consciousness critically evaluate information presented to them and take responsibility for their learning. Ignelzi (citing Kegan, 1994) noted that "there is a developmental mismatch between the meaning-making order of most college students—predominantly order 3—and the mental demands of contemporary learning culture—predominantly order 4" (p. 10).

King and Baxter Magolda (1996) posited that "the achievement of self-authorship and personal authority [that is, fourth order meaning making] should be heralded as a central purpose of higher education" (p. 166). To achieve this goal, the concept of "sympathetic coaching" that was introduced by Kegan (1994) is relevant. Sympathetic coaching involves provision of both challenge and support to assist individuals in the process of evolution. Ignelzi

(2000) made several specific suggestions for educators to help students move from third-order to fourth-order meaning making: (1) communicate that the student's order-three approach to meaning making is understood and valued; (2) create structured tasks that encourage self-authorship, such as discussion of ethical dilemmas, journal writing, and exercises requiring critical thinking; (3) use group work so that students hear meaning making used by others who are closer to order four and are encouraged to develop their own views; (4) support self-authorship with appropriate feedback and acknowledgment.

Self-authorship can be encouraged in an out-of-class setting as well. A leadership opportunity in a student organization that requires decision making and implementation of initiatives, a responsible work-study position, and an opportunity to work closely with others in a service activity all move the student toward critical thinking and independent decision making, especially when feedback and support are provided by advisers and mentors.

Learning Style Theory

Learning style is an important consideration in developing educated persons. Students learn uniquely, and the educator must acknowledge these differences in working with students both in and outside the classroom. Rather than focusing on one or two approaches to learning, the educator should strive to develop all of the various means that contribute to people's understanding of and interaction with their world. The theories of Kolb (1984) and Gardner (1987, 1993) are particularly informative.

Experiential Learning

Kolb's theory (1984), which stresses that learning is a cyclical process involving four components that build on each other (concrete experience, reflective observation, abstract conceptualization, and active experimentation; recall the discussion in Chapter Two), suggests that educators must be aware that the student's ability to use each skill varies. One of their goals, therefore, should be to assist students to become more facile in using each of these components. Evans, Forney, and Guido-DiBrito (1998) wrote that "to be effective, learners need the abilities represented by each of these four components of the learning cycle. They need to be able to involve themselves fully and without bias in learning experiences (CE), observe and reflect on these experiences from multiple perspectives (RO), formulate concepts that integrate their observations into theories (AC), and put such theories to use in making decisions and solving problems (AE)" (p. 209).

Kolb (1984) stressed the importance of developing each component to ensure that the individual can effectively use whichever adaptive mode is most appropriate to a particular situation and can move effectively from one component in the learning cycle to the next. Development "is characterized by increasing complexity and relativism in dealing with the world" (Evans et al., 1998, p. 212). Attention to development of the individual's adaptive modes of learning and acknowledgment of the strengths associated with each learning style are important when evaluating the extent to which a college environment has produced an educated person.

A number of writers have presented examples of learning activities designed to match Kolb's four learning-cycle components (1984; see Anderson & Adams, 1992; Murrell & Claxton, 1987; Smith & Kolb, 1986; Svinicki & Dixon, 1987). For example, concrete experimentation is enhanced by such experiential activity as simulation, fieldwork, and solving problems. Reflective observation is required in discussion, journal writing, and responding to thought questions. Abstract conceptualization is developed by using analytical papers, model building, and analogy. Finally, active experimentation is involved in case studies, projects, and laboratory work.

Knowledge of learning styles also suggests the importance of using various presentation techniques in educational programming and training sessions (Lea & Leibowitz, 1986). Introducing the concept of learning styles to students is another way of encouraging development. For instance, Claxton and Murrell (1987) presented information about learning styles in orientation programs to help students better understand their learning preferences and strengths. Other ways of enhancing development of Kolb's four components of learning (1984) are presented in Evans, Forney, and Guido-DiBrito (1998).

Multiple Intelligences

The educator has to be aware that intelligence comes in many forms (Gardner, 1987, 1993). For example, students who are not particularly gifted linguistically or mathematically may be quite accomplished musically or kinesthetically. Students will do well in a situation that requires intelligence in areas in which they excel and less well in others. Helping students find their niche is a responsibility that the educator should take seriously. In addition, development of each of Gardner's intelligences proceeds independently and at its own pace. Students should not be labeled as "not college material" because they do not quickly grasp traditional academic material that requires a particular type of intelligence. Rather, the educator should offer alternative types of assignments that enable students to use various intelligences (King, 1996).

Gardner (1993) also argued that educators must attend to development of each type of intelligence rather than focusing mainly on linguistic and logical-mathematical skills, as has been traditionally the case. He pointed out that typical educational approaches disadvantage students whose skills lie in, say, the bodily-kinesthetic or interpersonal arenas. In considering what it means to be educated, consideration should be given to developing a person's skills in each of the areas identified by Gardner.

Extracurricular activities are an opportunity for students to use intelligences that are not stressed in most classrooms. Activities might be performance in a musical group, dance, or theatre to involve musical, kinesthetic, or interpersonal intelligence. Kinesthetic intelligence can be showcased in intercollegiate or intramural sports. Interpersonal and intrapersonal intelligence is an advantage in a leadership position, group activity, or work setting that requires interaction with people. Artistic pursuits highlight spatial intelligence.

Experiences That Promote Critical Thinking and Cognitive Development

A variety of experiences and settings facilitate development of critical thinking, cognitive, and intellectual development besides the obvious learning that occurs as a consequence of the in-class experience of the student. Several of these are summarized in this section.

Student-Faculty Relationships

Students who are able to develop a relationship with a faculty member outside routine interaction in the classroom or laboratory report greater gains in cognitive development than students who do not develop such a relationship. According to Kuh, Douglas, Lund, and Ramin-Gyurnek (1994), students who report greater gains (1) perceive faculty as being concerned with teaching and student development; (2) have developed a close, influential relationship with at least one faculty member; and (3) report that their peers have had an important influence on their development.

The findings of Terenzini, Springer, Pascarella, and Nora (1995) support these conclusions. They concluded that a student's experiences with faculty members are extremely influential; "the more a student is exposed to the academic experience of college the larger the net positive impact on his or her growth in critical thinking" (p. 24). Among the activities they recommended to enhance this exposure was informal interaction with faculty members.

Faculty interaction itself may not be enough to enrich the intellectual environment for students. Pascarella, Duby, Terenzini, and Iverson (1983) reported that "the quality of interactions with faculty may play a more important role in the personal and intellectual development of commuter students than the simple frequency with which such interactions occur" (p. 401). They concluded that "individual faculty can have a potentially significant influence on student development by expanding their formal, pedagogical roles into less formal aspects of the student's institutional life" (p. 402). Faculty should be encouraged to engage in intellectual discussion with students, challenge them to apply what they have learned in class to a practical setting, and press them to carry out on their own investigation of a topic discussed in class.

A previous study by Pascarella and Terenzini (1980) reached essentially the same conclusions. They found that "with preenrollment differences among entering freshmen held constant, measures of the frequency of student/faculty informal contact are significantly and positively associated with freshman year academic performance, intellectual development, and personal development" (p. 527). They went on to observe that informal contact between students and faculty members that extends the content of the curriculum into the student's life is most valuable. Such contact is associated with "academic performance and intellectual gains" (p. 527).

According to Volkwein, King, and Terenzini (1986), transfer students' perceptions about the quality and strength of their relationships with faculty are associated significantly with measures of intellectual growth. Faculty concern about students seems to result in students' feeling more positive about their academic experience. In this study, faculty concern was defined as a student perception "of faculty as being genuinely interested in good teaching, being interested in student growth both inside and outside the classroom, and simply being available" (p. 425).

In a study of college students' intellectual development, Baxter Magolda (1992b) found that certain teaching strategies and types of faculty-student interaction were recommended by students, who sought the opportunity to know their professors, to be engaged in positive interaction with faculty, and desired a genuine relationship with faculty. Such teaching strategies as creating an active classroom, getting students involved in classroom discussion, and connecting learning to real life were recommended by students.

The implications for student affairs practice are clear. Methods must be identified so that students and faculty can continue their interaction once the formal classroom interaction has concluded. Twale and Sanders (1999) have suggestions for extending educationally purposeful interaction among faculty members, students, and student peers outside of the classroom. Among the suggestions are "group work, cooperative learning, presentations by stimulating guest lecturers, use of e-mail and list serve communication with students on and off campus, and controversial, educational programs staged in public campus areas including residence facilities" (p. 141).

Pedagogical Practices and Learning Experiences

Without question, student learning is enhanced by excellent teaching. Pascarella and Terenzini (1991) asserted that a variety of instructional techniques facilitate student learning, knowledge acquisition, and some dimensions of cognitive and psychosocial change. For instance, they noted that "classroom activities that require student participation—question and answer exchanges, topical discussions, assignments that call upon higher-order thinking, problem-solving activities, in-class presentations, and student involvement in decisions about course content and activities— appear to promote course involvement" (p. 651).

Astin (1993) identified a number of student experiences that seem to be associated with positive cognitive outcomes. Among them are "time devoted to studying and homework, tutoring, cooperative learning, honors or advanced placement courses, racial or cultural awareness workshops, independent research projects, giving class presentations, taking essay exams, having class papers critiqued by professors, use of personal computers, frequent student-faculty interaction, and frequent student-student interaction" (pp. 423–424).

Terenzini, Springer, Pascarella, and Nora (1995) found that certain student experiences appear to be related to the intrinsic value students find in learning: "Students' experiences with faculty members (in and after class interactions, seeking criticisms of one's work, working with faculty on a research project) and their instructors' effectiveness in teaching the social sciences are positively related to gains in this area" (p. 41). They also found that students' classroom experiences, such as participating in class discussion, trying to see how ideas fit together, and doing a paper or project requiring integration of ideas from numerous sources, were powerful predictors of the level of academic interest.

Actively engaging the student in the learning process also seems to be an important pedagogical technique. Such strategies as note taking, peer teaching, and various individualized learning approaches increased the student's active engagement in learning (Pascarella & Terenzini, 1991).

Volkwein, King, and Terenzini (1986) studied intellectual growth and faculty-student relationships among transfer students. They concluded that the faculty who are most effective in educating students are those who gave "meaningful out-of-class assignments, have intellectually stimulating class sessions that hold a student's attention, and encourage students to express their views in class. In addition, these faculty demonstrate a genuine interest in students and in helping them grow, are willing to spend time outside of class to discuss intellectual issues of interest to students, and demonstrate their interest in and enthusiasm for teaching" (p. 426). They added that these faculty behaviors are strongly associated with student intellectual growth and that the behaviors appear to be much more important than the mere frequency of student-faculty contact.

Peer Interaction

As important as the student's relationship with faculty is to achieving educational outcomes, so are students' relationships with each other. Indeed, Astin (1993) concluded that "the student's peer group is the single most potent source of influence on growth and development during the undergraduate years" (p. 398). Similarly, Twale and Sanders (1999) found that out-of-class peer interaction affects critical thinking. Given the strength of the peer influence, methods involving peer interaction that can positively influence student learning should be identified. Indeed, a number of such methods have been developed as a consequence of careful study in the field.

Whitt and others (1999) studied relationships at twenty-three colleges and universities. They concluded that "the importance—even the necessity—of involvement for student learning is so strong that any efforts to foster and enhance learning (inside or outside the classroom) must incorporate plentiful opportunities for active engagement and involvement" (p. 72). These opportunities, in their opinion, need to include student interaction with peers in and outside of class, both on course-related and non-course-related matters. They added that "peer interactions on non-course-related matters were the only interactions that had significant positive effects on objectively measured outcomes, and were associated with self-reported gains in all areas except understanding science for all 3 years of the study" (p. 72).

Notably, the findings of this study were not influenced by the student's place of residence, on or off campus. The authors recommended that special attention be paid to opportunity for first-year students to be engaged with their colleagues in "a wide variety of educationally purposeful activities" (Whitt et al., 1999, p. 72).

Whitt and colleagues concluded that "the results of this study provide substantial support for scholars who have argued for the central importance of peer interactions in shaping the nature and magnitude of college's impact on students" (p. 72). As a result, they suggested that "efforts to enhance student learning—including outcomes assessment—must focus on learning environments and activities on both sides of the classroom door" (p. 72).

Kuh and his colleagues (1994) also found that peers could exert a positive influence on a student's education experience. They concluded that peers teaching peers and participation in peer tutorial programs have a positive impact on learning for those who do the teaching (citing Goldschmid & Goldschmid, 1976). This is because students who teach other students must know the material—or come to know the material—more thoroughly than if they were only studying it for themselves (Kuh, Douglas, Lund, & Ramin-Gyurnek, 1994, citing Annis, 1983; Bargh & Schul, 1980; Pace, 1990). These studies point to specific programmatic interventions that have a positive effect on student learning.

Many different kinds of students commute to college (see Rhatigan, 1986), perhaps affecting the time available for frequent or meaningful peer and faculty interaction. Pascarella, Duby, Terenzini, and Iverson (1983) found that despite the disadvantages of the environment of a commuter institution, "the nature of a student's interactions with both faculty and other students may nevertheless play a significant role in their intellectual and personal growth during the first year of college" (p. 401).

The research on peer interactions is clear. To the extent that students are engaged with each other in educationally purposeful discussion, the better their education experience is. Developing such structures as peer tutoring and peer instruction, organizing a study group, and simply offering an opportunity for meaningful discussion are interventions that an institution can develop for and with students, with positive results.

Place of Residence

Students who live in a residence hall are potentially advantaged over their counterparts who live off campus. Terenzini and Pascarella (1997, p. 178) suggested that "considerable evidence suggests discernible differences in the social and intellectual climates of different residence halls on the same campus; halls with the strongest impacts on cognitive development and persistence are typically the result of purposeful, programmatic efforts to integrate students' intellectual and social lives during college—living-learning centers are not a neat idea, they actually work!" Schuh (1999) added, "Clearly, the development of living-learning centers and special assignment programs can have a positive influence on student learning" (p. 15).

Kuh, Douglas, Lund, and Ramin-Gyurnek (1994) cited a study by Pascarella and Terenzini, who found that first-year students in a living-learning residence evaluated their intellectual environment as being significantly stronger in intellectual press and sense of community than did students who lived in other residences. Their study also found that such students reported significantly greater gain in cognitive development compared with their counterparts in other campus residences.

Pascarella and others (1993) found that students who lived on campus exhibited greater gains in critical thinking than did similar students who commuted. They continued: "The findings suggest that living in college residences can have a potentially significant influence on students' intellectual as well as their personal development during college" (p. 219). According to Pace (cited by Kuh et al., 1994), students who live on campus benefit more in terms of intellectual development even though their participation in relevant activities as measured by the College Student Experience Questionnaire activities scale is not much higher than those who live off campus. This finding suggests that it may not be solely the activity or level of participation that promotes or fosters development, but the ongoing contact with peers and others that such activity can produce.

Effects of the Community College Experience

Nearly as many undergraduate students are enrolled in public two-year colleges as public four-year colleges in the United States (U.S. Department of Education, 1999b). Enrollment of freshmen in public two-year colleges has been greater than freshman enrollment in four-year public colleges for thirty years; these institutions offer educational opportunities for members of historically underrepresented groups (see U.S. Department of Education, 1999a). Typically, these students do not live on campus. In spite of some inherent inequities in educational opportunity, several aspects of community college attendance can help level the playing field for these students with their four-year college counterparts.

The nature of the community college experience affects members of certain groups differently. Specifically, men, women, and students of color are affected by whether they attend a two-year or a four-year college. For example, Pascarella and others (1994) found that "irrespective of ethnicity and other characteristics, women appear to derive greater cognitive benefits than men from four-year college attendance" (p. 19). The opposite is true for men. In this study, men derived somewhat greater cognitive benefits than women from two-year college attendance. First-year attendance at a two-year college had a more positive effect in terms of cognitive benefits on students of color than on white students. However, white students appeared to derive relatively greater cognitive benefits from four-year college attendance than do their nonwhite counterparts.

The findings of these studies also point to specific interventions that an institution can implement to enhance students' cognitive development. Chief among these would be to encourage students to enroll full-time rather than in a limited number of credits per term. For example, Pascarella, Bohr, Nora, and Terenzini (1994) found that full-time students in two-year nonresidential institutions derived greater critical thinking benefits than those enrolled part-time. Presumably, students who enroll in a more limited course schedule also work more hours for pay, the negative consequences of which are well documented in the literature (see Astin, 1993; U.S. Department of Education, 1998).

Developing Out-of-Class Experiences That Foster Student Learning

Students do not compartmentalize their experience. It has been argued elsewhere (see Kuh et al., 1991) that a holistic point of view should be applied to student growth and learning. Nevertheless, at times it can be useful to artificially compartmentalize student experience for the purpose of trying to identify certain experiences or interventions that can be blended into the campus environment. Several such concepts are identified in this section.

As was mentioned previously, full-time enrollment seems to make a difference in student learning. Pascarella and others (1994) concluded that "full-time enrollment may be a partial proxy for the fact that students attending college full-time are also more likely than their non full-time counterparts to become involved in the mutually reinforcing academic and social experiences that foster intellectual development" (p. 21). Among these experiences, they identify informal interaction with faculty and peers (discussed earlier) as well as involvement in clubs, organizations, and cultural events, and residing on campus.

In a study of students at twenty-three institutions, Pascarella and others (1996) found that critical thinking was affected by student involvement in clubs and organizations, attendance at a racial and cultural awareness workshop, and student perceptions of faculty concern for student development. As a consequence of their research, they concluded that "student affairs professionals and student affairs programs play a major role in student learning and cognitive development during college" (pp. 189–190). Pascarella and others (1996) then suggested a need for rethinking contemporary structural and functional relationships between academic and student affairs divisions in colleges and universities, a suggestion consistent with other recommendations in the literature (see Schuh & Whitt, 1999). They concluded that "if students develop intellectually as a consequence of an interconnected and holistic set of in-class and out-of-class influences, then administrative structures, program planning, and program implementation should be similarly interconnected and collaborative" (p. 190).

In a study of six hundred students at a single institution, Terenzini (1993) concluded that "students' class-related and out-of-class experiences both had effects on gains in critical thinking that were unique, statistically significant, and comparable in magnitude" (p. 9). Terenzini went on to report that "the evidence from this study quite clearly indicates that changes in students' critical thinking abilities are shaped, independently, by what happens to them both in and out of the classroom" (p. 10). The findings from this study suggest that collaboration among student affairs practitioners, faculty, and academic administrators is essential if student experiences are to be optimized.

We have suggested elsewhere in this chapter that living in a residence hall where educationally purposeful experiences are available can bestow an educational advantage on students. Inman and Pascarella (1998) reported, however, that living off campus does not necessarily mean that students are disadvantaged. They found that "under certain circumstances, students who commute to campus can exhibit cognitive gain similar in magnitude to their residential counterparts" (pp. 565–566). They recommended that the institution provide specialized support services and involvement opportunities for commuter students that accommodate their schedules and lifestyles. They concluded, "If student academic and support services accommodate the commuter students' needs, these students need not be at a disadvantage in terms of critical thinking development compared with their residential counterparts" (p. 566).

One specific experience that appears to have a positive effect on student learning is service learning. According to Eyler and Giles (1999, p. 80), a variety of conclusions about the contributions of service learning to academic learning can be drawn:

• A majority of service-learning students report that they learn more and are motivated to work harder in service-learning classes than in regular classes.

• A majority report that a deeper understanding of subject matter, understanding the complexity of social issues, and being able to apply material they learn in class to real problems are among the important benefits of service learning.

• High-quality community placement, where students have real responsibility and interesting and challenging work, resulted in student reports of more learning and the learning of specific skills.

• Students in classes where service and learning are well integrated through classroom focus and reflection are more likely to demonstrate greater issue knowledge, have a more realistic and detailed personal political strategy, and give more complete analysis of causes of and solutions to the problem at the conclusion of their experience than those in classes where the service was less well integrated into the course or no service was done.

They added that "students who are in service-learning classes where service and learning are well integrated through classroom focus and reflection are more likely to show an increase in their level of critical thinking demonstrated in problem analysis than those in classes where the service was less well integrated into the course or where no service was done" (p. 127). As has been reported elsewhere in the literature (See Astin & Sax, 1998), service learning is an extremely powerful experience for college students. In this case, the evidence is clear: service learning helps enrich the student's academic experience.

Terenzini (1993) concluded that "gains in critical thinking are not just a consequence of the instructional process. Rather, such gains are a result of class-related and out-of-class experiences" (p. 10). As a consequence, he observed that "academic and student affairs units have common goals, and the evidence of this study suggests that students are more likely to benefit educationally if these units work together, rather than separately, in pursuit of those common goals" (p. 10). Kuh, Douglas, Lund, and Ramin-Gyurnek (1994) made similar recommendations. They suggested that institutional members (faculty, staff, and student affairs practitioners) personally encourage students to take advantage of educationally purposeful experiences at their college. In their view, "the mere presence of involvement opportunities that appeal to a diversity of student needs and interests is not enough"(p. 65). They urge that an "ethos of learning" permeate the institution. Whitt and colleagues (1999) concurred. They observed: "Institutional and academic program planning processes, these findings suggest, are more likely to be successful and effective if they take into account the potential for simultaneous contribution of students' class-related and out-of-class experience on student learning. Gains in critical thinking appear to be a consequence of a variety of students' experiences, not just those that are part of the formal instructional program" (p. 72).

Accordingly, student learning is advanced if student experiences are viewed holistically, in-class and out-of-class experience are related and complement one another, and organizational structures are developed to ensure that faculty and student affairs staff can collaborate in attempting to advance student learning.

African American Students' Learning

African American students form an important cohort on American college campuses. In the most recent reporting year, they made up 10.5 percent of all students enrolled in higher education (U. S. Department of Education, 1999a). Nevertheless, the number and percentage of African American men, in particular, is "disturbingly small" (Cuyjet, 1997, p. 1). This section examines two reports of African American student learning that compare predominantly white institutions with historically black colleges and universities.

Pascarella and Terenzini (1996) studied students at eighteen four-year colleges and universities in fifteen states, including two historically black colleges (HBCUs). They found that "compared to their counterparts at predominantly White institutions, Black students at historically Black colleges demonstrate at least equal, and perhaps on some dimensions superior, cognitive development during the first 2 years of college" (p. 499). Why is this the case? Pascarella and Terenzini (1996) observed that "there may be much to learn from those historically Black colleges that are able to develop a supportive institutional climate for students without sacrificing academic standards or intellectual impact" (pp. 499–500).

In a study of cognitive effects on black students of attendance at two historically black institutions, students at these schools were compared with black students at sixteen predominantly white colleges (Pascarella et al., 1996). Controlling for a variety of precollege variables, no differences were found between the two groups in critical thinking, reading comprehension, or math skills. The authors observed about the results that "these findings are also important for predominantly White institutions that are concerned about the intellectual growth and achievement of their Black students. If supportive environments foster learning at HBCUs, how might similar climates for learning be fostered at White institutions? What should such environments include and what obstacles exist to their development?" (p. 185).

It is clear from these studies that predominantly white institutions have much to learn from their HBCU colleagues. In fact, Redd (2000) concluded that "the data show that black graduates from HBCUs, particularly males, can do just as well in employment and other areas as those from other institutions" (p. 4). The HBCU institutions are able to offer an equivalent academic experience for their African American students while offering a much more supportive environment. These institutions can serve as models for the kind of environment in which African American students can thrive.

Transfer Student Experiences

Transfer students are often a significant percentage of the enrollment of a campus. Accordingly, we report one study that examined factors that produced a rich learning experience for transfer students. Volkwein, King, and Terenzini (1986) concluded that "students' involvement in and enjoyment of the classroom experience also proved to have a strong relationship to both measures of intellectual growth, especially for the population from community colleges, suggesting that for transfer students at least, what happens in the classroom is what counts" (p. 425). In this study, effective faculty appeared to make a difference for students.

Volkwein and colleagues went on to describe effective faculty members: "Such faculty give meaningful out-of-class assignments, have intellectually stimulating class sessions that hold a student's attention, and encourage students to express their views in class. In addition, these faculty demonstrate a genuine interest in students in helping them grow, are willing to spend time outside of class to discuss intellectual issues of interest to students, and demonstrate their interest in and enthusiasm for teaching. These faculty behaviors are strongly associated with student intellectual growth and appear to be much more important than the mere frequency of student-faculty contact" (1986, p. 426).

Although the techniques used by these faculty members are particularly effective in working with transfer students, virtually all faculty in their interaction with undergraduate students could incorporate many of these techniques.

Negative Influences on Cognitive Development

Some experiences have a negative effect on student learning, cognitive development, and critical thinking. These experiences need to be identified so that they can be avoided or minimized by those developing interventions in the college environment.

Participating in intercollegiate athletics appears to have a negative influence on students. Pascarella and others (1996) found that male basketball and football players scored lower on reading comprehension and mathematics tests administered at the end of the first year than did male athletes in other sports or male non-athletes. The authors recommended that "any steps taken to ameliorate these negative consequences need to be taken *early* [authors' emphasis] in these students' collegiate careers" (p. 187).

Participation in social fraternities can have a negative influence on student learning (see Pike & Askew, 1990). Specifically, Pascarella and others (1996) found that fraternity membership had a negative effect on critical thinking. Their data also "revealed that men who were members of social fraternities had significantly lower end-of-first-year reading comprehension, mathematics, critical thinking, and composite achievement than their peers who were not affiliated with Greek organizations" (p. 188). They suggested, for example, that "rush and new-member activities, especially for White men, might be deferred to the second semester—or even the second year—of college" (p. 189).

Astin (1993) also identified several experiences that negatively affected student growth. He found that among these experiences are "watching television, taking multiple-choice exams, working full-time, working off campus, and commuting" (p. 424). He suggested that "discouraging or minimizing such activities will not only enhance learning but also reduce the dropout rate" (p. 424).

Summary, Conclusions, and Implications for Practice

The evidence is quite clear. Certain experiences have the effect of enhancing student learning, including critical thinking and cognitive development. We conclude this chapter by summarizing the literature and adding several additional thoughts about how student learning can be enhanced.

Going to college makes a difference. Pascarella and others (1994) concluded that "for four-year college students college attendance appears to not only have a net, positive impact on the development of critical thinking, but the more a student is exposed to the academic experience of college the larger the net positive impact on his or her growth in critical thinking" (p. 19). They added: "The findings also suggest that the positive effect on critical thinking for four-year college students is general rather than conditional. That is, it appears to be similar in magnitude for students with different precollege, ascribed, and other characteristics (e.g., precollege critical thinking and academic motivation, race, gender, age, work responsibilities, and kinds of courses taken)" (p. 18). It seems clear from this study and others (such as Pace, 1979) that graduating from college has a positive effect on student learning, including critical thinking and cognitive development.

Terenzini (1993) emphasized that "students' class-related and out-of-class experiences both make positive, statistically significant and unique contributions to freshman year-end critical thinking scores, even after controlling students' precollege characteristics" (p. 9). Pascarella (1989) confirmed this finding in another study. He concluded it is "the student's total engagement in the intellectual and social experience of college that positively influences the development of critical thinking ability. This reinforces the notion that intellectual or cognitive development in college may be the result of an integrated total experience rather than the outcome of involvement in specific, isolated experiences" (p. 25). The evidence from these studies and others suggests that a student's total experience is what is important. Bifurcating a student's experience is a mistake too often made by institutions of higher education. We urge colleges and universities to develop ways for academic affairs and student affairs to form a partnership to enhance learning (see Schuh & Whitt, 1999).

Marcia Baxter Magolda's comments (1992a) on improving the intellectual development of students are instructive as we conclude this chapter: "Articulating to faculty how student affairs efforts promote intellectual development would heighten their interest in integrative efforts. The ideas have pervaded our literature for years. The challenge is to organize them under the mission of intellectual development and take the initiative to join the campus community" (p. 213).

Implications for Faculty

To improve the learning environment for students, faculty can take the leadership on several initiatives. First, they can work to shrink the size of classes. Any classes that are offered using a large lecture format have to be subdivided to permit more personalized instruction for students. As institutions deepen their commitment to improving the quality of the instructional experience for undergraduates, faculty can assert that smaller classes will improve the student experience.

Active learning strategies are related to improved student learning in the classroom and laboratory. As a consequence, faculty would be well advised to develop active learning strategies for implementation in their work with students. Among these would be use of case studies in class, group learning experiences, poster activities, and applied demonstrations and presentations.

To measure the quality of the learning environment, faculty should develop a variety of assessment strategies to offer evidence of the efficacy of active learning as well as evidence of improved student learning. These strategies should be built into every course. Faculty can take on the leadership of these initiatives; if they and the leaders of their institutions assert that assessment of student learning is important, this will support instructional creativity and assessment of learning.

Implications for Faculty and Student Affairs

A number of collaborative activities can be undertaken jointly by faculty and student affairs staff. Here is a short list of such initiatives.

Faculty and student affairs staff need to redouble their efforts to meet the needs of historically underrepresented populations at their institution. Typically, these groups comprise students of color, returning adult learners, and part-time students. The focus of many colleges and universities has been on full-time, traditional-age students. This focus needs to be broadened; it must include specialized orientation, improved academic advising activities, and special academic support activities such as tutoring for academically disadvantaged students.

As has been mentioned in other chapters in this book, service learning is an activity that should be developed more fully at colleges and universities. Since a typical service-learning experience contains a classroom component complemented by field-based experiences, faculty can take the lead on developing the content-based portion of the experience while student affairs staff can work on field-based aspects of the experience. Service learning contributes greatly to the overall education of students, but to date this form of experience has not been developed adequately at many institutions. Faculty and student affairs staff can work together to make this happen.

Faculty and student affairs staff can partner on forming learning communities in the residence halls. Learning communities are a relatively recent phenomenon at many colleges and universities in the United States, although the concept builds on a long-standing model from England. This undertaking requires great cooperation between faculty members and student affairs staff, so that residence hall assignments and classes can be coordinated. The registrar also has to provide support. The learning community is a richly integrated experience for students, and it should be developed.

Finally, faculty and student affairs need to work together to strengthen faculty and student out-of-class relationships. Such initiatives might include, for example, faculty members providing better support for student clubs as advisers, or interacting more frequently with students who live in the residence halls by taking meals with them or visiting with them in their lounges. Faculty members and student affairs staff members can work on creating other experiences that afford meaningful interaction outside of the formal classroom relationship. A wealth of potential interactions are possible for faculty and students, and good cooperation between faculty and student affairs staff will make them happen.

Implications for Student Affairs

A variety of implications for student affairs help advance the college toward the goal of strengthening experiences that lead to an educated person.

As was suggested earlier, in the past colleges and universities paid scant attention to the needs of several populations of students, including transfer students. Community college enrollment has continued to grow dramatically, and student affairs should work not only to recruit these students for transfer admission but also, upon their arrival, to strengthen the quality of student support, including academic advising and career development assistance. These students are easy to identify. Through the targeted orientation program we have suggested, the students can be attracted to specific programs to address their needs. Improved academic advising and career development assistance is helpful in improving the experience of transfers, a group of students who have been taken for granted and overlooked for far too long. Directed attention and focus on these students can also help them take advantage of additional learning opportunities at their college or university.

Many institutions in the past have also not paid as much attention as they might to federally funded student support services, which could be a ready framework for rich student learning experiences. Student support services, a federal program, should be part of the student affairs portfolio at virtually every college or university; a team should be assembled to submit a proposal for funding to establish such an office on campus if one does not presently exist. Typically, these programs address the learning needs of first-generation students, who are frequently less advantaged than students whose parents have graduated from college. Until such a program is in place, an institution might want to organize a peer tutorial program as an interim measure. In this way, assistance can be given to all students who are at an academic disadvantage. Additionally, student tutors can benefit from their prolonged engagement with subject matter, which results in greater learning for them as well.

Student affairs administrators need to work with Greek letter organizations to demonstrate the benefits of deferring rush until the spring semester. Since participation in Greek social fraternities is associated with negative academic outcomes, students should wait before participating in the member recruitment process until their academic skills are better developed. It is unlikely that the Greek community will react favorably to this change at first, but in the end the students who join the organizations will be better informed and establish themselves more strongly academically. Retention by the organizations is likely to improve, as is the general satisfaction of members. Deferring rush is not easy, but students will benefit from this change in policy.

Finally, student affairs officers should begin to develop strategies whereby some scholarship support can be developed for students who might like to live in the residence halls but who simply cannot afford to do so. If financial assistance could be provided to these students, they could have the advantage of on-campus living as part of their education. As learning communities are developed and other enriched residential experiences are implemented focusing on enhanced learning environments, students who need financial help should not be precluded from participation in these programs.

Implications for Advancement Staff

Many of the initiatives identified here require additional resources. As a consequence, advancement staff can play an important role in developing funding sources (gifts or grants) to support these initiatives. Many institutions are undertaking a major change in their approach to student learning by implementing learning communities, improving and expanding service learning, seeking large federal grants, and developing new programs. It is difficult to do everything without an infusion of new funds. The role of the advancement staff is to find sources of funds to support these new initiatives.

Implications for Senior Institutional Officers

Faculty and student affairs partnerships to advance learning often do not come naturally or easily. Incentives should be put in place to assist in this development. Senior institutional officers can develop a series of incentives (travel grants, infrastructure support, and so on) that encourage partnership. Additionally, rewards can be instituted that recognize successful partnership in terms of assessment and evaluation of students' learning and the contributions of programs to student learning. Senior institutional officers also can use the strength of the symbols they have available to them to reaffirm the value of these partnerships and recognize those faculty and student affairs staff who develop and further such partnerships.

References

American College Personnel Association (ACPA). (1994). The student learning imperative: Implications for student affairs. Washington, DC: Author.

Anderson, J. A., & Adams, M. (1992). Acknowledging the learning styles of diverse student populations: Implications for instructional design. In L.L.B. Border & N.V.N. Chism (Eds.), *Teaching for diversity* (New Directions for Teaching and Learning, no. 49, pp. 19–33). San Francisco: Jossey-Bass.

Association of American Colleges (AAC). (1985). *Integrity in the college curriculum: A report to the academic community.* Washington, DC: Author.

Astin, A. W. (1993). *How college affects students.* San Francisco: Jossey-Bass.

Astin, A. W., & Sax, L. J. (1998). How undergraduates are affected by service participation. *Journal of College Student Development, 39,* 251–263.

Baxter Magolda, M. B. (1992a). Cocurricular influences on college students' intellectual development. *Journal of College Student Development, 33,* 203–213.

Baxter Magolda, M. B. (1992b). *Knowing and reasoning in college: Gender-related patterns in students' intellectual development.* San Francisco: Jossey-Bass.

Belenky, M. F., Clinchy, B. M., Goldberger, N. R., & Tarule, J. M. (1986). *Women's ways of knowing: The development of self, voice, and mind.* New York: Basic Books.

Bock, M. T. (1999). Baxter Magolda's epistemological reflection model. In P. G. Love & V. L. Guthrie, *Understanding and applying cognitive developmental theory* (New Directions for Student Services, no. 88, pp. 29–40). San Francisco: Jossey-Bass.

Bowen, H. R. (1977). *Investment in learning: The individual and social value of American higher education.* San Francisco: Jossey-Bass.

Brownlee, P. P. (1993). End paper: What does society need from higher education? In *An American imperative: Higher expectations for higher education* (pp. 61–63). Racine, WI: Johnson Foundation.

Chickering, A. W. (1969). *Education and identity.* San Francisco: Jossey-Bass.

Chickering, A. W., & Reisser, L. (1993). *Education and identity* (2nd ed.). San Francisco: Jossey-Bass.

Claxton, C. S., & Murrell, P. H. (1987). *Learning styles: Implications for improving educational practice* (ASHE-ERIC Higher Education Report, no. 4). Washington, DC: Association for the Study of Higher Education.

Crawford, J. S. (1989). *Perry levels and Belenky's findings: Their possibilities in the teaching of art and art history.* Paper presented at the Getty Conference on Discipline-Based Art Education, Austin. (ERIC Document Reproduction Service no. ED 310 698)

Crowley, P. M. (1989). Ask the expert: A group teaching tool. *Journal for Specialists in Group Work, 14,* 173–175.

Cuyjet, M. J. (1997). Editor's notes. In M. J. Cuyjet (Ed.), *Helping African American men succeed in college*. (New Directions for Student Services, no. 80, pp. 1–3). San Francisco: Jossey-Bass.

Dewey, J. (1985). *Democracy and education*. Carbondale: Southern Illinois University Press. (Original work published 1916)

Evans, N. J., Forney, D. S., & Guido-DiBrito, F. (1998). *Student development in college: Theory, research, and practice*. San Francisco: Jossey-Bass.

Eyler, J., & Giles, D. E., Jr. (1999). *Where's the learning in service learning?* San Francisco: Jossey-Bass.

Gardner, H. (1987). The theory of multiple intelligences. *Annals of Dyslexia, 37,* 19–35.

Gardner, H. (1993). *Multiple intelligences: The theory in practice.* New York: Basic Books.

Gose, B. (1995, February 10). "Women's ways of knowing" form the basis of Ursuline curriculum. *Chronicle of Higher Education,* p. A25.

Heath, D. (1968). *Growing up in college.* San Francisco: Jossey-Bass.

Ignelzi, M. (2000). Meaning-making in the learning and teaching process. In M. B. Baxter Magolda (Ed.), *Teaching to promote intellectual and personal maturity: Incorporating students' worldviews and identities into the learning process* (New Directions for Teaching and Learning, no. 82, pp. 5–14). San Francisco: Jossey-Bass.

Inman, P., & Pascarella, E. (1998). The impact of college residence on the development of critical thinking skills in college freshmen. *Journal of College Student Development, 39,* 557–568.

Kegan, R. (1982). *The evolving self: Problem and process in human development.* Cambridge, MA: Harvard University Press.

Kegan, R. (1994). *In over our heads: The mental demands of modern life.* Cambridge, MA: Harvard University Press.

King, P. M. (1978). William Perry's theory of intellectual and ethical development. In L. Knefelkamp, C. Widick, & C. A. Parker (Eds.), *Applying new developmental findings* (New Directions for Student Services, no. 4, pp. 35–51). San Francisco: Jossey-Bass.

King, P. M. (1996). Student cognition and learning. In S. R. Komives, D. B. Woodard, Jr., & Associates, *Student services: A handbook for the profession* (pp. 218–243). San Francisco: Jossey-Bass.

King, P. M., & Baxter Magolda, M. B. (1996). A developmental perspective on learning. *Journal of College Student Development, 37,* 163–173.

King, P. M., & Kitchener, K. S. (1994). *Development of reflective judgment: Understanding and promoting intellectual growth and critical thinking in adolescents and adults.* San Francisco: Jossey-Bass.

Kitchener, K. S., Lynch, C. L., Fischer, K. W., & Wood, P. K. (1993). Developmental range of reflective judgment: The effect of contextual support and practice on developmental stage. *Developmental psychology, 29,* 893–906.

Knefelkamp, L. (1984*). A workbook for the practice-to-theory-to-practice model.* Unpublished manuscript, University of Maryland, College Park.

Knefelkamp, L., Parker, C. A., & Widick, C. (1978). Jane Loevinger's milestones of development. In L. Knefelkamp, C. Widick, & C. A. Parker (Eds.), *Applying new developmental findings* (New Directions for Student Services, no. 4, pp. 69–78). San Francisco: Jossey-Bass.

Kolb, D. A. (1984). *Experiential learning: Experience as the source of learning and development.* Englewood Cliffs, NJ: Prentice Hall.

Kuh, G. D., Douglas, K. B., Lund, J. P., Ramin-Gyurnek, J. (1994). *Student learning outside the classroom: Transcending artificial boundaries.* (ASHE-ERIC Report no. 8). Washington, DC: George Washington University, School of Education and Human Development.

Kuh, G. D., Schuh, J. H., Whitt, E. J, & Associates. (1991). *Involving colleges.* San Francisco: Jossey-Bass.

Lamborn, S. D., & Fischer, K. W. (1988). Optimal and functional levels in cognitive development: The individual's developmental range. *Newsletter of the International Society for the Study of Behavioral Development, 14*(2), 1–4.

Lea, H. D., & Leibowitz, Z. (1986). The program developer as learner. In Z. Leibowitz & D. Lea (Eds.), *Adult career development: Concepts, issues, and practices* (pp. 50–62). Alexandria, VA: American Association for Counseling and Development.

Loevinger, J. (1976). *Ego development.* San Francisco: Jossey-Bass.

Love, P. G., & Guthrie, V. L. (1999). *Understanding and applying cognitive developmental theory.* (New Directions for Student Services, no. 88). San Francisco: Jossey-Bass.

Murrell, P. H., & Claxton, C. S. (1987). Experiential learning theory as a guide for effective teaching. *Counselor Education and Supervision, 27,* 4–14.

Newman, J. H. (1982). *The idea of a university.* Notre Dame, IN: University of Notre Dame Press. (Original work published 1958)

Ortman, P. E. (1993). A feminist approach to teaching learning theory with educational applications. *Teaching of Psychology, 20,* 38–40.

Pace, C. R. (1979). *Measuring outcomes of college.* San Francisco: Jossey-Bass.

Pagano, J. (1990). *Exiles and communities: Teaching in the patriarchal wilderness.* Albany: State University of New York Press.

Pascarella, E., Bohr, L., Nora, A., Zusman, B., Inman, P., & Desler, M. (1993). Cognitive impacts of living on campus versus commuting to college. *Journal of College Student Development, 34,* 216–220.

Pascarella, E., Bohr, L., Nora, A., & Terenzini, P. (1994). *Is differential expo-sure to college linked to the development of critical thinking?* Chicago: University of Illinois (ERIC Document Reproduction Service no. ED374729).

Pascarella, E. T. (1989). The development of critical thinking: Does college make a difference? *Journal of College Student Development, 30,* 19–26.

Pascarella, E. T., Duby, P. B., Terenzini, P. T., & Iverson, B. K. (1983). Student-faculty relationships and freshman year intellectual growth in a nonresidential setting. *Journal of College Student Development, 24,* 395–402.

Pascarella, E. T., & others. (1994). *Cognitive effects of two-year and four-year colleges: Some new evidence.* Chicago: University of Illinois. (ERIC Document Reproduction Service no. ED371678)

Pascarella, E. T., & Terenzini, P. T. (1980). Student/faculty relationships and freshman year educational outcomes. *Journal of College Student Development, 21,* 521–528.

Pascarella, E. T., & Terenzini, P. T. (1991). *How college affects students: Findings and insights from twenty years of research.* San Francisco: Jossey-Bass.

Pascarella, E. T., & Terenzini, P. T. (1996). Additional evidence on the cognitive effects of college racial composition: A research note. *Journal of College Student Development, 37,* 494–501.

Pascarella, E. T., Whitt, E. J., Nora, A., Edison, M., Hagedorn, L. S., & Terenzini, P. T. (1996). What have we learned from the first year of the national study of student learning? *Journal of College Student Development, 37,* 182–192.

Perry, W. G., Jr. (1968). *Forms of intellectual and ethical development in the college years: A scheme.* New York: Holt, Rinehart & Winston.

Pike, G., & Askew, J. (1990). The impact of fraternity or sorority membership on academic involvement and learning outcomes. *NASPA Journal, 28,* 13–19.

Points of view. (1989). Washington, DC: National Association of Student Personnel Administrators.

Redd, K. E. (2000). *HBCU graduates: Employment, earnings and success after college.* USA Group Foundation New Agenda Series, vol. 2, no. 4. Indianapolis, IN: USA Group Foundation.

Reisser, L. (1995). Revisiting the seven vectors. *Journal of College Student Development, 36,* 505–511.

Rhatigan, J. J. (1986). Developing a campus profile of commuting students. *NASPA Journal, 24*(1), 4–10.

Rudolph, F. (1990). *The American college and university: A history.* Athens, GA: University of Georgia Press.

Sanford, N. (1967). *Where colleges fail: A study of the student as a person.* San Francisco: Jossey-Bass.

Schuh, J. H. (1999). Student learning in college residence halls: What the research shows. In J. H. Schuh (Ed.), *Educational programming and student learning in college and university residence halls* (pp. 2–20). Columbus, OH: Association of College and University Housing Officers-International.

Schuh, J. H., & Whitt, E. J. (1999). (Eds.). *Creating successful partnerships between academic and student affairs.* (New Directions for Student Services, no. 87). San Francisco: Jossey-Bass.

Shoben, E. J., Jr. (1962). A rationale for modern student personnel work. *Personnel-O-Gram, 12*(3), 9–11.

Smith, D. M., & Kolb, D. A. (1986). *User's guide for the Learning Style Inventory.* Boston: McBer.

The student in higher education: Report of the committee on the student in higher education. (1968). New Haven, CT: Hazen Foundation.

Svinicki, M. D., & Dixon, N. M. (1987). The Kolb model modified for classroom activities. *College Teaching, 35,* 141–146.

Tedesco, J. (1991). Women's ways of knowing/women's ways of composing. *Rhetoric Review, 9,* 246–252.

Terenzini, P. T. (1993). *Influences affecting the development of students' critical thinking skills.* University Park, PA: National Center on Postsecondary Teaching, Learning and Assessment. (ERIC Document no. ED 372 666)

Terenzini, P. T., & Pascarella, E. T. (1997). Living with myths: Undergraduate education in America. In E. J. Whitt (Ed.), *College student affairs administration* (pp. 173–179). (ASHE Reader Series). Needham Heights, MA: Simon & Schuster.

Terenzini, P. T., Springer, L., Pascarella, E. T., & Nora, A. (1995). Academic and out-of-class influences on students' intellectual orientations. *Review of Higher Education, 19,* 23–44.

Twale, D., & Sanders, C. S. (1999). Impact of non-classroom experiences on critical thinking ability. *NASPA Journal, 36,* 133–146.

U.S. Department of Education (1998). *Profile of undergraduates in U.S. postsecondary education institutions: 1995–96.* Washington, DC: National Center for Education Statistics.

U.S. Department of Education. (1999a). *The condition of education 1999.* Washington, DC: National Center for Education Statistics.

U.S. Department of Education. (1999b). *Digest of Education Statistics.* Washington, DC: National Center for Education Statistics.

Volkwein, J. F., King, M. C., & Terenzini, P. T. (1986). Student-faculty relationships and intellectual growth among transfer students. *Journal of Higher Education, 57,* 413–430.

Whitt, E. J., Edison, M., Pascarella, E. T., Nora, A., & Terenzini, P. T. (1999). Interactions with peers and objective and self-reported cognitive outcomes across 3 years of college. *Journal of College Student Development, 40,* 61–78.

| Skilled Worker

"Plastics."

This piece of lucrative career advice, given to the young hero in the 1969 film *The Graduate,* embodied both the growing interpretation of a college education as career preparation and students' repudiation of careerism and assuming a place in a social and vocational order (May, 1990). However, in the years since *The Graduate* appeared, a higher proportion than ever of first-year students—almost 71 percent in 1989—identified increased earning power as the primary benefit associated with college (Astin, 1998). In 1990 and 1993 national polls, more than two-thirds of respondents agreed that job training is the main reason to go to college (Harvey & Immerwahr, 1995b), and nearly eight in ten respondents agreed that students should attend college to better their job prospects (Harvey & Associates, 1994).

These beliefs appear to be well founded. Among U.S. workers aged twenty-five and over, degree holders (associate's degree or higher) earned a higher median income than noncollege graduates and were less likely to be unemployed than workers possessing less than an associate's degree (*Digest of Education Statistics,* 1997). Indeed, the 2.2 percent unemployment rate among workers with a baccalaureate degree or higher was almost half that (4.2 percent) of the general population ("Money Income," 1996).

Additionally, an undergraduate degree has been estimated to yield a respectable 11.8–13.4 percent rate of return to the graduate (Leslie & Brinkman, 1988). Pascarella and Terenzini (1991) suggested similarly positive returns on a college education. They estimated that "a bachelor's degree confers about a 34 percentile point advantage in occupational status or prestige over and above graduating from high school" (p. 488).

In this chapter, we discuss various opportunities and experiences offered to help students develop career readiness and vocational awareness during college. We first outline historical precedents for institutional attention to students' vocational development in the curriculum and co-curriculum, and then we examine how various kinds of institutions address vocational matters. Next we discuss student development theories that are most relevant to career development. This discussion is followed by examples of intervention that intend to successfully advance a student's education in this realm. Finally, conclusions and implications for practice are offered.

Early Developments

Although many colonial college students subsequently entered the family business or inherited the family's wealth, the college curriculum decidedly did not include commerce, manufacturing, or agricultural studies. Individuals seeking to learn a trade instead apprenticed themselves to a master or learned skills on the job: "The young merchant must be trained in the counting room, the mechanic in the workshop, the farmer in the field" ("Original papers in relation to a course of liberal education," cited in Rudolph, 1962, p. 134). Teaching and the ministry were the career fields most directly related to a classical education (Rudolph, 1962).

Among the best-known features of the Yale Report of 1828 was the reaffirmation of a classical curriculum as appropriate preparation for a cultured life and its rejection of elective coursework that included sciences and "popular and practical" studies (Rudolph, 1962, p. 135). Although not all colleges affirmed the report and its humanistic curriculum, the Morrill Acts transformed higher education through, among other things, establishment of land grant institutions with their attendant technical and practical studies. Land grant institutions (Rudolph, 1962) also incorporated professional school education, minimizing the previous hierarchies of professions (for example, divinity and law) and vocations (agriculture, manufacturing, and the like). Less than a century after the first Morrill Act was passed, more than 20 percent of American postsecondary students attended a land grant college (Rudolph, 1962). This rise in institutional attendance was complemented by trends toward personnel assessment and vocational counseling.

In the early years of the 1900s, the emerging trait-and-factor theories of career matching (for instance, Parsons, 1909), the mental hygiene movement (Yarris, 1996), and the U.S. military's massive personnel operations during World War I gave rise to formal vocational assessment tools and a scientific approach to personnel selection. During World War I, the Army Alpha General Classification Test was used to match military personnel more efficiently with appropriate duty assignments (Kroll & Rentz, 1996). Counselors were systematically brought to campus to adapt and administer these tests with college and university students (Kroll & Rentz, 1996; Schneider, 1977; Thorndike, 1949).

As a followup to his wartime service conducting assessment and selection protocol in the Army Air Force, Thorndike (1949) developed a longitudinal database with information on more than ten thousand wartime Air Crew candidates, their initial test battery results, and their eventual career fields. This database was used to explore the validity of the tests as predictors of subsequent vocational choice (Thorndike & Hagen, 1959). Other trait-and-factor-based models and respective psychometric assessments followed (Holland, 1959, 1973; Super, 1983) and were increasingly used by career planning and placement staff in counseling college students. This emphasis on vocational matching and awareness among college students was also echoed in the postwar era 1949 "Student Personnel Point of View": "The college has a responsibility to see that these students [who are exploring themselves and career fields] have access to accurate, usable information about opportunities, requirements, and training for various occupations appropriate to their possible levels of vocational preparation. . . . When conducted with social imagination, [vocational] counseling can help to develop these leaders who will pioneer in new professions and in the extension of needed services for the country's welfare (*Points of View*, 1989, p. 32).

Complementing the career planning and placement services offered on many campuses are opportunities for students to engage in internship or other practical work experience. Not only does this experience give students a structured opportunity to try out a career field but it also promotes cooperation between the student affairs office and academic departments. Finally, an internship program represents an opportunity for an institution to develop and strengthen ties with companies and not-for-profit organizations. According to the Association of American Colleges (1985):

> There are many opportunities for imaginative and constructive interaction with the world beyond the campus. Trustees and graduates are a natural link with business, industry, government, the arts, and the professions, those segments of society that attract a substantial portion of the nation's talent. Surely there are creative ways to enrich the baccalaureate experience by tapping these resources beyond the campus. . . . These same external resources could be exploited in creating work-study programs, career education programs, and internships in government and business, and other experiences that unite rather than oppose the values of career and of liberal learning [p. 13].

Two-year community and junior colleges, the largest sector of higher education in terms of student enrollment (O'Banion, 1997), have played a central role in fostering vocational and career education. Although only a few private junior colleges existed in 1900 (Thornton, 1966), there were more than 200 two-year colleges by the end of the 1920s (Ratcliff, 1987; Thornton, 1966), 837 in 1967 (AACJC, 1988), and more than 1,200 by 1987 (AACJC, 1988). The number of public two-year colleges jumped from 244 in 1937 to 1,068 in 1987—a fourfold increase over only fifty years—while the number of private two-year colleges declined by half (AACJC, 1988). The community college's unique features include adapting and responding to the local area (Thornton, 1966) and encompassing the needs of local industry, through use of "environmental antennae" (Hammons, 1992, p. 82). The community college uses these antennae to monitor and assess changes to which it should and often does respond. Two-year colleges also create tailored opportunities to meet students' educational needs, from refreshing current technical and technological skills to undertaking a systematic occupational training program or preparing for transfer to a four-year college (Thornton, 1966).

Preparing career-ready and vocationally aware graduates has become a purpose commonly associated with colleges and universities. Bowen's wide-ranging taxonomy of higher education goals for college students (1977) included "economic productivity: Knowledge and skills needed for first job and for growth in productivity through experience and on-the-job training. Adaptability and mobility. Sound career decisions. Capacity to bring humanistic values to the workplace and derive meaning from work" (pp. 57–58).

Although all of this emphasizes student-level outcomes and individual development of skills and characteristics, Bowen (1977) also identified three roles for colleges and universities with reference to career counseling and placement of graduates: (1) guidance (focused interaction with peers, professors, and counselors); (2) brokerage (the institution's mediating role—most often concentrated in an institution's placement office—between students and prospective employers), and (3) credentialing (assigning grades, awarding a degree, and making recommendations available, which are to be a symbol of accomplishment as well as an alert to a prospective employer).

That students should emerge from college with a clearer vocational vision and a set of employment-relevant skills is generally reflected in the institutional mission and purpose statements as well. For example, the private, for-profit University of Phoenix offers "high quality education to working adult students. . . . The University provides general education and professional programs that prepare students to articulate and advance their personal and professional goals" (University of Phoenix Website, 2000). According to its mission statement, Emporia State University in Kansas intends to "educate and prepare for both the professions and advanced study" (Emporia State University Website, 2000).

Although the emphasis on career preparation and work readiness has become more prevalent among institutions in recent history, it is not without lingering controversy. One of the problematic characteristics outlined in the *Involvement in Learning* report (1984) was the excessive attention to vocationalism among colleges and universities. This echoes John Dewey's views on education, which suggest that the desired outcomes of education include greater self-understanding and self-directedness, enlargement of one's horizons, and improved ability to actualize one's plans. In this view, preparing students for a specific future role should be, at most, a "by-product" of education (Boisvert, 1998, p. 113). Interpreting

Dewey's writing on the appropriate purposes of education, Boisvert (1998) argued that education is not "the mere servant of industry, training people for fixed professions" (p. 113), in which development of a student's capacity to the fullest degree is secondary to meeting contemporary industry needs. Bowen (1977) echoed this view: "The relative emphasis on liberal and practical education fluctuates. At the moment, the balance seems to be swinging toward the practical side. Yet a preponderance of authority over the centuries gives higher priority to general human development than to practical training and warns against the persistent tendency to neglect broad human development in favor of training for practical pursuits" (p. 41).

Upton Sinclair (1923) also was suspicious of the close ties between college presidents and the industry leaders of the early twentieth century. Sinclair warned that by participating in this "interlocking directorate," (p. 18) college presidents had fundamentally betrayed their social responsibility by attending primarily to the needs of American industry rather than placing the education of students first.

This does not mean that incorporating so-called real-life experience over the course of education is necessarily problematic. Incorporating an experiential base within a curriculum becomes controversial when the intended outcomes shift from educating the student to meeting workplace or workforce needs. Boisvert (1998) also cautioned against the dangers to democracy that occur when vocational training is available to the nonelite, while liberal schooling is provided to the elite—yet both are characterized as education. Dewey, in 1916, argued that students' experiences, regardless of the context, should become the subject of education in order that all experience be reflected upon and serve as a basis for further learning: "As formal teaching and training grow in extent, there is the danger of creating an undesirable split between the experience gained in more direct associations and what is acquired in school. This danger was never greater than at the present time, on account of the rapid growth in the last few centuries of knowledge and technical modes of skill" (1916/1985, p. 13).

Proceeding from this philosophical and historical heritage, colleges and universities should pursue connection between the student's practical experiences—regardless of the source—and formal education. Additionally, offering practical experiences as part of a degree or co-curricular program should be a means to the desired end of education and learning, rather than a means to meeting an industry or company's needs for a skilled workforce. Dewey's summary (1916/1985) highlights this overall focus on emphasizing experiential fodder—regardless of the academic source—that contributes to a student's learning: "We cannot establish a hierarchy of values among studies. It is futile to attempt to arrange them in an order, beginning with one having least worth and going on to that of maximum value. In so far as any study has a unique or irreplaceable function in experience, in so far as it marks a characteristic enrichment of life, its worth is intrinsic or incomparable" (p. 248).

Related Student Development Theories

Psychologists, sociologists, and educators have all had a strong interest in vocational choice and career development throughout the twentieth century and now into the twenty-first. Beginning with the work of Frank Parsons (1909), numerous theorists have attempted to explain the process of career selection and the factors that influence it over the life span. In addition, general theories of psychosocial development and adult development frequently include career decision making as a developmental task that the individual must address and suggest how this process is facilitated. Cognitive structural approaches offer information concerning how an individual goes about career exploration.

Career Development Theories

Each of the career development approaches reviewed in the earlier chapter on student development guide the educator interested in assisting a student in becoming a skilled worker. Specific contributions and interventions suggested by each model are discussed in this section.

Trait-and-Factor Approaches

Although somewhat simplistic, trait-and-factor theories (Parsons, 1909; Paterson & Darley, 1936; Williamson, 1939, 1965) still have utility when working with students exploring career options. They underscore the importance of students' knowing themselves well, being familiar with the requirements of a potential occupation, and being able to determine when an occupation is a good match. Thus the process of career exploration involves self-exploration, including assessment of interests, personality traits, and aptitude using various inventories; review of occupational information; and analysis to determine a good fit between the person and the tasks associated with a particular occupation. Career counselors, advisers, and other student affairs practitioners with whom a student might consult can easily use this model to guide the student through the process of exploring career possibilities.

Sociological Theories

Sociological theories (see Herr & Cramer, 1988) remind us that the environment plays a significant role as individuals determine their career direction. Students should be aware of environmental influences such as parents, community, and economic conditions and consciously work to expand their options beyond those with which they are familiar or that seem most available (McDaniels & Gysbers, 1992). Structured career exploration activity, such as systematic investigation of career options, job shadowing, and informational interviewing can be of assistance in this process. Rather than following the path of least resistance by selecting a career that seems most familiar or accessible, as Osipow suggested is often the case (1969, cited in McDaniels & Gysbers, 1992), students need encouragement from faculty and student affairs mentors to consider options they may not have known about or thought were possible.

Developmental Theory

Super's developmental theory (1990, 1992) reinforces the complexity of career development and its evolution over time. It suggests the importance of helping students to understand that career decision making is not necessarily a one-time occurrence and that choices made at age twenty-two can be changed many times throughout one's lifetime. This theory also points out that work is only one aspect of a person's life and that career choices are influenced by other roles the individual takes on, such as parent or life partner. Too often, students fail to consider how to balance the many roles they take on; student affairs staff and faculty advisers can help them think through the implications of their responsibilities and choices.

Super (1990) proposed that career development is enhanced as individuals gain a clearer picture of their abilities, interests, and other personal qualities that contribute to an occupational self-concept and as they have an opportunity to experience various roles and gain feedback. Role playing, ranging from fantasy to career shadowing to part-time employment to internships to entry-level employment, can assist students in learning more about themselves in relation to possible career options. Super viewed this process as evolutionary across the life span. Exploration should begin in a basic way in elementary school, with youngsters being encouraged to explore their interests and abilities and to learn about various jobs. The process should continue in high school and college, with increasing sophistication. Stress should be placed on the intersection of various roles that contribute to one's career and to the developmental nature of one's career over the life course (McDaniels & Gysbers, 1992).

Personality Theory

Holland's theory of personality type and work environment (1985/1992) is easy to understand and useful to students engaged in career exploration. Determining their type and the types associated with various work environments can help students better understand their interests and which career possibilities may be a good fit. The concepts of congruency, consistency, and differentiation are useful when considering factors that influence career choice and satisfaction (McDaniels & Gysbers, 1992).

A number of instruments have been based on Holland's theory, notably the Vocational Preference Inventory (VPI; Holland, 1985), the Self-Directed Search (SDS; Holland, 1994), and the General Occupational Theme Scales of the Strong Interest Inventory (SII; Harmon, Hansen, Borgen, & Hammer, 1994). Holland also developed an occupational classification that was based on his codes, which includes 12,860 occupations (Gottfredson & Holland, 1989). These instruments can be useful to individuals engaged in career exploration.

Because of its clarity and face validity, Holland's (1985/1992) theory has been used as an organizing structure for many career exploration programs and courses. Several examples are high-lighted in Evans, Forney, and Guido-DiBrito (1998). They include career orientation programs (Calliotte, Helms, & Wells, 1975), career information services (Reardon & Minor, 1975), and other career counseling initiatives (Holland, Powell, & Fritzsche, 1994).

Social Learning Theory

Krumboltz's theory (1979, 1981) informs us that the individual is often not aware of factors influencing a career decision. Positive and negative reinforcement from significant others can have a tremendous impact on how students see themselves and the career options that might be available to them. An educator can help by encouraging students to examine the validity of the assumptions they have been conditioned to accept and to expand their thinking regarding possibilities.

In addition, educators must be sensitive to the impact that they themselves can have on the choices a student makes. Their comments, suggestions, and opinions, as well as those of family members and peers, can affect the options that a student considers and pursues. Giving students the opportunity to try out various work-related tasks through course work, internship, and summer employment can open up possibilities that the student may not have considered.

Theories of Psychosocial Development

Psychosocial theories focus on the developmental issues that people must address throughout their lives. Obviously, deciding on a career direction and becoming an effective worker are important concerns for most people. Erikson (1959/1980), Marcia (1966), and Chickering and Reisser (1993) all included career-related issues in their theories, directly or indirectly.

Erikson

Although Erikson (1959/1980, 1968) did not directly address the career decision-making process, work-related issues clearly play a role in his understanding of human development. Stage four of Erikson's model, industry versus inferiority, focuses on how children in school come to perceive themselves as workers. Since the extent to which each of Erikson's stages is successfully resolved influences the resolution of later stages, this aspect of self-concept affects one's identity and relationships with others. For example, individuals who see themselves as incapable of academic success may feel inferior to their peers and may avoid interacting with them around academic issues. Revisiting developmental issues related to industry would be a prerequisite for such students to enable them to succeed in college and identify a satisfying career. Creating an academic success center, tutoring program, or opportunity for counseling to explore the developmental issues related to industry can help the student fully achieve positive self-concepts in this area and effectively address other issues that build on this task.

In midlife, adults must determine how to contribute to society in a meaningful way that allows them to leave their mark. Failure to do so leaves a void in one's life. Erikson (1959/1980) referred to this stage as generativity versus stagnation. People often choose to mentor a younger employee or student as a way of fulfilling their need to be generative. Engaging in a major work-related project that makes a professional contribution is another option. The concept of generativity is particularly relevant for senior faculty and staff as they attempt to find ongoing significance in their work. It may also be salient for a student who enters or returns to college at midlife to find a more meaningful way to contribute to society. In working with individuals at midlife, it is important to acknowledge their need for generativity and make opportunities for them to contribute to society meaningfully.

Marcia

Marcia (1966) viewed career choice as one of the three major areas that determine identity resolution. He suggested that the degree to which a person has experienced a crisis period related to vocational decision making as well as the level of commitment the person has made to a choice affects how the person's identity is resolved. Experiencing both crisis and commitment is necessary if identity achievement is to occur.

Thus, in working with a student concerned about identity issues, a student affairs professional or faculty member might want to explore with the student how much he or she has actively addressed career decision making and how certain the student is about his or her tentative career choice. On the basis of the student's response, experiences can be suggested that pose an opportunity for active exploration, such as visiting the career center on campus or testing out career possibilities through an internship or summer job.

Chickering

Developing purpose is one of the seven vectors of development that Chickering and Reisser (1993) identified. They suggested that a sense of purpose is achieved when a person has a clear career goal, has made a commitment to specific interests and activities, and has made a strong commitment to significant people in his or her life. Another part of developing purpose is making and staying with a decision, even when it is unpopular. Chickering and Reisser viewed purpose in broad terms, including lifestyle and avocational decisions as well as career choice.

Chickering and Reisser (1993) stressed the importance of integrating work and classroom learning in the development of purpose. Studies indicate that involvement in extracurricular activities (Hood, Riahinejad, & White, 1986; Hunt & Rentz, 1994; Williams & Winston, 1985) and significant involvement in work and studies (Niles, Sowa, & Laden, 1994) are related to accomplishment in this vector of development. The educator must create an opportunity for meaningful work and extracurricular experiences in which learning is emphasized.

Adult Development Theories

Theories addressing adult development are concerned with how people grow and change over the course of the life span. Career plays an important role in this process for many people. Life stage (Levinson, 1978; Vaillant, 1977), life events and transition (Fiske & Chiriboga, 1990; Hultsch & Plemons, 1979; Schlossberg, 1989; Schlossberg, Waters, & Goodman, 1995), life course (Elder, 1995; Neugarten, 1976), and integrative theories (Baltes, 1987; Perun & Bielby, 1980) of adult development all contribute to our understanding of the role of career in adult development.

Life Stage Theories

Life stage theorists view development as occurring in a series of stages that are frequently, but not always, age-linked. In these theories, career issues are often the focus of a particular stage. For instance, George Vaillant (1977) accepted the stages Erikson (1959/1980) presented but added a stage he labeled *career consolidation,* which he saw occurring around age thirty. Vaillant suggested that at this time of life, individuals focus on establishing themselves in their career by becoming an expert in their field, demonstrating their competence, and obtaining higher status or greater recognition from their supervisors and colleagues. These motivations might lead the adult student to return to school to gain additional skills or seek an advanced degree. Understanding the importance attached to such a decision can help faculty and student affairs staff work effectively with adult students.

Levinson (1978) saw creation of a life structure as the basis for adult development. The most important factors in this process are relationships with others, including one's co-workers, supervisors, family, and friends. He saw people going through a series of stages, alternating between periods of stability and periods of transition. Career issues, such as making an initial career choice, taking the steps to carry out that choice, establishing oneself in a career, reevaluating one's career and making modifications deemed necessary, and planning for retirement, are tasks that Levinson felt people need to address as they move through their lives. He associated each task with a specific stage occurring at a particular time period. Early adulthood (ages twenty-two to twenty-eight), for example, is characterized by two developmental tasks that help to shape the person's later life: forming a mentoring relationship with an older adult (usually a person in one's work setting) and creating a dream (that is, a fantasy about what one wants to accomplish in one's life). Each task can have a significant effect on a career decision.

Educators should keep in mind the particular career issues associated with periods of a person's life as they advise and work with students. A model such as Levinson's (1978) can also be used as a basis for workshops to help students understand issues they will face at various points in their careers.

Life Events and Transition Theories

Unlike the life stage theorists, who focus on commonalities across the life span, life events and transition theorists stress individual variability in human behavior. They see development as centering on the events and transitions that people experience during their lives, each of which requires some type of response and adaptation (Merriam & Caffarella, 1999; Schlossberg et al., 1995). Life events are viewed as more important than age in understanding behavior (Fiske & Chiriboga, 1990). For these theorists, career development is not linear, but rather a process affected by the events that occur in a person's life and how the person interprets those events.

Hultsch and Plemons (1979) identified two categories of life event: cultural and individual. Cultural events include the societal and historical happenings that form the context in which the person's life is lived, such as changing economic conditions or political upheaval. Many such events can certainly influence career decision making or job availability. Individual events are specific to each person; career choice is included as well as other transitions a person might face, such as marriage, death of a significant other, and so forth. Schlossberg (1989) categorized these events as anticipated, unanticipated, nonevents (expected events that do not occur, such as not securing a job that one expects to be offered), or sleeper events (those with an unclear beginning, such as growing dissatisfied with a job).

Many factors influence how a person experiences a life event. Merriam and Caffarella (1999) listed timing, cohort specificity, and probability as particularly important. With regard to timing, the impact of an event varies depending on whether it occurs when the person (or society) thinks it should happen. For instance, securing one's first full-time job is much easier at age twenty-one than at age forty-five. Cohort specificity refers to whether an event affects only one generation or several, and in different ways. For example, the Great Depression had a major impact on several generations, notably those who were adults at the time who could not secure employment as well as their children, who could not attend college because of their family's financial situation. Probability, the likelihood of an event happening, also affects how an event is experienced. If the odds of a person getting into an elite graduate school are viewed as poor, for instance, the nonoccurrence of this event has much less negative impact than if admission is pretty much assumed.

Dealing with a life event is a process that takes time and may result in either growth or decline (Schlossberg et al., 1995). Schlossberg and colleagues suggested that coping with a transition is influenced by the ratio of assets and liabilities an individual has related to four factors: the situation (timing, control, duration), the self (personal, demographic, and psychological characteristics), support (intimate relationships, family, friends, institutional agents), and strategies (modifying the situation, controlling its meaning). An educator working with students who are experiencing career-related transition can assist them in evaluating their coping process by reviewing these factors and helping them explore alternatives.

Life Course Theories

As with the theories discussed in the previous section, life course theories focus on life events. Rather than viewing events as psychological phenomena, however, they are viewed through a sociological lens. The emphasis is on how "dynamic worlds change people and how people select and construct their environments" (Elder, 1995, p. 102). Elder defined the social life course as "the interweave of age-graded trajectories, such as work and family careers, that are subject to changing conditions and future options, and to short-term transitions, ranging from birth and school entry to retirement" (p. 103). The ordering of events, transitions, and social roles is of primary concern in this perspective. Four concepts are particularly noteworthy in shaping a person's life course: historical change, human agentry, linked lives, and timing.

Historical change refers to social forces that occur at a particular point or place in history. For instance, the Vietnam War was instrumental in decisions that many young men made about attending college in the 1960s, and these decisions affected their careers significantly. Likewise, growing up on a reservation greatly influences the career decisions of many American Indian youths who wish to remain in that setting.

Human agentry underscores the fact that people make choices that affect their lives. For example, deciding to give up a job when one's life partner is offered a position in another part of the country can greatly influence a person's career path. Yet it is an active decision that many people make.

The concept of linked lives suggests that people's lives are intertwined; "personal actions have consequences for others, and the actions of others impinge on the self" (Elder, 1995, p. 112). The example in the preceding paragraph illustrates this idea.

Finally, the timing of events influences the life course. In addition to historical timing, which was discussed earlier, social timing is important. Neugarten (1976) noted that every society has norms concerning when certain events are supposed to occur. She hypothesized that events that occur when they are "supposed to" are less stressful than those that occur off-time. Elder (1995) also pointed out that the effects of a particular event vary across the life course. For example, being laid off from a job at age thirty is a much different experience than a layoff at fifty-five.

Helping students understand that the environment around them, be it societal conditions or norms or the significant people in their lives, greatly affects their career decisions is an important role that the educator can assume, along with helping students realize that individuals play an active role in their career decisions by how they make meaning of a situation they experience and how they choose to respond to it.

Integrative Theories

Integrative theories underscore the complexity of adult development and are helpful when an educator is assisting students in unraveling the many factors that influence career decision making and career development through life. Looking at how roles intersect and the differing influence of various roles over time can be quite useful to students who consider career choice as something accomplished at one point in time.

Baltes (1987) pointed out that no two people's experiences come together in exactly the same way. As a result, a career decision is always unique and shaped by factors related to each individual. The educator is cautioned not to assume that a decision-making process effective for one student necessarily works for all students. Nor is the same decision appropriate for all students. For example, two equally bright students, each accepted by a competitive graduate school, might make differing, though personally appropriate, decisions about enrolling on the basis of such factors as family circumstances, need for emotional support, financial considerations, or other salient matters.

Perun and Bielby (1980) contended that the rate of movement of each aspect of development varies; nor are these rates the same for each person. The entire process is also influenced by the historical time in which it occurs. No two career paths, then, progress in the same manner. Students should be cautioned not to compare their progress with that of their peers or family members, but rather, consider what is right for them as individuals.

Perun and Bielby (1980) also suggested that some of the change that happens in a person's life is inevitable and some of it is chosen. Asynchrony occurs when one or more dimensions are off-time in relation to others. Asynchrony creates stress, but it also triggers change. For instance, a man who goes back to obtain an undergraduate degree at age forty-five while his children are in high school is likely to experience stress because the timing of his educational trajectory and his family trajectory are out of sync. Perun and Bielby noted that "synchronous movement through developmental progressions is contingent. . . on timing schedules established by the social structure with individuals experiencing rewards and punishments both intra-psychically and socially relative to their lives' congruity with externally prescribed age norms" (pp. 105–106). The social structure is likely to punish a man who puts his own educational needs before those of providing for his children. Faculty and student affairs staff can help students experiencing such a situation to understand that they have a right to make their own decisions, regardless of what those around them are saying or thinking.

Cognitive Structural Theories

How a student interprets a situation depends on the person's level of cognitive development. Cognitive structural theories help the educator understand how students at different levels make meaning of the process of career choice, and offer guidance regarding how to communicate with students as they explore this process. Designing workshops to match the student's developmental level also increases the effectiveness of such interventions.

Perry

Knefelkamp and Slepitza (1976) used Perry's model (1968) to examine the career decision-making process. They noted that understanding the shift from external to internal locus of control that takes place as an individual progresses through the model is helpful in making sense of how the student views this process. For example, dualistic thinkers are likely to believe that there is one right career for them and that the career counselor, who is the expert, is able to tell them what that career is. Students who view career choice in this way need the support of a structured approach, with the counselor offering guidance concerning where and how to seek information. However, they also benefit from the challenge of hearing that career decision making is a complex process that cannot be accomplished in one visit to the career center.

A multiplistic thinker, in contrast, expects the career counselor to present a process for making a decision and has trouble determining if one choice is better than another. A counselor working with a student in multiplicity is likely to spend considerable time helping that student examine and evaluate information.

Relativistic thinkers see the counselor as someone from whom information can be obtained and with whom ideas can be discussed, but they realize that they alone are ultimately responsible for making their own decision. They are also able to evaluate the advantages and disadvantages of various options and recognize that decisions made in college are tentative and can later be reevaluated. Working with a relativistic thinker requires much less structure; the counselor may simply provide feedback and ask questions to guide the student's thinking.

Career exploration workshops can be designed to take into account the developmental level of the students. Touchton, Wertheimer, Cornfeld, and Harrison (1977) based such a workshop on the work of Knefelkamp and Slepitza (1976), incorporating challenge and support components to address the needs of students at the various levels in Perry's model of cognitive development (1968).

Belenky, Clinchy, Goldberger, and Tarule

In their study of the cognitive development of women, Belenky and her colleagues (1986) noted the influence of connection with others in how women processed information. They advocated teaching that emphasizes cooperative learning, acceptance, and respect for students' experiences. These concepts also apply when working with students in a career exploration group or course. Small-group work, team projects, experiential learning, and self-reflection can be used effectively in career exploration.

Baxter Magolda

Like Perry (1968), Baxter Magolda (1992) found that cognitive development progresses through stages of increasing complexity. She identified three factors that enhance the intellectual development of the student: validating the student as knower, situating learning in the student's experience, and defining learning as jointly constructed meaning. All of these principles can be incorporated into the career exploration process. An educator can do so by assuring students that their viewpoint with regard to career choice is heard and valued, by having students share their career-related experiences, and by working with students rather than directing their activities.

Baxter Magolda (1992) noted that different types of experience are appropriate for students at various stages of cognitive development. Absolute knowers benefit from peer interaction and the opportunity to assume responsibility. For example, a career workshop might include an activity for students to complete outside the group and an expectation that they share the results with their peers. Transitional knowers value practical experience; students at this stage can be encouraged to secure hands-on work and leadership experience. Independent knowers should be encouraged to process and reflect on their experiences (internship, a part-time job) both informally and in a more structured setting such as a class. Contextual knowers benefit from freedom and encouragement to make their own decisions and to take risks, particularly with regard to new experiences such as travel abroad or previously unconsidered employment options.

King and Kitchener

Certainly, career decision making qualifies as an ill-structured problem as defined by King and Kitchener (1994), in that there is no clear answer as to what type of work is right for any particular person. As is true of other cognitive structural theories, King and Kitchener's stages progress from simple to complex understanding of how problems such as career decision making are solved. Prereflective thinkers assume that there is one right answer concerning what career they should pursue and are unable to weigh factors that might contribute to a decision. Individuals using quasi-reflective thinking can see that there may be uncertainty associated with career decision making and have trouble making and justifying choices. Reflective thinkers understand that they are responsible for making their own choices and that any decision must take into consideration a number of factors, all of which could change in the future.

Counselors working with students at varying levels of reflective judgment should allow students to grapple with the complex problem of career decision making and should give guidance and practice in evaluating factors that influence choices (King, 1996). They also need to help students understand that a career decision, like any other ill-structured problem, can be reevaluated when new information becomes available.

Experiences That Enhance Development of Worker Skills

Four practical interventions are available to support achievement of skills that fall under the general umbrella of skilled worker. Included in this set are working for pay while being enrolled in higher education, participating in a cooperative education program, serving an internship, and participating in a service-learning activity. Each activity has an effect on a student's experience and is discussed in this section of this chapter.

Lewis and Williams (1994) presented a useful overview of practical experiences. Internship and practicum experience have been a part of professional education experience for years, and often part of the curriculum in such academic disciplines as medicine, education in the form of student teaching experiences, and social work. Lewis and Williams described cooperative education as a process whereby students alternate full-time, off-campus employment with periods of full-time study on campus. This approach has been used in engineering and other applied disciplines, although cooperative education can also include working off campus and taking classes during the same academic term. More recently, service learning has been seen as a viable form of experiential learning. Lewis and Williams pointed out that "service learning provides a way to link class work and community service. The concept expands upon the idea of volunteerism by including a reflective component, by emphasizing the transfer of learning between the server and the served, by encouraging students to view problems in a larger social context" (p. 8).

Ryan and Cassidy (1996) asserted that "experiential education can significantly enrich the education of students by demanding that they take an active role and personal responsibility for what they are and are not learning. Concerned with both the content and process of learning, programs which successfully allow for students to change, grow, and learn in dramatic ways are carefully designed and include principles of academic rigor" (p. 23).

Working for Pay

Stern, McMillion, Hopkins, and Stone (1990) observed that a variety of factors have increased the pace of learning that is required at work. They posited that employees without good academic skills are unable to keep up with new technologies and product development. They suggested that one way the need for people to develop teamwork, problem-solving skills, and a positive work ethic can be addressed is by integrating work experience with courses in school. They concluded, "If properly designed, such experience can give students practice in the actual process of learning at work" (p. 356).

Working for pay is an increasingly common experience among college students. Stern and colleagues (1990) observed that a growing proportion of students hold paid jobs. They believe that this experience represents an opportunity for students to use work as a deliberate learning experience to help them develop a capacity for learning in a work setting.

Working for pay, although affected by the type and amount of work, has an effect on students while they are enrolled in college. Pascarella and Terenzini (1991) offered a summary of the value of work. They concluded that research evidence suggests that if students work during their college experience, especially if the work is in a job related to a student's major or initial career aspiration, the experience has a positive effect on career, career attainment, and the level of responsibility achieved early in the person's career. Work, however, does not always have a positive influence on student outcomes. Citing Ehrenburg and Sherman's 1987 study, Stern, McMillion, Hopkins, and Stone (1990) concluded that the number of hours of employment in an off-campus job was negatively associated with persistence, but that students who spent more hours working on campus were likely to graduate and also enter graduate school. About student work in general, the researchers offered four conclusions:

1. Students who work during college earn more money in the first few years after graduation.
2. Students who work do not get lower grades than nonworkers.
3. Students who work are more likely to drop out or take longer to complete their academic programs.
4. Working has a more positive correlation with performance in school when the job is more closely related to school (p. 374).

Astin (1993) concluded that working in a part-time job on campus increases a student's chances of being elected to a student office, tutoring other students, and attending a recital or concert. He suggested that the positive effect on the student of part-time work on campus is consistent with his theory of involvement: "Compared to students who spend an equal amount of time working off campus, students who are employed on campus are, almost by definition, in more frequent contact with other students and possibly with faculty (depending on the type of work). Apparently, this greater degree of immersion in the collegiate environment and culture more than compensates, in terms of outcomes, for the time that students must devote to a part-time job on campus. Similar trade-offs are simply not available to the student whose part-time job is located off campus" (pp. 388–389).

Astin (1993) also found that part-time work off campus is positively associated with completing a bachelor's degree and self-reported cognitive and affective growth. Working full-time off campus, however, has a negative effect on students, according to his research.

The conclusions of Kuh, Douglas, Lund, and Ramin-Gyurnek (1994) paralleled the findings of Astin (1993) just mentioned. They found that working part-time on campus had a positive effect on persistence, educational attainment, and practical competence, especially if the work was directly related to an academic major or vocational aspiration. Humanitarianism was positively affected if the job was nonwork-study. On the other hand, they concluded that part-time, off-campus work had a negative impact on student satisfaction but a positive relationship to practical competence, especially if the work was related to a student's academic major or vocational aspiration.

Work can have a number of effects on a student, according to Horn and Malizio (1998). They found that the students who in their study reported working put in an average of twenty-five hours per week. Students at a four-year institution reported working fewer hours per week than those attending a two-year college. Students who worked fewer hours, according to Horn and Malizio, "were much less likely to report that work limited their class choices, their class schedules, the number of hours they could take, or access to the library" (1998, p. 24). They concluded that "borrowing enough to reduce the number of hours a student needs to work to no more than 15 hours per week may increase a student's chances of completing her or his degree" (p. 25).

Cooperative Education

Van Gyn, Cutt, Loken, and Ricks (1997) asserted that "the basis of the cooperative education movement is, most certainly, the education of the student, but over time the focus and interest have shifted to more tangible, pragmatic employment outcomes associated with this curriculum model" (p. 70). The value of cooperative education, according to Derousi and Sherwood (1997), is well documented. They concluded that these assignments reduce the employer's cost of recruiting and training. For students, they are an opportunity to gain experience while developing career awareness and determining the suitability of a career aspiration.

Stern, McMillion, Hopkins, and Stone (1990) compared and contrasted cooperative experiences with college work-study programs. As with work-study, cooperative education students are able to support themselves in part through paid employment. Cooperative education is not limited by financial aid eligibility, however. Additionally, cooperative education is related to the student's career field, and the student often receives some form of academic credit for the experience. Stern and colleagues concluded that one big challenge facing such a program is to maximize the benefits of the work experience while minimizing the negative effects of cooperative education (such as the student's working an excessive number of hours). Smith-Eggeman and Scott (1994) found that one of the benefits of participating in cooperative education is that the experience "had an enhancing effect on a student's achievement of the development task of freeing interpersonal relationships" (p. 19). Stern, McMillion, Hopkins, and Stone (1990) also concluded that jobs with characteristics such as autonomy, challenge, and substantive complexity promoted emotional and cognitive development.

Internship

Internship is defined as "structured and career-relevant work experiences obtained by students prior to graduation from an academic program" (Taylor, 1988, p. 393). It serves two functions, according to Feldman and Weitz (1990): internship increases both the student's access to career opportunities and the amount and quality of data the student has when making a career decision.

Lee and Caffarella (1994) noted that supervision for an intern can come from one or more sources, among them a full mentoring relationship or intermittent conferring with one or more supervising experts. The internship experience has to be integrated to provide the richest experience possible. Accordingly, Lee and Caffarella (1994) recommended a wrap-up experience with an in-class reaction panel to enhance knowledge synthesis and richness.

Internship has also been shown to benefit both the internship provider and the student participant. Derousi and Sherwood (1997) found that in 89 percent of fifty-four agencies studied, as a result of having an intern the agency was able to accomplish much more than would have been possible otherwise. Internship is also an effective way to promote access to certain professions for a member of a historically underrepresented group (Fisher, 1992).

Taylor (1988) studied the effects of internship on students. A variety of positive outcomes were identified, leading to the conclusion that interns have a distinct advantage over their peers in the labor market. Taylor identified the benefits to the intern as a higher level of satisfaction and stronger intention to remain on their first job, less job anxiety and higher performance on that same job, higher employment ratings, and receipt of more job offers. To these conclusions, Astin (1993) added: "Participation in a college internship program has its strongest effect on self-reported growth in job skills. It also produces modest positive correlations with college GPA, graduating with honors, completion of the bachelor's degree and most satisfaction outcomes" (p. 380).

Service Learning

Service learning is another programmatic intervention that appears to assist the student in applying classroom learning to a practical setting. Kendall (1991) characterized service-learning programs as emphasizing accomplishment of tasks that meet human needs in combination with conscious educational growth. Service learning, in his view, combines tasks needed in the community with intentional learning goals and with conscious reflection and critical analysis. Service-learning programs, according to Kendall, boast features that foster learning about larger social issues undergirding the human needs they are trying to help address, and that emphasize reciprocity between the learners and the people being served.

Astin (1996) concluded that "participation in service-based programs favorably affects persistence in college, interest in graduate study, critical thinking skills, leadership skills, and a commitment to promoting racial understanding" (p. 16). In a comprehensive study of service learning, Eyler and Giles (1999) reported a number of positive effects of service learning on student participants. Since their findings are extremely comprehensive and detailed, space does not permit a complete summary. Nevertheless, they found that service learning has a positive effect on students in these areas: reduced stereotyping and intolerance, personal development, interpersonal development, community and college connection, understanding and applying knowledge, critical thinking, and effective citizenship. The reader is referred to their book to examine their findings in detail. There is no question from this study that service learning has a number of powerful effects on those who choose to participate in this experience.

Conclusions and Implications for Practice

Clearly, preparing college students to become skilled workers has evolved over time. In the colonial period, preparation for joining the workforce was not nearly as important an objective of higher education as it is in contemporary times, where workforce development is an important objective for many institutions of higher education. In some respects, the development of this trend has reflected a broadening of the curricular offerings of institutions of higher education, rather than substitution of vocationally oriented curriculum for classical curriculum. To be sure, today's students who desire a classical educational experience can find it, although some subjects are not particularly common (for example, Latin and Greek). For those who wish to pursue an academic course of study that leads directly to employment (such as engineering or nursing), these experiences are readily available.

An ample theoretical background is available for those who wish to build vocational experiences for students on a theoretical foundation. Clearly, from a historical perspective, the vocational counseling movement that was triggered by World War I has experienced growth in momentum over time. Virtually any structured experience for students to prepare them for a vocation can be framed by one or more theories.

The opportunities that are available for students in the area of practical experience related to worker training are plentiful. They include working part-time on campus, participating in a cooperative education or internship program, and service learning. The empirical evidence for these experiences is valuable and clear: such experiences add richness to students' educational experiences and serve them well as they enter the world of full-time work. Those who advise students about working for pay off campus should exercise caution, however, in their conversation with students, and urge them to work a limited number of hours. The evidence suggests that if a student works more than fifteen to twenty hours per week, the responsibilities of work can have a negative effect on the student's academic pursuits. Students are best advised, if at all possible, to work fifteen hours per week or fewer, on campus, and in an area that complements their academic interests.

Implications for Faculty

Much of what students learn that enables them to become a skilled worker is a product of their interaction with faculty. Several implications for practice are appropriate for faculty.

Faculty can form partnerships with elementary and secondary schools, business, and industry to improve the quality of economic life for the geographic area served by the institution. Faculty members have tremendous expertise, and it can be used to improve the quality of the economic environment for citizens in the area. In specific terms, partnerships can focus on cooperative and internship experiences for students, which is helpful to the region in at least two ways. First, students can be prepared for positions with firms in the geographic area served by the institution. This preparation can focus on the culture of the firm, specific techniques necessary for students to be successful in applying their knowledge to practical circumstances, and understanding the daily routine of the workplace. Second, partnerships can be useful in recruiting students to become full-time employees of firms in the area. Whether a student teacher, engineering student, business student, or otherwise, participants develop valuable skills and can become part of the backbone of the future workforce for the region served by the college or university.

Faculty members also can be recruited by advancement staff to serve on a panel of expert consultants who can be helpful to the region in terms of its economic development. Faculty members can use consulting experience to enrich practical application of their work. These consulting experiences, in turn, can lead to a transactional relationship between the faculty member as consultant and the organization with which he or she consults. Through various economic development civic organizations, the availability of the faculty for such assignment can be publicized in the region served by the institution. A corollary to this experience is that faculty can include students in their consulting activity. The advantage of the strategy is obvious. Students can learn practical application of the discipline they are studying, and simultaneously be helpful in the consulting process.

Implications for Faculty and Student Affairs

A number of initiatives can be undertaken jointly by student affairs staff and faculty. One such initiative could be to develop an undergraduate research assistantship organized by student affairs, with student recipients selected by and working with faculty members. Funding for a program could come from financial aid sources, or from grants secured by faculty. Regardless of the source of funding, undergraduates could work with faculty along a variety of dimensions, including research projects or consulting activities, as has already been suggested here. An undergraduate research assistantship can be a positive experience for a student, and a significant source of help for faculty.

Faculty and student affairs professionals can also work together to infuse service learning in academic courses. For the process to work, service learning generally requires a partnership between faculty and student affairs. Faculty organize the courses, and student affairs provides the infrastructure for the off-campus experience. Thus the partnership formed to advance service learning also affords wonderful experiences for students through the collaboration developed by student affairs and faculty.

Faculty and student affairs administrators can work together to link various majors to specific occupations and work opportunities. In good economic times, potential students may skip college for employment opportunities. In the short run, this action may be economically advantageous for potential students, but in the long run it works to their economic disadvantage. The economic value of the college experience has to be reinforced. This can be done by demonstrating how certain majors lead to specific areas of employment, especially in the liberal arts. Career services can assist in this area and collaborate with faculty. Workshops such as "What Can I Do with a Major in ____?" can be held for current and prospective students. Such an activity can help to attract prospective students to college, especially a young person who is torn between enrolling in college or seeking employment right out of high school.

Implications for Student Affairs

Two implications for student affairs can be helpful in advancing the concept of the skilled worker. First, the office of career services might appoint an advisory board made up of a group of people from the community who represent important employers. The board could include someone from the local school district and several employers from the private sector, among them manufacturing and the service sector. Such a board is an important link between the college and the community.

Second, the division of student affairs must develop employment on campus for students that can be linked to their academic course of study. Students should be discouraged from working off campus for long hours since that can distract them from their academic work. The rate of pay probably has to be increased on campus; a careful survey of potential employment opportunities on campus must be conducted. Regardless of the effort needed, however, providing meaningful work for students on campus should be a top priority for student affairs.

Implications for Institutional Advancement Staff

Institutional advancement staff can use the information in this chapter about developing skilled workers in several ways. First, they can produce organized, systematic reports on the contribution of the college to the economic development of the region. Too often, these contributions are not well known, and when press releases and reports are issued systematically the importance of the institution to the economic health of the region is better understood.

Institutional advancement staff also can work closely with economic development agencies in the region to make resources available for studies of economic development needs and potential solutions. Drawing on resources at the institution, these studies can be useful in identifying how the institution can be of assistance to the region as well as underscoring the tremendous resource the institution already represents to the region.

Implications for Senior Executive Officers

Senior officers of the institution need to strengthen their relationship with community leaders. These initiatives should include establishing routine contact with the office of the mayor, the local legislative delegation, and economic development groups. Specifically, the contacts can include a briefing on college activities, a proposal for linking campus resources to an economic development initiative, and development of learning experiences for students off campus.

References

American Association of Community and Junior Colleges (AACJC). (1988). *Community College Fact Book.* New York: ACE/Macmillan.

Association of American Colleges. (1985). *Integrity in the college curriculum: A report to the academic community.* Washington, DC: Author.

Astin, A. W. (1993). *What matters in college?* San Francisco: Jossey-Bass.

Astin, A. W. (1996, March–April). The role of service in higher education. *About Campus, 1*(1), 14–19.

Astin, A. W. (1998). The changing American college student: Thirty-year trends, 1966–1996. *Review of Higher Education, 21,* 115–135.

Baltes, P. B. (1987). Theoretical propositions of life-span developmental psychology: On the dynamics between growth and decline. *Developmental Psychology, 23,* 611–626.

Baxter Magolda, M. B. (1992). *Knowing and reasoning in college: Gender-related patterns in students' intellectual development.* San Francisco: Jossey-Bass.

Belenky, M. F., Clinchy, B. M., Goldberger, N. R., & Tarule, J. M. (1986). *Women's ways of knowing: The development of self, voice, and mind.* New York: Basic Books.

Boisvert, R. D. (1998). *John Dewey: Rethinking our time.* Albany: State University of New York Press.

Bowen, H. R. (1977). *Investment in learning: The individual and social value of American higher education.* Baltimore: Johns Hopkins University Press.

Calliotte, J. A., Helms, S. T., & Wells, E. A. (1975). *The education and vocational orientations of UMBC freshmen.* Baltimore: University of Maryland, Counseling Center.

Chickering, A. W., & Reisser, L. (1993). *Education and identity* (2nd ed.). San Francisco: Jossey-Bass.

Derousi, P., & Sherwood, C. S. (1997). Community service scholarships: Combining cooperative education with service learning. *Journal of Cooperative Education, 33*(1), 46–54.

Dewey, J. (1985). *Democracy and education*. Carbondale, IL: Southern Illinois University Press. (Original work published 1916)

Digest of Education Statistics. (1997). Washington, DC: U.S. Department of Labor, Bureau of Labor Statistics.

Elder, G. H., Jr. (1995). The life course paradigm: Social change and individual development. In P. Moen, G. H. Elder, Jr., & K. Lüscher (Eds.), *Examining lives in context: Perspectives on the ecology of human development* (pp. 101–139). Washington, DC: American Psychological Association.

Emporia State University Website. Retrieved Jan. 14, 2000, from http://www.emporia.edu/esu/mission.htm.

Erikson, E. H. (1968). *Identity: Youth and crisis*. New York: Norton.

Erikson, E. H. (1980). *Identity and the life cycle*. New York: Norton. (Original work published 1959)

Evans, N. J., Forney, D. S., & Guido-DiBrito, F. (1998). *Student development in college: Theory, research, and practice*. San Francisco: Jossey-Bass.

Eyler, J., & Giles, D. W., Jr. (1999). *Where's the service in service-learning?* San Francisco: Jossey-Bass.

Fairweather, J. S. (1996). *Faculty work and public trust: Restoring the value of teaching and public service in American academic life*. Boston: Allyn and Bacon.

Feldman, D. C., & Weitz, B. A. (1990). Summer interns: Factors contributing to positive developmental experiences. *Journal of Vocational Behavior, 37*, 267–284.

Fisher, M. A. (1992). Developing diversity: Bringing more minorities into advancement through internships. *CASE Currents, 18*(4), 14–17.

Fiske, M., & Chiriboga, D. A. (1990). *Change and continuity in adult life*. San Francisco: Jossey-Bass.

Gottfredson, G. D., & Holland, J. L. (1989). *Dictionary of Holland occupational codes* (2nd ed.). Odessa, FL: Psychological Assessment Resources.

Hammons, J. O. (1992). To acquire stature: "To thine own self be true." In B. W. Dziech & W. R. Vilter (Eds.), *Prisoners of elitism: The community college's struggle for stature* (New Directions for Community Colleges, no. 78, pp. 77–86). San Francisco: Jossey-Bass.

Harmon, L. W., Hansen, J. C., Borgen, F. H., & Hammer, A. L. (1994). *Strong Interest Inventory: Applications and technical guide*. Stanford, CA: Stanford University Press.

Harvey, J., & Associates. (1994). *First impressions and second thoughts: Public support for higher education.* Washington, DC: American Council on Education.

Harvey, J., & Immerwahr, J. (1995a). *The fragile coalition: Public support for higher education in the 1990s.* Washington, DC: American Council on Education.

Harvey, J., & Immerwahr, J. (1995b). *Goodwill and growing worry: Public perceptions of higher education.* Washington, DC: American Council on Education.

Herr, E. L., & Cramer, S. H. (1988). *Career guidance and counseling through the life span.* Glenview, IL: Scott, Foresman.

Holland, J. L. (1959). A theory of vocational choice. *Journal of Counseling Psychology, 6*(1), 35–44.

Holland, J. L. (1973). *Making vocational choices: A theory of careers.* Upper Saddle River, NJ: Prentice Hall.

Holland, J. L. (1985). *Vocational Preference Inventory (VPI): Professional manual.* Odessa, FL: Psychological Assessment Resources.

Holland, J. L. (1992). *Making vocational choices: A theory of vocational personalities and work environments* (2nd ed.). Odessa, FL: Psychological Assessment Resources. (Original work published 1985)

Holland, J. L. (1994). *The Self-Directed Search (SDS) technical manual.* Odessa, FL: Psychological Assessment Resources.

Holland, J. L., Powell, A. B., & Fritzsche, B. A. (1994). *The Self-Directed Search (SDS) professional user's guide.* Odessa, FL: Psychological Assessment Resources.

Hood, A. B., Riahinejad, A. R., & White, D. B. (1986). Changes in ego identity during the college years. *Journal of College Student Personnel, 27,* 107–113.

Horn, L. J., & Malizio, A. G. (1998). *Profile of undergraduates in U. S. postsecondary education institutions: 1995–96.* (NCES 98–084). Washington, DC: U.S. Department of Education.

Hultsch, J. A., & Plemons, J. K. (1979). Life events and life span development. In P. B. Baltes & O. G. Brim (Eds.), *Life-span development and behavior* (vol. 2, pp. 1–36). New York: Academic.

Hunt, S., & Rentz, A. L. (1994). Greek-letter social group members' involvement and psychosocial development. *Journal of College Student Development, 35,* 289–295.

Involvement in learning: Realizing the potential of American higher education. (1984). Washington, DC: U.S. Department of Education, National Institute of Education, Study Group on the Conditions of Excellence in American Higher Education.

Kendall, J. C. (1991). Combining service and learning: An introduction for cooperative education professionals. *Journal of Cooperative Education, 27*(2), 9–25.

King, P. M. (1996). Student cognition and learning. In S. R. Komives, D. B. Woodard, Jr., & Associates, *Student services: A handbook for the profession* (3rd ed., pp. 218–243). San Francisco: Jossey-Bass.

King, P. M., & Kitchener, K. S. (1994). *Developing reflective judgment: Understanding and promoting intellectual growth and critical thinking in adolescents and adults.* San Francisco: Jossey-Bass.

Knefelkamp, L. L., & Slepitza, R. (1976). A cognitive-developmental model of career development: An adaptation of the Perry scheme. *Counseling Psychologist, 6*(3), 53–58.

Kroll, J., & Rentz, A. L. (1996). Career services. In A. L. Rentz & Associates, *Student affairs practice in higher education* (2nd ed., pp. 108–142). Springfield, IL: Charles C. Thomas.

Krumboltz, J. D. (1979). A social learning theory of career decision making. In A. M. Mitchell, G. B. Jones, & J. D. Krumboltz (Eds.), *Social learning and career decision making* (pp. 19–49). Cranston, RI: Carroll.

Krumboltz, J. D. (1981). A social learning theory of career selection. In D. H. Montross & C. J. Shinkman (Eds.), *Career development in the 1980s: Theory and practice* (pp. 43–66). Springfield, IL: Charles C. Thomas.

Kuh, G. D., Douglas, K. B., Lund, J. P., & Ramin-Gyurnek, J. (1994). *Student learning outside the classroom: Transcending artificial boundaries* (ASHE-ERIC Higher Education Report no. 8). Washington, DC: George Washington University, School of Education and Human Development.

Lee, P., & Caffarella, R. S. (1994). Methods and techniques for engaging learners in experiential learning activities. In L. Jackson & R. S. Caffarella (Eds.), *Experiential learning: A new approach* (New Directions for Adult and Continuing Education, no. 62, pp. 43–54). San Francisco: Jossey-Bass.

Leslie, L. T., & Brinkman, P. T. (1988). *The economic value of higher education.* New York: ACE/Macmillan.

Levinson, D. J. (1978). *The seasons of a man's life.* New York: Ballantine.

Lewis, L. H., & Williams, C. J. (1994). Experiential learning: Past and present. In L. Jackson & R. S. Caffarella (Eds.), *Experiential learning: A new approach* (New Directions for Adult and Continuing Education, no. 62, pp. 5–16). San Francisco: Jossey-Bass.

Marcia, J. E. (1966). Development and validation of ego-identity status. *Journal of Personality and Social Psychology, 3,* 551–558.

May, W. F. (1990). Public happiness and higher education. In P. J. Palmer, B. G. Wheeler, & J. W. Fowler (Eds.), *Caring for the commonweal: Education for religious and public life* (pp. 227–247). Macon, GA: Mercer University Press.

McDaniels, C., & Gysbers, N. C. (1992). *Counseling for career development: Theories, resources, and practice.* San Francisco: Jossey-Bass.

Merriam, S. B., & Caffarella, R. S. (1999). *Learning in adulthood* (2nd ed.). San Francisco: Jossey-Bass.

"Money income in the United States: 1995." (1996). (Current Population Reports, series P-60). Washington, DC: U. S. Department of Commerce, Bureau of the Census.

Neugarten, B. (1976). Adaptation and the life cycle. *Counseling Psychologist, 6*(1), 16–20.

Niles, S. G., Sowa, C. J., & Laden, J. (1994). Life role participation and commitment as predictors of college student development. *Journal of College Student Development, 35,* 159–163.

O'Banion, T. (1997). *A learning college for the 21st century.* Phoenix: Oryx.

Parsons, F. (1909). *Choosing a vocation.* Boston: Houghton Mifflin.

Pascarella, E. T., & Terenzini, P. T. (1991). *How college affects students: Findings and insights from twenty years of research.* San Francisco: Jossey-Bass.

Paterson, D. G., & Darley, J. G. (1936). *Men, women, and jobs: A study in human engineering.* Minneapolis: University of Minnesota Press.

Perry, W. G., Jr. (1968). *Forms of intellectual and ethical development in the college years: A scheme.* New York: Holt, Rinehart & Winston.

Perun, P. J., & Bielby, D.D.V. (1980). Structure and dynamics of the individual life course. In K. W. Beck (Ed.), *Life course: Integrative theories and exemplary populations* (pp. 97–119). Boulder, CO: Westview.

Points of View. (1989). Washington, DC: National Association of Student Personnel Administrators.

Ratcliff, J. L. (1987). "First" public junior colleges in an age of reform. *Journal of Higher Education, 58,* 151–180.

Reardon, R. C., & Minor, C. W. (1975). Revitalizing the career information service. *Personnel and Guidance Journal, 54,* 169–171.

Rudolph, F. (1962). *The American college and university: A history.* New York: Random House.

Ryan, M., & Cassidy, J. R. (1996). Internships & excellence. *Liberal Education, 82*(3), 16–23.

Schlossberg, N. K. (1989). *Overwhelmed: Coping with life's ups and downs.* Lexington, MA: Lexington.

Schlossberg, N. K., Waters, E. B., & Goodman, J. (1995). *Counseling adults in transition* (2nd ed.). New York: Springer.

Schneider, L. D. (1977). Counseling. In W. T. Packwood (Ed.), *College student personnel services* (pp. 340–367). Springfield, IL: Charles C. Thomas.

Sinclair, U. (1923). *The goose-step: A study in American education.* (Vols. 1–4). Girard, KS: Haldeman-Julius.

Smith-Eggeman, B., & Scott, N. A. (1994). The relative influence of cooperative education on college students' development of interpersonal relationships. *Journal of Cooperative Education, 29*(3), 14–22.

Stern, D., McMillion, M., Hopkins, C. & Stone, J. (1990). Work experience for students in high school and college. *Youth & Society, 21,* 355–398.

Super, D. E. (1983). Assessment in career guidance: Toward truly developmental counseling. *Personnel and Guidance Journal, 61,* 555–562.

Super, D. E. (1990). A life-span, life-space approach to career development. In D. Brown, L. Brooks, & Associates, *Career choice and development: Applying contemporary theories to development* (2nd ed., pp. 197–261). San Francisco: Jossey-Bass.

Super, D. E. (1992). Toward a comprehensive theory of career development. In D. H. Montross & C. J. Shinkman (Eds.), *Career development: Theory and practice* (pp. 35–64). Springfield, IL: Charles C. Thomas.

Taylor, M. S. (1988). Effects of college internships on individual participants. *Journal of Counseling Psychology, 32,* 539–550.

Thorndike, R. L. (1949). *Personnel selection: Test and measurement techniques.* New York: Wiley.

Thorndike, R. L., & Hagen, E. (1959). *Ten thousand careers.* New York: Wiley.

Thornton, J. W., Jr. (1966). *The community junior college* (2nd ed.). New York: Wiley.

Touchton, J. G., Wertheimer, L. C., Cornfeld, J. L., & Harrison, K. H. (1977). Career planning and decision-making: A developmental approach to the classroom. *Counseling Psychologist, 6*(4), 42–47.

University of Phoenix Website. Retrieved Jan. 14, 2000, from http://www.uophx.edu/uop/ourunive.htm.

Vaillant, G. (1977). *Adaptation to life.* Boston: Little, Brown.

Van Gyn, G., Cutt, J., Loken, M., & Ricks, F. (1997). Investigating the educational benefits of cooperative education: A longitudinal study. *Journal of Cooperative Education, 32*(2), 70–85.

Williams, M. E., & Winston, R. B., Jr. (1985). Participating in organized student activities and work: Differences in developmental task achievement of traditional-aged college students. *NASPA Journal, 24*(2), 38–48.

Williamson, E. G. (1939). *How to counsel students: A manual of techniques for clinical counselors.* New York: McGraw-Hill.

Williamson, E. G. (1965). *Vocational counseling.* New York: McGraw-Hill.

The Wingspread Group on Higher Education. (1993). *An American imperative: Higher expectations for higher education.* Racine, WI: Johnson Foundation.

Yarris, E. (1996). Counseling. In A. L. Rentz & Associates, *Student affairs practice in higher education* (2nd ed., pp. 143–174). Springfield, IL: Charles C. Thomas.

Chapter Nine

Life Skills Manager

A college or university typically offers a broad complement of programs to address numerous academic support and success issues, such as career planning, study skills, and leadership development. An increasing number of programming efforts, however, focus on what would traditionally be considered aspects of the student's personal life. They include money management and wellness programs designed to help students develop dispositions, habits, and awareness that enhance their long-term well-being in areas such as health and personal finance. These outcomes relate directly to the personal realm of the student's life (as contrasted with the public realm that encompasses being a student or a citizen) and are somewhat less directly connected with the realm of academic success that characterizes most traditional student affairs programs. Nonetheless, as economic self-sufficiency and consumer choices become more complex, and as connections between health, well-being, and leisure activities are documented, the college or university increasingly devotes attention to these important concerns in students' lives.

Additionally, in an age characterized by ready offers of consumer credit to students; an increasing number of part-time, largely self-supporting students; and adult students balancing multiple financial and personal demands, more life issues traditionally regarded as highly personal or private have become issues for discussion and consideration on the college campus.

There is little mention of these and other "life skill management" considerations within higher education literature, with the notable exception of student affairs statements and Bowen's

Investment in Learning (1997). In the second commissioned statement of student affairs philosophy and purposes in 1949, the authors included specific references to financial self-sufficiency and recreational interests. With respect to personal finance, the authors stipulated: "The student achieves understanding and control of his [sic] financial resources. Learning how to live within his income, how to increase that income, and how to find financial aids that are available are part of an understanding of the student's economic life. Such an understanding of money values must be achieved in balanced relationships to physical energy, curricular, and social demands" (1949 statement, *Points of View*, 1989, p. 31).

In this relatively early specification of student outcomes, a concern for the student's financial well-being, a highly personal realm, was clearly specified. These authors went on to promote recreational and leisure activities as an important emphasis for the college or university, at which campus "the student develops lively and significant interests . . . fostering a program of recreational and discussional activities that is diversified" (1949 statement, *Points of View*, 1989, p. 31). To promote development of these interests, the college or university is to offer "a program of recreational activities designed to promote lifetime interests and skills appropriate to the individual student" (1949 statement, *Points of View*, 1989, p. 37). In more general terms, the 1987 commissioned statement specified a number of responsibilities that the college or university owes students, including "[establishing] programs that encourage healthy living and [confronting] abusive behaviors" as well as "[providing] opportunities for recreation and leisure-time activities" (1987 statement, *Points of View*, 1989, p. 17).

Bowen's *Investment in Learning* (1997) devoted an entire chapter to influences and outcomes related to health and leisure, consumerism, and family life. Among the "practical competencies" he associated with these aspects of development were consumer efficiency, which was characterized by "sound choice of values relating to style of life. Skill in stretching consumer dollars. Ability to cope with taxes, credit, insurance, investments, legal issues, and so on. Ability to recognize deceptive sales practices and to withstand high-pressure sales tactics" (p. 58).

Leisure, according to Bowen (1997), was to be "fruitful" (p. 58), constructive, or productive in nature. Among other things, fruitful leisure included "wisdom in allocation of time. . . . Lifelong education, formal and informal, as a productive use of leisure. Resourcefulness in overcoming boredom, finding renewal, and discovering satisfying and rewarding uses of leisure time" (p. 58). Leisure time, then, was regarded as an opportunity for development and not as an invitation to idleness. Elsewhere, Bowen discussed higher education as preparing students to face the quotidian aspects of everyday life, such as "preparing individuals to cope with the ordinary affairs of life; dealing with interpersonal problems within the family; using the health care system; getting proper legal advice; coping with bureaucracy; managing investments, insurance, and taxes; buying and selling real estate; and so on" (p. 40).

Within other statements discussing desirable student-level outcomes from higher education, there is more or less oblique reference to aspects of the student's life that traditionally fall into such a highly personal realm as life skills or life management, such as those enumerated just above by Bowen. For example, the 1968 study group on *The Student in Higher Education* considered one of the three primary student needs to be connecting "the relevance of higher learning to the quality of his [sic] own life and to see that life in relation to the new kinds of judgments he now makes" (pp. 10–11). In many ways, this assertion echoes and supports Chickering's final vector of developing integrity, in which the student's behavior and decisions become consistent with espoused values (Chickering & Reisser, 1993).

Another generalized reference to student outcomes was contained in a contributed essay to the *American Imperative* volume, in which Bosworth cautioned that "we should not concentrate so exclusively on teaching young Americans to work in an increasingly complex, technologically driven world, that we neglect to teach them how to live in such a world" (1993, p. 57). Clearly, this statement reflects a concern that higher education not simply respond to demands for skilled and technologically sophisticated workers while ignoring ramifications of this same evolving and changing workplace for students' private lives and personal choices.

Such concern for students' development of awareness and agency in their personal lives are less widely articulated in various statements on desired student outcomes from higher education. However, it certainly is not an unimportant consideration and speaks to a central, perhaps tacit humanistic concern: that a college or university attend to and support individual students as they make quite personal decisions regarding how to live their private lives. The growing prominence of wellness initiatives, consumer awareness, and financial education programs on campus attests to this concern being increasingly addressed through overt, deliberate strategies.

In the first section, we summarize relevant student development theories and link them to issues of life skills management. That section is followed by discussion of studies that demonstrate the influence of the college experience on life skills management. Suggestions for practice conclude the chapter.

Student Development Theory

Student development theories, specifically those theories that are psychosocial in nature, yield important information about how individuals develop life skills. Indeed, psychosocial theories, such as those of Erikson (1959, 1968) and Chickering and Reisser (1993), have as their central focus the development of life skills, which these theorists labeled "developmental tasks." Adult development theorists extended consideration of life skills development across the life span. Perun and Bielby's integrative theory (1980); the life events and transition theory of Schlossberg, Waters, and Goodman (1995); and the life course theory of Elder (1995) all have implications for the educator working with students to develop life skills.

Psychosocial Theories

The developmental tasks associated with adolescence and adulthood are the focus of psychosocial theory. Erikson (1959, 1968) and Chickering and Reisser (1993) have identified key life skills that become a part of each person's repertoire as he or she grows and develops, and factors that influence development of these skills. Because Chickering's theory significantly contributes to understanding the development of life skills, we discuss its implications in greater detail here than has been the case with specific theories in other chapters.

Erikson

A number of the stages of development that Erikson (1959, 1968) identified specifically address development of life skills. Although autonomy, initiative, and industry are developmental tasks that the individual normally addresses during childhood, the extent to which the person does so successfully influences the ability to live a productive adult life. Individuals who have not completely resolved issues related to these tasks are likely to face situations in college that require them to reexamine their basic attitudes. For instance, a developmental crisis is likely to arise for a student who doubts his ability to function independently in the world when he moves away to college and must take responsibility for his own finances, eating habits, and personal management tasks. Similarly, a student who has always relied on her parents to tell her to do her homework, to take her to band practice, and to get her up in the morning faces significant challenges in the college environment.

Because of the external demands placed on college students to be autonomous, take initiative, and work diligently to accomplish their goals, an individual who attends college is likely to successfully resolve the developmental tasks that Erikson suggested are the foundation for the tasks he or she will face later in life. These early tasks contribute to a strong sense of identity, which allows one to confront life challenges, and later to generativity, which involves caring for and educating the younger generation, typically through parenting.

Opportunities for students to work independently, take on a leadership role, and achieve goals they have set might include a study-abroad program, student government, service learning, or participation in a theatrical production. More directly, programs designed to introduce students to the challenges of living on their own, financial planning, and wellness concepts are valuable in developing life skills. Such initiatives could be part of comprehensive developmental programming in a residence hall, for example, as well as a relevant academic course.

Chickering

Many of Chickering's vectors deal directly with development of life skills (Chickering & Reisser, 1993). His vectors build on each other, resulting in a strong sense of self that enables the individual to carry out life tasks confidently and responsibly. Vectors that specifically contribute to life skills development are developing competence, managing emotions, moving through autonomy toward interdependence, establishing identity, developing purpose, and developing integrity.

Developing Competence. Foundational to managing one's life is a sense of competence. Competence develops in three areas: the intellectual, physical and manual, and interpersonal. As important as the skills themselves is having confidence in one's ability to handle the challenges that arise within each domain. Intellectual competence centers on knowledge and skills related to particular subject matter and the ability to reason abstractly and analytically. These skills are important in managing one's life and making decisions concerning finances, personal affairs, and lifestyle. Physical and manual competence is increased through pursuit of recreational activities and sports, attention to wellness, and involvement in artistic and manual activity. Pursuits such as these in college set a direction for leisure interests later in life and help to create the foundation for a healthy lifestyle. Interpersonal competence involves effective communication and the ability to work with others. Such skills enable the individual to conduct personal business that involves interaction with others. They are also important in good parenting.

Managing Emotions. The vector of managing emotions focuses on a person's ability to recognize, accept, and appropriately express and control such emotions as anger, depression, and anxiety. They are a part of life and effective management of daily living involves the ability to handle them appropriately. Being able to acknowledge and share such positive emotions as love, caring, and joy also contributes to personal well-being.

Moving Through Autonomy Toward Interdependence. Chickering's third vector involves both emotional and instrumental independence. Emotional independence, defined as "freedom from continual and pressing needs for reassurance, affection, or approval from others" (Chickering & Reisser, 1993, p. 117), is a key factor in being able to make independent decisions concerning all aspects of one's life.

Instrumental autonomy relates to cognitive processes such as decision making, problem solving, and taking control of one's life. Becoming financially independent and living on one's own contribute to development of these skills, which certainly carry over into later life. Recognition of interdependence—awareness of one's interconnectedness with others—is also a part of this vector.

Establishing Identity. Chickering and Reisser's discussion of identity (1993) includes reference to many life skills. Being comfortable with one's body and appearance is one component that certainly contributes to the type of leisure activity in which a person might choose to engage, how active he or she may be in recreational pursuits, and the attention that he or she gives to health and wellness. A clear sense of self also helps the person determine the lifestyle he or she wishes to pursue and imparts direction as to how to establish such a style of life. Comfort with one's racial, ethnic, and sexual identity enables the person to evaluate and select avocational pursuits, leisure activities, and personal commitments in line with these aspects of identity. Self-esteem and self-confidence as well as the personal stability and integration associated with a clear identity are the basis for setting a life course and carrying out the tasks needed to accomplish one's personal goals. These tasks might include managing one's financial and material resources, handling personal affairs, and actively engaging in avocational interests.

Developing Purpose. In addition to establishing vocational goals, developing purpose includes making a significant commitment to meaningful personal interests and involvement. The individual with a clear sense of purpose is able to make and stick to a decision, even in the face of opposition. The lifestyle one wishes to pursue, as well as family-related influences, affects the decision-making and goal-setting processes involved in developing purpose. The extent to which an individual's life purpose is established in college affects the manner and clarity with which personal interests are pursued in later life.

Developing Integrity. The vector of developing integrity centers on establishing values and using them as a guide in decision making and behavior. The actions of individuals who have developed integrity are congruent with the values they espouse. Individuals also act in a manner in which their own interests are balanced with the needs of others and a sense of responsibility to society. Part of effectively managing one's life is determining how to take care of oneself while at the same time caring for one's family, friends, community, and society as a whole.

Environmental Influences on Life Skills Development. Chickering and Reisser (1993) identified a number of factors within the college environment that contribute to developing life skills. They noted that clear and consistent institutional objectives help students clarify their own reasons for attending a college and define their purposes while at college. They also pointed out that institutional objectives have a strong value component that encourages students to consider their personal values in relation to these overarching values.

Chickering and Reisser (1993) hypothesized that a small college offers more opportunity for the student to develop identity and integrity since fewer students compete to engage in meaningful experiences and activities. They noted that "situations provoking examination of values and consideration of the consequences of one's actions" (p. 269) are more likely to occur for students in a smaller college. The challenge for educators working in a larger college or university is to create small subenvironments that permit similar opportunity. A learning community, house system, student interest group or organization, or departmental club can be a way to accomplish this goal.

Chickering and Reisser (1993) also stressed the significant role played by faculty-student relationships in student development. As they stated it, "When student-faculty interaction is frequent and friendly and when it occurs in diverse situations calling for varied roles and relationships, development of intellectual competence, sense of competence, autonomy and interdependence, purpose, and integrity are encouraged" (p. 269). Faculty involvement can take the form of advising a student organization, including students in a research project, and participating in a learning community, as well as taking the time to meet and talk with students outside of class.

The curriculum can also have a powerful impact on developing life skills. Chickering and Reisser (1993) stressed the importance of attending to both the process and the content of the curriculum. They advocated for coursework that is relevant; recognizes individual differences; allows "encounters with diverse perspectives that challenge preexisting information, assumptions, and values" (p. 270); and includes activities that help students to incorporate diverse views and values into their belief system.

Effective teaching strategies are necessary to deliver a meaningful curriculum. According to Chickering and Reisser (1993), competence, autonomy, identity, and purpose are all fostered "when teaching calls for active learning, encourages student-faculty contact and cooperation among students, gives prompt feedback, emphasizes time on task and high expectations, and respects diverse talents and ways of knowing" (p. 272).

Friendships and student communities are important venues for a student to develop life skills (Chickering & Reisser, 1993). Living independently in a residence hall requires that students manage their time and resources. They have opportunities to take on leadership positions, which help them develop a better sense of who they are and what is important to them. Interacting with others encourages development of identity and purpose in comparing one's own interests, goals, and values with those of one's friends. Chickering and Reisser suggested that a community fosters optimum development when it encourages frequent interaction among students, presents the possibility of collaboration, is small enough that everyone can become involved, includes individuals from diverse backgrounds, and serves as a reference group.

As a final point, Chickering and Reisser (1993) stressed that collaborative initiatives between student affairs professionals and faculty increase the likelihood of a program successfully influencing the development of students in all areas. When student affairs professionals view themselves as student development educators rather than strictly as providers of ancillary services, they are much more likely to affect student growth meaningfully. Chickering and Reisser suggested that "using student development concepts to evaluate everything done outside the classroom can facilitate both large and small changes" (p. 278). Collaborative initiatives between faculty and student affairs professionals, such as service learning, a leadership development program, or study abroad, connect cognitive and affective components of learning to encourage development of competence, purpose, identity, and integrity. These skills carry over into the way in which students manage life after college.

Adult Development Theories

Adult development perspectives—such as those of Perun and Bielby (1980); Schlossberg, Waters, and Goodman (1995); and Elder (1995)—examine dimensions of development, life events, and the roles that individuals adopt throughout their lives. In particular, these theorists consider how the environment contributes to development of life skills.

Perun and Bielby

Perun and Bielby (1980) viewed adult development as a series of "temporal progressions—sequences of experiences or internal changes each of which follow some timeline" (Bee, 1996, p. 75). These progressions include some internal dimensions, such as physical and intellectual development, and some external components, such as family or work roles. Each dimension of development progresses at its own rate for each individual (Perun & Bielby). Although some aspects of development are inevitable, individuals have choice in other areas. For example, intellectual development is pretty much a process of internal maturation, but development of such life roles as whether to marry and have a family and how the individual progresses through these roles, is very much within the control of the individual.

However, the historical time and social context in which the person lives also influence development. The specific college environment to which a student is exposed certainly influences the particular life skills that are viewed as important and actively pursued. A college where participation in intramural sports is highly valued encourages students to develop physical competence and center their leisure pursuits around sports participation, while another institution that has a strong and visible fine arts program is likely to draw students into activities centering on music, theatre, and art.

Perun and Bielby (1980) also introduced the concept of asynchrony. This phenomenon occurs when one or more aspects of development are off-time in relation to others. Asynchrony often results in stress, but it can also trigger further developmental change. Many adult students experience asynchrony as they attend college later in life than is considered normal in U.S. society. These students are often faced with challenge in balancing life issues (managing finances, parenting children, juggling work and student roles, and so on).

Educators need to recognize the various aspects of development individuals are experiencing and help them find a balance among these dimensions. If they are to develop positive life skills, students must be encouraged to see that they do have control over many aspects of their lives. The educator might also wish to examine institutional values and mission with regard to what is being conveyed concerning how individuals should live their lives.

Schlossberg

Life events and transition theorists, exemplified by Schlossberg, Waters, and Goodman (1995), suggest that the life course is determined by the significant individual events (marriage, educational opportunity) and cultural events (economic conditions, social movements) a person experiences. The extent to which life skills are developed is influenced by the challenges individuals encounter and how they resolve the transitions they face. Variables associated with the situation, the degree of support the person has, the individual's personal qualities, and the strategies used to address the transition all affect the outcome. If a transition is addressed successfully, the individual is better prepared to effectively handle the next significant life event he or she faces.

For instance, a significant life event sometimes faced in college is moving into one's first apartment. This transition from living in a supervised environment to living independently can foster development of important life skills, namely, managing one's own living situation, paying bills, and making decisions about the lifestyle one wants to pursue. How this transition is managed can lead to success or failure in many areas of one's later life. The outcomes are affected by a number of factors, among them how fully the transition is anticipated and planned for, the student's sense of responsibility and ego development, the support from parents in making the move, and the meaning made of the situation (for instance, whether it is viewed as an opportunity or an impossible hurdle).

Schlossberg, Waters, and Goodman's theory (1995) offers a helpful structure for working with students experiencing transition. By asking students questions that enable them to analyze the supports and challenges they face in the situation, coping strategies can be developed that enhance the possibility of successful outcomes. These in turn lead to development of life skills that are valuable to students in the future.

Elder

The life course perspective of Elder (1995) focuses on the external roles that the individual plays during her or his life and factors that influence how the life course evolves. Elder's theory emphasizes "the social pathways of human lives, their sequence of events, transitions, and social roles" (p. 103). Elder stressed that individuals have agency; they plan and make choices that affect their life course. The situations in which they find themselves and the meaning they make of these situations, however, influence their decisions. For instance, one student attending a college where the tuition is unexpectedly raised by the board of regents may see this action as an insurmountable barrier to returning to school in the fall, while another may decide that the problem can be overcome by securing a part-time job. As Chickering and Reisser (1993) pointed out, the student's level of instrumental autonomy can influence how the student sees this situation; in turn, this life skill might be enhanced by actively addressing the environmental challenge.

"Linked lives" is another significant concept introduced by Elder (1995). He pointed out that our actions have consequences for the individuals with whom we interact and that we are also influenced by the actions of others. For instance, if a student's parents allow her to charge all of her expenses to their credit card and pay all of her bills, it will be difficult for her to develop money management skills and she may struggle with this task once she is out of college.

Elder (1995) also stressed the influence on development of social forces, place, and historical time, noting that the life course is established by the individual within the parameters set by the larger society. These factors certainly have influenced the extent to which women have been expected and encouraged to develop instrumental autonomy concerning management of finances and pursuit of an independent life role. Colleges in the 1950s and earlier, for example, had established parietal rules to "protect" women; those students were rarely encouraged to pursue a career or take an interest in family finances. Today, preparing women for such endeavors is expected.

The sociological perspective presented by Elder (1995) reminds educators of the important influence of the environment on development of life skills as well as the fluid nature of development resulting from changing societal norms and expectations. People, place, and time have a powerful impact on development of life skills, and the educator should intentionally examine those influences.

Effect of the College Experience on Life Skills

One of the major questions in higher education is who benefits from a college education. Some would argue that the benefits primarily accrue to the graduate, through a variety of outcomes (primarily, a higher economic standard of living and enhanced capacity for managing one's life and resources). Others point to the benefits to society as a whole by having highly educated citizens who are likely to vote, volunteer their time in their community, and lead healthy lives as being of primary importance.

Directly or indirectly, this debate can be illustrated by federal financial aid policies. For at least two decades, the primary form of federal financial aid has been loans—to students, their parents, or both—to be paid back, presumably out of future earnings (Hearn, 1998). This approach to financial aid suggests that a college education is regarded disproportionately by policy makers as a private benefit. On the other hand, governments and institutions still make grants to students, perhaps in part as recognition of the public good accruing from a college education. Actually, the debate is somewhat artificial in that graduation from college benefits individuals—that is, the graduates and their families—as well as society as a whole. Geske and Cohn (1998) concluded that "the overall level of returns to investment in higher education indicates that, in general, such an investment is profitable both for the individual and for society" (p. 28).

Released in 1998, *Reaping the Benefits: Defining the Public and Private Value of Going to College* gave examples of specific benefits related to college attendance. The authors indicated that "the goal of this report is to categorize or catalogue these benefits, providing a more accurate and inclusive picture than is commonly understood. This may help to broaden public understanding of the value of higher education, and thereby lead to more rational, and longer-term, consideration of governmental and societal investment in collegiate learning" (Institute for Higher Education Policy, 1998, p. 3).

In the aggregate, the college experience offers substantial advantages for college graduates, positioning them to manage their lives in ways that have profound effects. Life skills management, perhaps more than any other general outcome of higher education, is a function of the seamless learning experience of the student (see Kuh et al., 1991). That is, a broad combination of collegiate experiences contributes to this outcome.

A substantial number of reports suggest that the overall college experience has an especially powerful influence on life skills management. Identifying these outcomes is valuable from a variety of perspectives. Students need to be reminded that the college experience can have a profound effect on how they lead their lives. This information can be used as a rationale to encourage them to participate in as complete a college experience as possible. Parents, in contemplating ever-increasing tuition bills, can take comfort in the knowledge that their student is engaging in a life-changing experience. Other important stakeholders, such as legislators, taxpayers, and benefactors, may find the potency of the college experience in changing people's lives reassuring as they review their investment in and commitment to higher education.

This section examines reports of the effects that college has on some of these life management outcomes among graduates. The specific outcomes that are discussed in this section are economic benefits, health management, public social benefits, and parenting and family outcomes. Evidence of successful life skills management is most clearly seen in retrospect, in studying adults representing various educational backgrounds that identify aspects of their personal and family lives; this evidence is heavily used in this section. However, the college or university experience also can foreshadow the postcollege decisions that students make regarding how they will live their lives and create opportunities within their communities and for their families.

Economic Benefits

Graduating from college has a dramatic effect as to which individuals participate in the workforce and what they earn. We have pointed out elsewhere in this volume that college graduates tend to have higher earnings than those with less education. Higher income also appears to be related to a number of life skills management issues.

Labor Force Participation and Employment

Better-educated people are more likely to participate in the workforce (that is, receive pay for work) than those who are less well educated. Holders of a bachelor's degree in 1998 participated in the labor force at a higher rate than those with less education (National Center for Education Statistics, 2000a).

Women with more education are more likely to participate in the labor force than less educated women. Clery, Lee, and Knapp (1998) reported that from 1970 to 1990, participation of women with less than a high school education in the labor force rose only slightly—from just 43 percent to 46 percent—while labor force participation by women with four years of college increased from 61 percent to 81 percent.

People with more education also had a lower level of unemployment (National Center for Education Statistics, 2000a). The unemployment rate for all persons twenty-five or older by education in 1998 is illustrated in Table 9.1. Not only do individuals with a bachelor's degree earn more than those with less education (Table 9.2), but they also begin their careers earning more than those with less education and over time continue to earn more. These summary findings are depicted in Table 9.3.

Table 9.1. Unemployment Rate for Persons over Twenty-Five Years of Age by Education Level.

Education Level	Unemployment Rate (%)
All education levels	3.4
Less than high school graduate	7.1
High school graduate, no college	4.0
Some college, no degree	3.2
Associate's degree	2.5
Bachelor's degree or higher	1.8

Source: National Center for Education Statistics (2000a), p. 435.

Table 9.2. Average Earning of Year-Round, Full-Time Workers Age Twenty-Five and Older According to Gender.

	Males	Females
Total	*$41,118*	*$27,162*
Level of Education		
Less than ninth grade	$20,461	$13,349
Ninth to twelfth grade, no diploma	$24,377	$16,188
High school graduate or equivalent	$31,081	$21,383
Some college, no degree	$35,639	$24,787
Associate's degree	$38,944	$26,903
Bachelor's degree	$61,008	$39,271

Source: Clery, Lee, and Knapp (1998, p. 4).

Table 9.3. Mean Annual Earnings of First and Last Full Year of Employment After Attainment, Number of Years in the Labor Force, and Number of Months Employed Among 1980 High School Sophomores Working Consistently, by Highest Level of Education and Gender.

| | Annual Earnings | | | |
	First Full Year	Last Full Year	Years in Labor Force	Months Employed
High school diploma or GED, no postsecondary experience				
Total	$13,886	$23,523	10.0	117.0
Male	$14,106	$25,601	10.0	117.0
Female	$13,452	$19,333	10.0	116.9
High school diploma or GED, some postsecondary experience				
Total	$11,075	$23,873	10.0	117.0
Male	$11,357	$26,799	10.0	117.0
Female	$10,711	$20,106	10.0	116.9
Certificate or associate's degree				
Total	$20,854	$24,270	6.7	78.2
Male	$22,410	$26,969	6.5	76.0
Female	$19,446	$21,868	6.9	80.1
Bachelor's degree*				
Total	$24,733	$30,749	5.5	63.1
Male	$26,778	$34,104	5.4	62.0
Female	$22,602	$27,259	5.6	64.2

* Includes respondents who obtained a bachelor's degree by 1992.

Source: Clery, Lee, and Knapp (1998), p. 19.

Other Economic Benefits

A variety of economic benefits can be attributed to attaining at least a bachelor's degree. They include greater likelihood of family wealth and decreased likelihood of participation in a public assistance program.

Wealth. Individuals who possess more education typically have greater household wealth than those with less education do. One federal study (Eller, 1991) underscores this conclusion using a variety of measures of wealth. According to the study, householders with a college education (or more, as in a graduate or professional degree) are more likely to have higher net worth than individuals with less education. Moreover, a higher percentage of such individuals have interest-earning accounts in financial institutions; own stocks, bonds, and mutual fund shares; own a business or practice a profession; own motor vehicles and a home; have rental property; own U.S. Savings Bonds; or have an IRA or Keogh account. As a consequence of these holdings, such individuals have higher net worth than those with less education.

Participation in Public Assistance Programs. The opposite of higher earnings, which is linked to completing college, is receiving public assistance such as welfare or other subsidies to cover basic living expenses. As individuals complete more education, their likelihood of receiving such assistance is reduced. For example, in 1994, 14.3 percent of persons aged twenty-five to thirty-four with nine to eleven years of education received Aid to Families with Dependent Children (AFDC). For individuals with sixteen or more years of education, 0.4 percent of the same cohort received such assistance (National Center for Education Statistics, 1996).

Other reports have revealed similar information. According to the U.S. Bureau of the Census (1989), individuals with sixteen years of education or more are less likely to participate in cash assistance programs (AFDC, General Assistance, Supplemental Security Income) than those with less education. Those with more education who do participate in such programs do so for a shorter period of time, and the proportion of their income from these sources is less than for those with less education (especially people who have completed less than twelve years of schooling).

Worker Productivity. According to Decker, Rice, Moore, and Rollefson (1997), "the productivity of the U.S. work force is a primary determinant of the standard of living of the U.S. population" (p. vii). They asserted that education is a key factor in accelerating worker productivity, concluding: "Education appears to play an important role in worker productivity in all industrialized countries. The industrialized countries with the highest productivity levels tend to have highly educated work forces, and the convergence in productivity among these countries generally parallels that in education attainment" (p. x). What this finding means is that as workers are more highly educated, they are more productive and the general standard of living is increased.

Health Management

People who have a college education tend to lead a healthier life than those with less education. Whether this outcome is (1) a consequence of the greater degree of affluence that the college educated generally attain, (2) explained by self-selection to college, or (3) accounted for in some other way is unclear. But it is clear that college educated individuals simply are healthier. The U.S. Department of Health and Human Services (1998) concluded that "for almost all health indicators considered, each increase in either income or education increased the likelihood of being in good health" (n.p.). The department went on to report that individuals with lower income or education are less likely to have health insurance coverage or receive preventive care and are more likely to report unmet health care needs. This report was confirmed by the U.S. Bureau of the Census (1999), which showed that people with greater education are more likely to have health insurance than people with less education. Finally, the U.S. Department of Health and Human Services concluded that "adults with less education tend to die younger than more-educated adults" (1998, n.p.).

Collins and LeClere's work (1996) substantiated this conclusion: "The education of a responsible adult family member may influence several health characteristics in this report. Persons in families with higher levels of education are likely to be more aware of preventive health issues such as nutrition, smoking, alcohol, drugs and timely medical intervention. These differences in health status, hospitalization, and disability may be noted. In addition, higher educational levels are most likely to correlate with higher income levels and hence higher levels of health insurance and access to preventive medicine" (p. 5).

These authors found that people with a higher level of education were less likely to be limited in physical activity and were less likely to report that they were in fair or poor health. Additionally, more highly educated people reported fewer days with restricted activity per year, fewer days being disabled in bed, fewer lost work days per year, and fewer lost school days per year. Collins and LeClere (1996) concluded that "the trend of higher rates of negative health characteristics among those in families in which the education of the responsible adult family member is less than 12 years is evident for both sexes and for white persons and black persons" (p. 9).

Teenage Childbearing

Women with education tend to defer childbearing until after their teenage years. According to Pamuk and others (1998), "In every race and ethnic group analyzed, there was an inverse relationship between the respondent's mother's education level and the proportion of women who had a teenage birth. Women whose mothers had more education were less likely to become a teenage parent" (p. 58). A variety of negative outcomes are associated with children who are born to teenagers, including high infant mortality, abuse, neglect, and a poor rate of high school completion (Pamuk et al., 1998). An HHS report stated that "low birth weight and infant mortality rates were higher among the children of less-educated mothers than among children of more-educated mothers" (U.S. Department of Heath and Human Services, 1998, n.p.).

Prenatal Care

According to Pamuk and others (1998), mothers who were at least twenty years of age with a college education had a higher rate of prenatal care when pregnant than those with less education. White mothers with at least sixteen years of education were 1.4 times as likely to have prenatal care as white mothers with fewer than twelve years of education. The same was true for black mothers, who also were about 1.4 times as likely to receive prenatal care as black mothers with fewer than twelve years of education. In every racial and ethnic group, mothers with more education were more likely to receive prenatal care than those with less education. Prenatal care typically results in better care for mothers and their children.

Health Risks and Habits

As is the case with prenatal care, individuals with more education tend to suffer less from chronic health problems than those with less education. Pamuk and others (1998) concluded that the more educated are less likely to die from chronic disease, injury, or communicable disease than those with less education. Adults with less education are more likely to die at a younger age than adults with more education (U.S. Department of Health and Human Services, 1998).

For adults aged twenty-five to forty-four, both men and women with thirteen or more years of education are less likely to die as a consequence of homicide than those with less education (Pamuk et al., 1998). They are also less likely to die as a consequence of suicide, according to the same study.

Health habits also seem to be related to educational level. Among people twenty-five years of age or older, those with sixteen years of education are less likely to smoke than those with less education (Pamuk et al., 1998). They are also less likely to be chronic users of alcohol or to be overweight, compared to those with less education (Pamuk et al.).

Well-educated people also seem to possess more information about health care. For example, people with more education reported having more knowledge about AIDS than those with less education. According to Collins and LeClere (1996), "Persons in families with higher levels of education are likely to be more aware of preventive health issues such as nutrition, smoking, alcohol, drugs, and timely medical intervention" (p. 5).

Physical Activity

The educated also are likely to engage in physical activity. According to Stephens and Caspersen (1994), people with less education are more likely to be sedentary than those who are well educated. Leisure-time physical activity is consistently more common among people with more education than those with less education (Stephens & Caspersen). Astin (1993) found a positive correlation between physical activity, primarily through intramural sports, and students' physical health. He also indicated that students report positive psychological health when engaged in sports or exercise.

Public Social Benefits

Public social benefits "are benefits that accrue to groups of people, or to society broadly, that are not directly related to economic, fiscal, or labor market effects" (Institute for Higher Education Policy, 1998, p. 17). A variety of benefits accrue to society in general as a consequence of having educated citizens who make productive and generative life decisions.

Incarceration and Criminal Activity

As level of education increases, people are less likely to be engaged in criminal activity and, as a consequence, be incarcerated. College graduates are less likely than those with less education to be incarcerated in a state prison (Bureau of Justice Statistics, 1993).

Charitable Activity

Perhaps owing in part to their economic advantage, college graduates are more likely to make donations to a charitable cause than those with less education. College graduates devote a larger percentage of their income to cash contributions than those who are not graduates (Bureau of Labor Statistics, 1999).

Civic Activities

College graduates also are likely to be involved in civic activities. They are more likely to register to vote (Day & Gaither, 1998) and to vote in congressional and presidential elections than those with less education (National Center for Education Statistics, 2000c, indicator 22–1). They are also more likely to be members of an organization such as a community group or church, participate in community service activity, and attend public meetings than those with less education (National Center for Education Statistics, 1998).

Cultural Activities

Individuals with a college degree are likely to participate in various artistic activities, according to the National Endowment for the Arts (1999). The attendance rate for college graduates was greater than for those with less education at performances of jazz, classical music, opera, musical and nonmusical plays, and ballet. Visits to an art museum, historic park, or an arts and crafts fair were also more frequent. College graduates also are more likely to have read literature in the preceding twelve months. These individuals also spend more money on reading than individuals without a college degree (Bureau of Labor Statistics, 1999).

Parenting and the Family

One of the most powerful effects of the college experience is on parenting skills. This section highlights selected effects that college experience has on parenting skills.

Reading Activities in the Home

Parents who are college graduates are likely to be engaged with their children in a variety of activities that improve their readiness for schooling. A number of reports reinforced this conclusion. Children aged three to five whose parents had completed a bachelor's degree (or had more education than that) are more likely to have been read to in the past week or visited a library in the past month than children whose parents' highest education level was a high school diploma or less (National Center for Education Statistics, 1999). The value of this activity is quite important in child development. The U.S. Department of Education asserted that "family participation in reading activities provides valuable development experiences for young children. In addition to developing an interest in reading, children who are read to, told stories, and visit the library may start school better prepared to learn than other students. Engaging young children in reading activities at home also enables parents and other family members to become actively involved in their children's education at an early age" (National Center for Education Statistics, 1999, p. 74).

The number of children's books in the home varies by maternal education and family receipt of welfare, according to Denton and Germino-Hausken (2000). Mothers with less education and families reporting receipt of welfare were more likely to report having fewer books in the home (zero to twenty-five) than mothers with more education and families that reported receiving no welfare. This pattern is also found for the number of children's records, audiotapes, or CDs in the home (Denton & Germino-Hausken, 2000). In this case, then, the level of parents' education might be seen as an indirect effect, in that a college graduate tends to earn a higher income than someone who does not have a degree. As a consequence, the college-educated parent is able to provide educational opportunities for his or her children, such as buying books for them, which may not be possible for a parent with less income.

Family Activities

Families where the mother has completed a greater amount of education also are engaged more often in exercise, sports, and games than parents with less education. *America's Kindergartners* (Denton & Germino-Hausken, 2000) indicated that children who grew up with mothers who had a high school diploma, a GED, or less education played sports, exercised with family members, and played games with family members less often than children whose mothers had some college or had earned a bachelor's degree or higher.

In general, children of better-educated parents are more likely to engage in literacy-development skills than children whose parents are less well educated. The mother's level of education seems to be related to the activity; mothers with a college degree or a graduate or professional degree have children who participate in literacy activities more frequently than children whose mothers have a high school diploma or less education. The literacy activities were being read to; being told a story; being taught letters, words, or numbers; being taught songs or music; doing arts and crafts, visiting a library; recognizing all the letters; counting to twenty or higher; writing one's name; and reading or pretending to read storybooks (Nord, Lennon, & Liu, 1999).

As children grow, the influence of parental education manifests itself in other ways. At times, parental education may be seen as an indirect effect. Such may be the case in the rate of student participation in extracurricular activities in high school, where children of a family with higher socioeconomic status (SES) are more likely to participate in such activities than those from a family with lower socioeconomic status. In one study, the participation of low SES students in extracurricular activities was consistently lower than that of high SES students in each type of activity, with the exception of vocational or professional clubs. Low SES students were almost twice as likely to participate in these clubs, among them Future Farmers of America (FFA) or Future Teachers of America (FTA; National Center for Education Statistics, 1995).

This participation gap is a cause for concern, especially if extracurricular activities can be a means of integrating at-risk students more fully into the school community, thereby increasing their chances of school success (National Center for Education Statistics, 1995). The report concluded that "it is clear that participation [in school activities] and success are strongly associated as evidenced by participants' better attendance, higher levels of achievement, and aspirations to higher levels of education" (n.p.).

Well-educated parents are more likely to participate in the school activities of their children than parents with less education. Regardless of whether children live in a two-parent family or with a single parent, the proportion of children whose mothers or fathers are highly involved in their school increases in proportion to the parents' education level. Among children living in a two-parent family, 31 percent have a mother who is highly involved in their school if the mother has less than a high school education, while 70 percent have a highly involved mother if she has a graduate degree or professional school experience (National Center for Education Statistics, 1998). Similarly, 10 percent of children in a two-parent family whose father has less than a high school education have a highly involved father, while 41 percent whose father has graduate or professional school experiences have a highly involved father (National Center for Education Statistics, 1998).

One of the most powerful effects of a college education has to do with the educational achievement of children. Children of college graduates are less likely to drop out of high school (National Center for Education Statistics, 1999) than are children of high school graduates. In fact, the dropout rate for children of parents with less than a high school degree is approximately five times worse than for those whose parents have a college degree.

Students with parents who are college graduates are more likely to persist to a bachelor's degree than students whose parents do not hold a college degree (National Center for Education Statistics, 1998). According to Nunez and Cuccaro-Alamin (1998), "first-generation students persisted in postsecondary education . . . at lower rates than their non-first-generation counterparts" (p. iii). Some would argue that student persistence may be a function of family income. This may be true, but family income also is directly related to family educational level. Whether the level of parental education is a direct or indirect effect, the fact remains that the children of college graduates are more likely to continue their education to a bachelor's degree or beyond than the children of parents who do not have a college degree.

Suggestions for Practice

The total educational experience, as suggested in this chapter, yields considerable benefits for those who have graduated from college. These include, on average, better financial circumstances, better physical health, a variety of public social benefits, and a more favorable environment for their children. In proposing suggestions for practice, we feel integration of the student experience is a logical place to begin the discussion. This section includes suggestions for faculty and for student affairs practitioners.

Suggestions for Faculty

A major role of faculty is to plan and deliver an institution's curriculum (Gaff, 1997). As a consequence, faculty have a powerful influence over what students learn in college. They can develop a curriculum that includes courses that speak specifically to the outcomes identified in this chapter (such as promotion of personal health, financial management, family management, and so on) by developing or requiring courses that specifically address these general topical areas. Elective courses for students including these topics and others can enhance a student's educational experience by speaking to many of the life management skills the person needs to be a self-sufficient, contributing member of society.

Faculty are also encouraged to incorporate practical experiences that accelerate the student's development of skills in these areas through courses already offered. The curriculum may not have room for students to take additional courses in management of self and family, but courses in the general educational curriculum or core requirements can easily include practical experience that accelerates student development in many of these areas. For example, a course in the social sciences could include steps that individuals might take to manage their families in the future; a course in the sciences could offer examples related to diet and exercise. Assignments related to budgeting, investing, and projecting income and expenses are appropriate in a business class. As service learning is integrated into additional courses, the practical application of many of these concepts in field experience is possible. Service learning also increases a student's awareness of and focus on public needs and priorities that are advanced largely by ongoing investment of the individual's time and energy.

Suggestions for Student Affairs Administrators

Opportunities abound for programming in the various areas discussed in this chapter. For example, in the residential setting, students can be prepared to undertake a number of life management skills: managing households, dietary planning, financial management, and so on. As an illustration, the University of California, Davis, has developed an excellent program designed to help students with the transition from residence hall living to off-campus living (Kuh et al., 1991). Typically, students make this transition between their freshman and sophomore years at Davis, but such a program could be offered to students at any time prior to their decision to live off campus.

Developing students' health management skills could result from interesting partnerships formed among food services, health services, and campus recreation. An arrangement could be developed where food service, student health service, and campus recreation each contribute information about health care management, exercise, and proper diet. Specific initiatives such as smoking cessation programs and alcohol and drug education (particularly with respect to social norming) can be undertaken jointly by units such as the student health service, counseling center, recreation, and wellness services. Parental support groups and cooperative child care centers should be available for the student who is already a parent and is concerned with enrichment for his or her child and further development of parenting skills. Development of parenting skills can be encouraged in many ways: a formal program, pamphlets and flyers, information placed on a bulletin board, and so on.

Asset and debt management are concerns that can also be addressed by the student affairs practitioner. Many college students incur debt as a consequence of attendance (National Center for Education Statistics, 2000b), but Solomon (cited by Geske & Cohn, 1998) asserted that the college-educated are more sophisticated or efficient investors. Financial aid offices increasingly are offering programs of advice and counsel to students on managing their college debt. A concomitant area worthy of discussion is management of credit cards and credit card debt. Partnerships can be formed for such activities, involving the financial aid office, residence halls, student activities, and perhaps other offices such as those of the campus legal counsel and controller. Formal programs and individual counseling are logical interventions to help students deal with these issues. In addition, specific training for student organization officers in handling the funds of their group is an important initiative (Dunkel & Schuh, 1998). Understanding stewardship, both personal as well as for the larger good, is an important aspect of the college experience. Consequently, training in this area is essential. Some college graduates will earn their living by managing money in a professional sense; many others will also serve as the treasurer of an organization where money management skills are important.

Finally, and perhaps most important, development of life management skills is an outcome of college that can be pointed out to students regularly. From orientation programs to interaction with academic advisers and with student affairs staff, students can be reminded that an important part of their college education is preparing themselves for a variety of life activities. Making specific experiences available for students to help them sharpen the skills identified in this chapter sustains the advantages of a college education. College-related experience has enriched the lives of college graduates for decades with respect to enhancing skills needed to manage personal matters and assets; targeted inputs further enrich these robust experiences.

References

Astin, A. W. (1993). *What matters in college?* San Francisco: Jossey-Bass.

Bee, H. L. (1996). *Journey of adulthood* (3rd ed.). Englewood Cliffs, NJ: Prentice Hall.

Bosworth, S. W. (1993). What does society need from higher education? (Contributed paper). In *An American imperative: Higher expectations for higher education* (pp. 54–57). Racine, WI: Johnson Foundation.

Bowen, H. R. (1997). *Investment in learning: The individual and social value of American higher education.* Baltimore, MD: Johns Hopkins University Press.

Bureau of Justice Statistics. (1993). *Survey of state prison inmates, 1991* (report no. NCJ 136949). Washington, DC: U.S. Department of Justice.

Bureau of Labor Statistics. (1999). *Consumer expenditure survey, 1999.* Washington, DC: Author.

Chickering, A. W., & Reisser, L. (1993). *Education and identity* (2nd ed.). San Francisco: Jossey-Bass.

Clery, S. B., Lee, J. B., & Knapp, L. G. (1998). *Gender differences in earnings among young adults entering the labor market* (report no. NCES 98–086). Washington, DC: U.S. Department of Education.

Collins, J. G., & LeClere, F. B. (1996). *Health and selected socioeconomic characteristics of the family: United States, 1988–90* (series 10, no. 195). Washington, DC: Centers for Disease Control, National Center for Health Statistics.

Day, J. C., & Gaither, A. I. (1998). *Voting and registration in the election of November 1998* (Current population reports P20-523RV). Washington, DC: U.S. Department of Commerce.

Decker, P. T., Rice, J. K., Moore, M. T., & Rollefson, M. R. (1997). *Education and the economy: An indicators report* (report no. NCES 97-269). Washington, DC: U.S. Department of Education.

Denton, K., & Germino-Hausken, E. (2000). *America's kindergartners* (report no. NCES 2000–070). Washington, DC: U.S. Department of Education, National Center for Education Statistics.

Dunkel, N. W., & Schuh, J. H. (1998). *Advising student groups and organizations.* San Francisco: Jossey-Bass.

Elder, G. H., Jr. (1995). The life course paradigm: Social change and individual development. In P. Moen, G. H. Elder, Jr., & K. Lüscher (Eds.), *Examining lives in context: Perspectives on the ecology of human development* (pp. 101–139). Washington, DC: American Psychological Association.

Eller, T. J. (1991). *Household wealth and asset ownership: 1991* (Current Population Reports, Household Economic Studies, no. P70–34). Washington, DC: U.S. Department of Commerce.

Erikson, E. H. (1959). Identity and the life cycle. *Psychological Issues, 1,* 1–17.

Erikson, E. H. (1968). *Identity: Youth and crisis.* New York: Norton.

Gaff, J. G. (1997). Tensions between tradition and innovation. In J. G. Gaff, J. L. Ratcliff, & Associates, *Handbook of the undergraduate curriculum* (pp. 608–627). San Francisco: Jossey-Bass.

Geske, T. G., & Cohn, E. (1998). Why is a high school diploma no longer enough? In R. Fossey & M. Bateman (Eds.), *Condemning students to debt: College loans and public policy* (pp. 19–36). New York: Teacher's College Press.

Hearn, J. C. (1998). The growing loan orientation in federal financial policy. In R. Fossey & M. Bateman (Eds.), *Condemning students to debt* (pp. 47–75). New York: Teachers College Press.

Institute for Higher Education Policy. (1998). *Reaping the benefits: Defining the public and private value of going to college.* Washington, DC: Author.

Kuh, G. D., Schuh, J. H., Whitt, E. J. & Associates (1991). *Involving colleges.* San Francisco: Jossey-Bass.

National Center for Education Statistics. (1995). *Extracurricular participation and student engagement* (report no. NCES 95–741). Washington, DC: U.S. Department of Education.

National Center for Education Statistics. (1996). Indicator 36: Welfare participation, by educational attainment. In *The condition of education, 1996.* Washington, DC: U.S. Department of Education.

National Center for Education Statistics. (1998). *Factors associated with fathers' and mothers' involvement in their children's schools* (report no. NCES 98–122). Washington, DC: U.S. Department of Education.

National Center for Education Statistics. (1999). *The condition of education 1999* (report no. NCES 1999–022). Washington, DC: U.S. Department of Education.

National Center for Education Statistics. (2000a). *Digest of education statistics 1999* (report no. NCES 2000–031). Washington, DC: U.S. Department of Education.

National Center for Education Statistics (2000b). *Low-income students: Who they are and how they pay for their education* (report no. 2000–169). Washington, DC: U.S. Department of Education, National Center for Education Statistics.

National Center for Education Statistics. (2000c). *The condition of education* (report no. 2000-062). Washington, DC: U.S. Department of Education.

National Endowment for the Arts. (1999). *Demographic characteristics of arts attendance: 1997* (research note no. 71). Washington, DC: National Endowment for the Arts, Research Division.

Nord, C. W., Lennon, J., & Liu, B. (1999). *Home literacy activities and signs of children's emerging literacy, 1993 and 1999* (report no. NCES 2000–026). Washington, DC: U.S. Department of Education, National Center for Education Statistics.

Nunez, A. M., & Cuccaro-Alamin, S. (1998). *First-generation students: Undergraduates whose parents never enrolled in postsecondary education* (report no. NCES 98–082). Washington, DC: U.S. Department of Education, National Center for Education Statistics.

Pamuk, E., Makuc, D., Heck, K., Reuben, C., & Lochner, K. (1998). *Socioeconomic status and health chartbook. Health, United States, 1998.* Hyattsville, MD: U.S. Department of Health and Human Services, National Center for Health Statistics.

Persky, H. R., Sandene, B. A., & Askew, J. M. (1998). *The NAEP 1997 arts report card: Eighth-grade findings for the National Assessment of Educational Progress* (report no. NCES 1999–486). Washington, DC: U.S. Department of Education, National Center for Education Statistics.

Perun, P. J., & Bielby, D. D. (1980). Structure and dynamics on the individual life course. In K. W. Back (Ed.), *Life course: Integrative theories and exemplary populations* (pp. 97–119). Boulder, CO: Westview.

Points of view. (1989). Washington, DC: National Association of Student Personnel Administrators.

Schlossberg, N. K., Waters, E. B., & Goodman, J. (1995). *Counseling adults in transition* (2nd ed.). New York: Springer.

Stephens, T., & Caspersen, C. J. (1994). The demography of physical activity. In C. Bickered, R. J. Shepherd, & T. Stephens (Eds.), *Physical activity, fitness and health: International proceedings and consensus statement* (pp. 204–213). Champaign, IL: Human Kinetics.

The student in higher education: Report of the Committee on the Student in Higher Education. (1968). New Haven, CT: Hazen Foundation.

U.S. Bureau of the Census. (1989). *Characteristics of persons receiving benefits from major assistance programs* (Current Population Reports, series P-70, no. 14). Washington, DC: U.S. Department of Commerce.

U.S. Bureau of the Census. (1993). *Education: The ticket to higher earnings* (report no. SB/93–7). Washington, DC: U.S. Department of Commerce.

U.S. Bureau of the Census. (1999). *Health insurance coverage: 1998. Current Population Survey, March 1999.* Washington, DC: Author.

U.S. Department of Health and Human Services. (1998, July 30). *HHS News: Health in America tied to income and education.* Washington, DC: Author.

Part Three

Where We Go from Here

In the final part of this book (Chapters Ten and Eleven), we offer recommendations for practice and for further research. Our recommendations give the practitioner ideas and suggestions about steps that might be taken to advance campus-based work and topics for further inquiry.

In Chapter Ten, Recommendations for Practice, our thinking is informed by the work of Karl Weick (1984) and Ernest Pascarella and Patrick Terenzini (1991). In each case, those authors recommend that numerous initiatives designed to change and improve the quality of campus life be undertaken, rather than an occasional large-scale, complex program. Building on their ideas, we suggest that new initiatives be designed to match the needs of students who are enrolled in a specific college or university; that special attention be paid to the transition process that students undergo as they begin their career at a new college or university; and that learning opportunities be conceived as an integrated, rather than random, student educational experience.

We conclude this book with a chapter of recommendations for future research. We encourage institutions to engage in careful self-assessment, using questions raised by the Wingspread Report (Wingspread Group on Higher Education, 1993) as a place to begin the conversation. We also recommend that institutional agents identify factors and conditions on their campus that contribute to a high-quality out-of-class learning experience for the student. We acknowledge the work of Kuh, Douglas, Lund, and

Ramin-Gyurnek (1994) and recommend that an institution examine how it organizes and expends resources to help students achieve their goals and study how student learning can best be linked to institutional goals. We also suggest that the institution examine the impact of specific experiences on student learning and growth.

References

Kuh, G. D., Douglas, K. B., Lund, J. P., & Ramin-Gyurnek, J. (1994). *Student learning outside the classroom: Transcending artificial boundaries.* ASHE-ERIC report no. 8. Washington, DC: George Washington University, School of Education and Human Development.

Pascarella, E. T., & Terenzini, P. T. (1991). *How college affects students.* San Francisco: Jossey-Bass.

Weick, K. E. (1984). Small wins: Redefining the scale of social problems. *American Psychologist, 39,* 40–49.

Wingspread Group on Higher Education. (1993). *An American imperative: Higher expectations for higher education.* Racine, WI: Johnson Foundation.

Chapter Ten

Recommendations for Practice

In this chapter, we offer recommendations for the student affairs practitioner interested in systematically enriching the undergraduate educational experience. In addition, we discuss recommendations for students, since they play a major role in choosing learning experiences and maximizing their progress toward selected outcomes. In many cases, parents can also extend supportive guidance to students by encouraging their active engagement in on-campus and related learning experiences. We draw upon relevant philosophical and theoretical elements as well as research findings (presented in earlier chapters) in developing these recommendations.

Two Approaches to Developing New Program Initiatives

The thinking of Weick (1984) and Pascarella and Terenzini (1991) is particularly helpful in framing development of new initiatives. Weick asserted that in going about social change, we find large-scale problems difficult to manage because they appear to be overwhelming. He suggested that a more viable approach is along the lines of small wins. Weick defined a small win as "a concrete, complete, implemented outcome of moderate importance. By itself, one small win may seem unimportant. A series of small wins at small but significant tasks, however, reveals a pattern that may attract allies, deter opponents, and lower resistance to subsequent proposals" (p. 43).

Thinking about small wins in program development, an institution may have as an overall goal the desire to change the student culture to one in which academic achievement is more highly valued, but it also knows that this could be a major undertaking. Student culture could be changed, using the approach of small wins, by initiating a number of small programs. For example, organizing a number of honorary societies and recognition ceremonies for students whose achievement is noteworthy could be a step toward placing greater emphasis on academic achievement. Each organization or ceremony could be conceived of as a small win; taken together, they have an effect on changing the culture of the institution by reinforcing the idea that academic achievement is valued.

Pascarella and Terenzini (1991) presented a similar approach toward achieving institutional goals. They indicated that rather than have a large, campuswide program designed to achieve a single institutional goal, the goal should be pursued through a variety of institutional activities. They observed that "rather than seeking single large levers to pull in order to promote change on a large scale, it may well be more effective to pull more levers more often" (p. 655). In the case of trying to change a student culture so that academic achievement is more widely appreciated and valued, instead of holding a single large recognition ceremony that would recognize students who have experienced academic success, a number of smaller ceremonies, perhaps organized by department or college, might be more effective. Using the concepts of Weick (1984) and Pascarella and Terenzini (1991), then, can be an excellent way of conceiving how to bring about institutional change.

Institutional Character and Institutional Fit

Desired student outcomes outlined in previous chapters may be prioritized differently according to the institution; structured learning opportunities can vary as well (for example, a disproportionate orientation toward workforce preparation as opposed to a broad-based education for students). This variety depends on the type of institution, institutional history and legacy, and contemporary determination of the institution's strengths or niche. It is critical for an institution to communicate information such as the student-level outcomes emphasized and the kinds of learning opportunity employed. It is equally important for students to seek a match with the college or university that they will attend.

Although some students base an enrollment decision largely on the perception of an intuitive match with a college or university, particularly upon a campus visit, the decision-making process can be supplemented by a variety of informational sources. Academically well-prepared students may experience a disorienting barrage of mailings during their high school years; less well-prepared students do not receive these targeted mailings. For all students, exploring institutional Websites uncovers descriptive and potentially comparative information. Institutional mission and vision statements (as well as corresponding statements from internal units) can impart a sense of the institutional priorities and selected learning foci. Using photos, maps, and animation, many Websites also offer a virtual tour of the campus, which is particularly valuable for a student for whom a campus visit is not feasible. This virtual information searching is becoming widely available to students as more schools and public libraries offer free Web access.

For many students, cost and proximity are the overriding factors in choosing a college or university. However, understanding the institution and its desired outcomes for students is no less important. Learning more about a targeted college or university is critical to the extent that students may then compare the desired student outcomes and learning opportunities with their own priorities for education. Additionally, students may be more likely to undertake the educational and developmental challenges offered if they experience a sense of support and shared expectations that come with a favorable student-institutional fit. If they are instead uncomfortable or do not perceive a match between their needs and the institution's offerings, their meaningful involvement in educational processes may be compromised.

Many students also have an opportunity to experience a college or university campus early on, since almost all sponsor exhibits, lectures, and entertainment open to the public. High school students can also explore dual-enrollment options that may be available, allowing them to take one or more college-level courses in addition to (or instead of) high school courses. Public institutions and some private colleges also offer various programs geared to adult students such as part-time auditing of a course, an experience that can also be used to explore one's potential fit with the campus. Institutional representatives should increase their awareness of these early and informal explorations. A follow-up offer of information and assistance to a student can serve as a form of validation of this early attempt at determining priorities and potential fit.

Integrated Learning Opportunities

Collaboration by units across campus and into the surrounding community can be a rich and mutually reinforcing educational experience for students that can approximate the "seamless" learning environment described by Kuh (1996). As students take courses in which they learn about and analyze aspects of citizenship (for instance, political science), social organizations (sociology), and natural resource stewardship (ecology), a campus can also link opportunities for student engagement and integrated application of course material. In this case, it may include participating in a coalition to protect the quality of a local watershed, or at the least attending a local meeting at which the relevant issues are debated, or working to extend the potential reach of a community-supported agriculture program. Ideally, these engagements would be supplemented with structured reflection and discussion components so the experience becomes a basis for further learning and so the students have an opportunity to benefit vicariously from each other's learning. Faculty members may be particularly well placed to engage in these reflections with students, since these applied and integrated learning experiences offer the faculty member a chance to revisit and reinforce key themes in the relevant discipline with students. Student reflections upon a learning experience are also valuable for the faculty member to assess student learning and application of the targeted material.

Traditional opportunities for student engagement and leadership have included participation in a student self-governance body or other campus-based organization. Yet citizenship, for example, encompasses much more than fulfilling the formal responsibility associated with an elected or appointed position, which suggests that integrated learning opportunities should extend into the surrounding community in which the campus is located. The campuses, or a designated cooperative unit, can engage the local community in a mutually beneficial way to give students a meaningful learning opportunity and give local entities a valuable source of volunteer personnel.

Such outreach can benefit students developmentally as well. Students from an underrepresented background, and particularly younger ones, often do not find cultural or social familiarity on a predominantly white campus and instead may experience isolation (or hypervisibility). By forming academically sanctioned links for involvement within the local community, agency, or program, the consequent learning opportunity promotes affiliation and validation for students. The campus-community connection is a way to extend the campus into the community rather than causing students to depart the campus to pursue desired belonging and affirmation.

With respect to campus-community connection, perhaps the community college, with its predominance of adult students, is best positioned to capitalize on the learning potential of the prior and continuing community-based engagement of students. Community college students are often involved in local governance, neighborhood coalitions, and affiliative groups, as well as being people with long-standing ties and commitment to the community. Building on the learning potential of such community engagement on the part of the community college student represents an educational experience as well as real-life empowerment and engagement that extend beyond one's enrollment at the college.

Additionally, career preparation needs are also served by integrated learning experiences. Particularly when a reflection component is included, students learn more about themselves, their skills and values, and potential career interests. Traditional cooperative work experience and academically linked internship with an employing organization certainly promotes acquisition of skills and dispositions. The institution must be sensitive, however, to the situation of able students who cannot financially afford to devote a semester to a "plum" internship, especially one that requires temporary relocation.

Student Initiatives and Commitment

For many students, maximizing their learning opportunities may include creating new and somewhat unorthodox opportunities; the college or university should be prepared to recognize the educational potential in such creations, acknowledge the student's initiative, and work to support student learning in this situation, too. Educationally purposeful student involvement encompasses more than having a student participate in a sanctioned event or hold a formal campus leadership role. Astin (1984) outlined the developmental benefits of student involvement; valuable aspects of this involvement may include a nontraditional, self-initiated leadership role. For example, an educator can reflect with student leaders involved in campus dissent on what was learned, as in the course of articulating a principled position and supporting rationale, or motivating other students and organizing participation, or networking with relevant information sources or external advocacy sources.

Learning can also result when dissenting students engage in discussion with college or university administrators as they present their concerns; dissenting student leaders are often called to deal with the potential or actual consequences of their dissent. In this situation, faculty members and key administrators who can view the student's engagement as an opportunity for learning and not primarily as an embarrassment or attention-seeking behavior are perhaps best positioned to help the student reflect on the experience during dissenting activity as well as the aftermath. With reflection, dissent experience can result in a student's strong sense of agency and purpose as well as recognition of accomplishment in articulating and voicing key concerns and interacting with senior representatives of a campus.

To maximize the likelihood of achieving the student-level outcomes discussed in earlier chapters, educators (including student affairs professionals at any level) should identify the outcomes desired for students at their particular campus, and then identify what kind of course, program, or educational opportunity promotes those outcomes. Once such an informal or formal "audit" of existing elements or building blocks has been performed, the educator can think creatively about how to combine or arrange the blocks so that integrated and more comprehensive learning opportunities result. The educator may decide to create or revise other blocks in this process as well, but he or she can only plan so much.

As illustrated in the examples of student involvement, some learning experiences may follow from current issues or work being conducted on the campus or in the community, while others may well be student-initiated and run. In the latter case, the student affairs professional or faculty member can be quick to comprehend a learning opportunity and build upon existing teacher-student or adviser-student relationships to offer the opportunity for reflective conversation with students. An educator seeking to design and incorporate these integrated learning experiences draws together existing elements on the campus and frames one version or one type of experience. Yet he or she should also be open to following the student's ideas for a learning experience and setting—one that matters and provides real enrichment for the particular student. In this way, the educator continues to heed Parker's advice (1977) to "read" and "flex," offering specific opportunities as a starting point yet realizing that learning can be accomplished in multiple settings and thus is not necessarily tied to preformed experience that may not connect with the learner.

Of course, undergraduate learning outcomes should also be assessed to ascertain whether and how desired outcomes have been achieved. Models for assessment have proliferated in recent years, so a variety of approaches using numerous assessment methods have become available to educators for review and guidance (see Upcraft & Schuh, 1996; and Schuh & Upcraft, 2001, for comprehensive sources). Although a number of programs may show hypothetical promise for realizing key outcomes for students, scrutinizing the program and examining relevant data can establish the occurrence of learning and lead to subsequent improvement of learning experiences.

References

Astin, A. W. (1984). Student involvement: A developmental theory for higher education. *Journal of College Student Personnel, 25,* 297–308.

Kuh, G. D. (1996). Guiding principles for creating seamless learning environments for undergraduates. *Journal of College Student Development, 37,* 135–148.

Parker, C. A. (1977). On modeling reality. *Journal of College Student Personnel, 18,* 419–425.

Pascarella, E. T., & Terenzini, P. T. (1991). *How college affects students.* San Francisco: Jossey-Bass.

Schuh, J. H., & Upcraft, M. L. (2001). *Assessment practice in student affairs: An applications manual.* San Francisco: Jossey-Bass.

Upcraft, M. L., & Schuh, J. H. (1996). *Assessment in student affairs: A guide for practitioners.* San Francisco: Jossey-Bass.

Weick, K. E. (1984). Small wins: Redefining the scale of social problems. *American Psychologist, 39,* 40–49.

Chapter Eleven

Recommendations for Further Research

In this book, we have endeavored to examine important student-level outcomes from college, along with their respective foundations in student development literature and programmatic practices that have been shown to yield progress toward achieving the outcomes. This integrative exploration leads to the conclusion that higher education in general makes efforts to pursue these outcomes and enjoys a measure of success in using targeted programmatic efforts. In the preceding chapter, we presented a list of recommendations for practice. Conducting systematic, careful assessment of this kind of intervention is an essential activity in generating the kind of hard data that contemporary society demands of an institution in demonstrating effectiveness.

In this chapter, we offer suggestions for the institution that is examining its learning environments and seeking to build upon integrated learning that can happen in various settings within a college education. Because institutions function differently by type, and with differing organizational and leadership milieus (see, for instance, Birnbaum, 1990), not all of the suggestions are likely to be effective at all institutions. You are encouraged to review and adapt the suggestions that follow as needed, and also to design additional research interventions that enable extended conversation and focused work to proceed at your campus.

Self-Assessment

One critical step is for a college or university to engage in self-assessment activity, preferably formal activity. It is most important that the activity offer opportunities for the campus community to discuss core values and key educational goals for its students. The Wingspread Report (Wingspread Group on Higher Education, 1993), for example, published an institutional self-assessment checklist designed to help a college or university think about itself in alternative ways. Several of the recommendations included in the checklist represent promising areas for further inquiry and further conversation at college or university sites. For example, these items excerpted or paraphrased from the report can guide a conversation beginning with examining core values, moving to student learning, and finally exploring lifelong learning:

Taking Values Seriously (p. 29)

- How does an institution's core curriculum of required courses respond to the needs of our students for a rigorous liberal education, enabling them to "live rightly and well in a free society?" Where does it fall short?
- In what ways does our institution model the values and skills expected in our community? Where and how does it fall short?
- How do our institutions and their programs promote development of shared values, especially civic virtues?

Putting Student Learning First (p. 30)

- How recently has the institution reviewed its programs to assure that they match the institution's mission and the needs and goals of the students who are admitted?
- In what ways could institutions do a better job of helping students to attain higher levels of both knowledge and skills?
- How do institutions encourage and assist students to develop the basic values required for learning?

Creating a Nation of Learners (p. 31)

- How are programs organized to develop and support a capacity for student lifelong learning?
- How often are employers—and graduates—surveyed to determine how and under what circumstances graduates succeed or fall short?

This set of questions could easily form the core of a number of institutional inquiries about the effectiveness of student experiences, academic and otherwise, that can be framed by the institutional outcomes desired for the student. Certainly, these are not the only questions an institution can ask of itself and its stakeholders, but they identify serious issues worthy of further investigation.

Assessing Goal Achievement

Kuh, Douglas, Lund, and Ramin-Gyurnek (1994) mapped an ambitious agenda of questions that, with modification, are also applicable to the content of this volume. We adopt three of their questions and offer some suggestions in turn. The first question asks, How do institutional factors and conditions affect achievement of the goals of higher education identified in this volume? A potential framework for researchers and campus representatives addressing themselves to this question could be the work of Kuh, Schuh, Whitt, and Associates (1991), who identified institutional factors and conditions that made for high-quality out-of-class student learning and development. Using a similar methodological approach, investigators could examine the institutional factors and conditions that seem to create an environment whereby students are more likely to meet the goals that have been established for their educational experience. We assume it is rare for any student to actually achieve all the goals identified, but we suspect that some institutions are more successful than others. Using an institution as the unit of analysis, why is this the case? Are students at some institutions more likely to approach goal achievement than at others, and if so, why? What can other institutions learn from these leading institutions?

Second, as Kuh, Douglas, Lund, and Ramin-Gyurnek (1994) inquired, how can an institution organize and expend its resources to help students achieve their goals? The financial challenges faced by institutions of higher education have been reported frequently in the literature (see Clotfelter, 1996; Stringer, Cunningham, Merisotis, Wellman, & O'Brien, 1999), yet each institution spends all that it raises (Bowen, 1996). Are there ways to target these resource allocations so that a more meaningful experience for the student is disproportionately supported? Can institutional expenditures be targeted so as to have the greatest impact on learning and create a rich learning environment? Since student learning is connected to virtually every aspect of a campus and its many cost centers, these questions are a potentially fruitful avenue of inquiry for researchers and for examination by campus financial officers and other administrators.

Finally, Kuh, Douglas, Lund, and Ramin-Gyurnek (1994) asked, How can student learning best be linked to institutional goals? Is this linkage most often assumed to be with formal curricula, with arrays of out-of-class experience, or both? In terms of specifying linkage, are there organizing principles that can be used to inform strategies to achieve these goals? Through a planning process, there are specific opportunities and steps that an institution can take to knit aspects of student learning more deeply into institutional priorities and goals. We think institutions are well served in engaging local conversation and conducting local studies to identify promising strategies that weave student learning and its pursuit into the fabric of the institution.

Determining Impact at the Institutional Level

Conversation and inquiry at the local institutional level can also be guided by attention to several principles related to student learning that have been highlighted in the preceding chapters. We know from the studies cited in this volume that certain student experiences seem to have great potency in helping the student learn and grow along specified dimensions related to broad goals of higher education. Among these experiences are:

- Participation in a learning community
- Service-learning experience
- Internship
- Student-faculty interaction framed by academic experiences such as discussing coursework outside of class
- Working on campus in an endeavor related to a student's academic area of interest

Much (although not all) of the research on these programs and opportunities has involved aggregate samples of students representing a range of institutions (see, for example, Astin, 1993; Astin & Sax, 1998), or meta-analyses of many previous studies (such as Pascarella & Terenzini, 1991; or Pascarella, Terenzini, & Blimling, 1994). These contributions to the literature have been crafted beautifully and are important in advancing the knowledge base on these important topics. But we suggest that this work be taken in two additional directions. First, we think that more institutions ought to be investigating their local situation to determine whether the potency of these student experiences mirrors the large-scale studies reported in the literature. Second, if the local outcomes are different, how so?

For example, does having a specific type of internship (such as one with a local school district) result in the student becoming more skilled as a potential employee? Does participation in service learning (perhaps participating in a local program designed to help youngsters from a low socioeconomic background learn how to read) contribute disproportionately to development of civic values? These questions and others appear to have great potential for local inquiry to determine the extent to which the experiences of students at a specific college mirror the extant literature on student learning and growth.

We also know that certain relationships have a substantial influence on a student's growth. Among these are relationships with their peers and with faculty (Astin, 1993). As already mentioned, we think that local inquiries are useful to determine if the experiences of students on a given campus are similar to the national data, and what sort of factors contribute to student learning and goal achievement. We suspect that such might be the case, but without empirical evidence our conclusions are not much more than an informed hunch. It would be useful for investigators to determine why these relationships are so powerful; in localized studies these factors and influences can be explored in depth.

Studies Examining Differential Impact

Another avenue of inquiry might involve a cross-disciplinary focus. We have identified a number of general outcomes of the higher education experience for students. What we have not identified, however, is the extent to which these outcomes hold true across all disciplines. For example, are students who participate in a traditional educational experience (such as a major in the liberal arts or humanities) likely to demonstrate outcomes similar to those of people majoring in a professional program (nursing, education, engineering)? If so, why are some courses of study more potent than others? If not, are these outcomes so universal that a student's course of study does not have an influence on these outcomes?

Astin (1993) produced some results along these lines using a large sample of students across institutions. An individual institution may benefit from exploring how a specific major, program, or educational experience affects students so that if some experiences or majors are found to be more successful than others, interventions can be designed for students who would not normally have such an experience.

Finally, students themselves, when disaggregated by demographic characteristics, may be affected differently by certain experiences. We know from the experiences cited (such as interaction with faculty outside the classroom) that some conditions are especially influential in affecting student growth. The individual institution can investigate the potency of certain experiences for subgroups of students, using such demographic factors as ethnicity, gender, and age to frame the study. Are men more affected than women by participation in service learning? If so, does the difference in effect apply more to older or younger men? Are students of color more influenced by participation in a learning community than students of the majority culture, and if so, why? Does campus work (many of the opportunities for which are premised on a set of student financial need characteristics) affect some subsets of students differently than others? These questions and others have great potential for an institution that is interested in designing and implementing the most powerful learning experiences possible for its students.

Conclusion

In the final analysis, we have endeavored to make the case that institutional representatives are well positioned to design and evaluate educational experiences for students when they know as much as possible about the home institution, its students, the educational program, and its overriding educational goals. We fear that too many institutions have seen this kind of introspection as a peripheral activity rather than a central one. Our view is the opposite. We maintain that a college or university must understand fully how the educational experiences it offers influence students. Until it does so, the institution is unable to refine and develop educational opportunities so that the impact of the total collegiate experience is the best possible for students along the dimensions we have identified.

References

Astin, A. W. (1993). *What matters in college? Four critical years revisited.* San Francisco: Jossey-Bass.

Astin, A. W., & Sax, L. J. (1998). How undergraduates are affected by service participation. *Journal of College Student Development, 39,* 251–263.

Birnbaum, R. (1990). *How colleges work: The cybernetics of academic organization and leadership.* San Francisco: Jossey-Bass.

Bowen, H. R. (1996). What determines the costs of higher education? In D. W. Breneman, L. L. Leslie, & R. E. Anderson (Eds.), *ASHE reader on finance in higher education* (pp. 113–127). Needham Heights, MA: Simon & Schuster.

Clotfelter, C. T. (1996). *Buying the best: Cost escalation in elite higher education.* Princeton, NJ: Princeton University Press.

Kuh, G. D., Douglas, K. B., Lund, J. P., & Ramin-Gyurnek, J. (1994). *Student learning outside the classroom: Transcending artificial boundaries* (ASHE-ERIC report no. 8). Washington, DC: George Washington University, School of Education and Human Development.

Kuh, G. D., Schuh, J. H., Whitt, E. J., & Associates. (1991). *Involving colleges.* San Francisco: Jossey-Bass.

Pascarella, E. T., & Terenzini, P. T. (1991). *How college affects students.* San Francisco: Jossey-Bass.

Pascarella, E. T., Terenzini, P. T., & Blimling, G. S. (1994). The impact of residential life on students. In C. C. Schroeder, P. Mable, & Associates, *Realizing the educational potential of residence halls* (pp. 22–52). San Francisco: Jossey-Bass.

Stringer, W. L., Cunningham, A. F., Merisotis, J. P., Wellman, J. V., & O'Brien, C. T. (1999). *Cost, price and public policy: Peering into the higher education black box.* Indianapolis, IN: USA Group Foundation.

Wingspread Group on Higher Education. (1993). *An American imperative: Higher expectations for higher education.* Racine, WI: Johnson Foundation.

Name Index

Subject Index

A

Absolute knowing: and career development of, 271; in epistemological theory, 61

Academic—student affairs collaboration, 114, 116–120, 121–126, 127, 171, 220

Access: for disabled students, 89, 90; for diverse and underrepresented populations, 11–25

Accessibility, of campus environment, 89, 90

Adult development theory, 32, 38–44; asynchrony concept in, 299; and career development, 53; integrated model in, 43–44; life course perspective in, 41–43, 300–301; life events and transition perspective in, 39–41, 299–300; and life skills development, 298–301; life stage perspectives in, 38–39; and social role taking, 41; and timing of life events, 41–43

African American educational institutions: early, quality of, 11; citizenship education in, 186; cognitive gains in, 239; cohesive environment of, 97; as environment models, 240; primary focus of, 12; segregated, 11–12

African American students: college adjustment of, 168; female, autonomy development of, 162; programming and support for, 127

Alverno College, citizenship education in, 185

American Association of Higher Education's principles of learning, 124

American College Personnel Association (ACPA): Statement of Ethical Principles and Standards, 135; Student Learning Imperative, 113, 122–123, 187

American Indian Higher Education Consortium, 16, 17

Americans with Disabilities Act (ADA), 90

Antebellum state universities, 6–7

Architectural environment, and student behavior, 89

Army Alpha General Classification Test, 255

Artifacts, in institutional culture, 100

Asian American students, 72

Association of American Colleges (AAC), 256; "Integrity in the College Curriculum," 216

Athletic participation, student development impacted by, 85, 164–165, 241

Autonomy development: of African American women, 162; and class standing, 162; and interpersonal relationships, 160; and parents' marital status, 161–162; and parent-student relationship, 160–161; and self-efficacy, 160